E=N=E=R=G=Y

ENERGY—THE LIFE OF
John J. McKetta Jr.

Elisabeth Sharp McKetta

The University of Texas, Austin

Distributed by Tower Books, an imprint of the University of Texas Press

Image credits:
Lignin: https://commons.wikimedia.org/wiki/File%3ALignin_structure.svg
by Karol Głąb
All other images by Elton Graugnard

Requests for permission to reproduce material from this work should be sent to:
    Permissions
    University of Texas Press
    P.O. Box 7819
    Austin, TX 78713-7819
    http://utpress.utexas.edu/index.php/rp-form

♾ The paper used in this book meets the minimum requirements of
ANSI/NISO Z39.48-1992 (R1997) (Permanence of Paper).

LIBRARY OF CONGRESS CATALOGING-IN-PUBLICATION DATA

Names: McKetta, Elisabeth Sharp, author.
Title: Energy : the life of John J. McKetta Jr. / Elisabeth Sharp McKetta.
Description: First edition. | Austin : The University of Texas, 2017. | Includes
    bibliographical references and index.
Identifiers: LCCN 2017000458
    ISBN 978-1-4773-1290-2 (cloth)
    ISBN 978-1-4773-1291-9 (library e-book)
    ISBN 978-1-4773-1292-6 (non-library e-book)
Subjects: LCSH: McKetta, John J., 1915– | Chemical engineers—United States—
    Biography.
Classification: LCC TP140.M35 M354 2017 | DDC 660.092 [B] —dc23
LC record available at https://lccn.loc.gov/2017000458

CONTENTS

Foreword by William H. Cunningham   vii

Author's Note   ix

INTRODUCTION   1

ONE═COAL (*Childhood*)   7

TWO═GRAPHITE (*Coal Mining*)   29

THREE═BLOOD (*College*)   39

FOUR═MERCURY (*Industry + Graduate School*)   51

FIVE═HONEY (*Love + Marriage*)   65

SIX═CHALK (*A Young Professor in Texas*)   75

SEVEN═PETROLEUM (*Research + The Laboratory*)   91

EIGHT═PAPER (*What Started the Encyclopedia*)   105

NINE═LIMESTONE (*Administration + The House on the Lake*)   121

TEN═AIR (*Piloting + Policy*)   149

ELEVEN═PISS & VINEGAR (*Reputation + Retirement*)   165

TWELVE═COFFEE (*Generosity + Centenarianhood*)   175

AFTERWORD   203

Notes   207

Thanks═Copper   213

Index   215

FOREWORD

John McKetta has lived an extraordinary life. He has been a coal miner, an engineer, an educator, a senior university administrator, chair of the National Energy Policy Commission, and an energy adviser to five presidents of the United States. Now over one hundred years old, Johnny continues to bring a smile to the many people who are lucky enough to interact with him on a regular basis.

I met Johnny shortly after I joined the University of Texas at Austin faculty in 1971. He had already achieved iconic status: a popular professor, beloved by his students and alumni; a former president of the American Institute of Chemical Engineers; a former dean of the School of Engineering; a member of the National Academy of Engineers; a former executive vice chancellor of the University of Texas System, charged with opening and selecting presidents for four new universities within the system. I remember, like it was yesterday, calling the legendary John McKetta when I was a very young, very inexperienced, and very unimportant business school administrator and asking him if he would be willing to consider giving a talk on energy policy to a group of executives. His only response was, "Bill, tell me where and when." I later learned that his enthusiastic response was typical of Johnny's reaction whenever anyone from the university needed his help.

Johnny retired from the faculty in 1990 after forty-four years of dedicated service. I was startled in 1995 when Johnny created the "McKetta Challenge." With engineering precision, he calculated every dollar the university had paid him over his long career as a professor—$984,000. He made an unprecedented offer to contribute that amount back to the university if his former students would match it. The money would be used to create a chair in chemical engineering. After his donation and all the students' matching gifts, more than $2.2 million was raised for the John J. McKetta Chair in Engineering. The contributions greatly exceeded the challenge. More recently, Johnny's former students raised

$28 million to name the Department of Chemical Engineering in his honor.

Every university should be so lucky as to have a John McKetta. He continues to this day to be an enormous source of enthusiasm and support for our university community and our alumni. For many Longhorns, especially graduates of the McKetta Department of Chemical Engineering, Johnny's name is synonymous with the excellence that is central to the mission of the University of Texas at Austin. Johnny has never let his success and renown go to his head. He is humbled by the accomplishments of his colleagues. He is quick to give credit to others.

Known for calling many of his former students on their birthdays, known for driving orange cars and for throwing chalk at sleeping students, known for writing four hundred technical articles and creating a sixty-nine-volume encyclopedia of chemical processing and design, known for national and international leadership on energy policy, John McKetta will be long remembered at the university he has graced with his presence.

Many of the legendary stories about Johnny in this biography have often been told. But great and inspiring stories should always be retold. His is a story about overcoming unimaginable hardship, achieving at the loftiest heights of his profession, embracing his students as his family, and always moving forward with great optimism and energy.

I have been both lucky and blessed to have enjoyed Johnny's friendship and counsel for almost fifty years.

William H. Cunningham
Former President, The University of Texas at Austin
Former Chancellor, The University of Texas System

AUTHOR'S NOTE

This is the life story of Dr. John J. McKetta Jr., born in 1915, a Ukrainian American coal miner who rescued himself from the coal mines and went on to become the world's foremost energy expert, a university dean, and one of America's most widely known and beloved professors. This is the myth. Who is the man?

In this book I try to answer this question. But don't be fooled: the myth is part of the man. His life is too much of a fairy tale to pretend you can be a great human without a myth. This rags-to-riches story traces how he worked, loved, and played his way into becoming the godfather of modern chemical engineering, dedicating his life to helping students reach their dreams, and helping his country produce and use energy well. His story spans the twentieth century and goes on today. At the time of this writing, he is alive and well at age one hundred.

When I was asked by my family to write this book, and when the McKetta Department of Chemical Engineering offered its support, I knew it would be a project that involved many people and many archives. All his life, John McKetta has kept records, as if he knew that his life was significant and would be useful for people to study. His archives are stored at the University of Texas, and they include artifacts ranging from department coffee mugs to World War II ration cards to letters from his wife (in a file called "Letters from de Pink") to his famous energy lectures to notes from presidential first ladies.

As I've studied his life, interviewing former students and colleagues and examining his extensive files, my wishes for his biography have become more personal. His records and all the words from his students reveal a person who lived an exemplary life: generous, empathetic, self-trusting, and astonishingly disciplined. And just as his life was shaped by the century in which it took place (and his contributions helped shape the century, too), my research on his life is shaped by the era in which I live. In this time, there is a great deal of interest in scientific research on happiness. "What makes a good life?" researchers are asking, and popular culture follows suit. Part of that research has been a systematic study of centenarians, and there have been links drawn between happiness and long lives. I am interested in the relationship between his happiness, his productivity, and his longevity. There will be other biographies, I hope, that look more deeply at his contributions to science, to world energy use, or to the University of Texas. In this biography I try to answer the question of what made his life so *good*.

E=N=E—R=G=Y

John J. McKetta Jr. at his one hundredth birthday celebration.

INTRODUCTION

Under a well-tailored suit and usually a necktie (and in the days when he went to parties alongside his wife, Pinky, a clip-on plastic name tag that read, "My wife did not pick out this tie"), John J. McKetta Jr. always wears orange underpants. You think this is a naughty detail to put into a biography. It isn't. Nearly any adult who has ever met Johnny at a university function, lecture, or party in Austin, Texas, where he has lived out most of his one hundred years, has seen his underpants. He has even flashed them in lectures for a burnt-orange peek at his University of Texas pride.

Above his necktie: a Slavic face, combed-back hair, baby-blue eyes. It is a face that, when it turns on a person, focuses completely. One of his former students said, "When he talks to you, you feel like you are the only person in the world. For ten seconds, one minute, twenty minutes, you have one hundred percent of him. He's not looking over your shoulder to see who more important is there."[1] He is a figure who has straddled two eras: the blackened-hand days when all the men he knew mined coal and ate their sandwich lunch from a bucket, and the electric-lit-office days when all university department members ate lunch together in the faculty lounge, talking about their research and their dreams. In the coal mines, he saw death at closest quarters. He spent his days in fear. And I, his granddaughter, wanted to understand what he learned in the mines and how it translated into his life as a chemical engineering professor, dean, encyclopedia editor, presidential energy adviser, world traveler, centenarian, and great patriarch.

In the summer of 2014, when I was thirty-five and newly the mother of two, I began investigating my grandfather's life: his extensive filing system, as well as interviews with his colleagues, descendants, former students, and also—recorded on my smartphone—interviews with the man himself. Collecting stories about John J. McKetta is easy because everybody has one. When I first began researching him in the study hall named after him in the McKetta Department of Chemical Engineering at the University of Texas at Austin, I had to have a key made so that I could read his archives during weird hours when I had child care. Kevin Haynes, a baseball-capped man wearing a Hawaiian shirt and cradling a broken arm in a sling, wrote me a permission slip to get a key. He sized me up, probably to see how much I do or do not look like my grandfather, and then he said, "Your grandfather is a special man. Every time I see Johnny, he asks me the same question. He's been doing it for twenty years. 'Got a question for you, son. Why am I so handsome and you are so damn ugly?'"

Johnny McKetta is a man with an impish sense of humor, rock-solid habits and discipline, an enormous number of friends, few apparent secrets. Or whatever should have been a secret he made sure to share readily, to detonate its mystique, to create (voilà!) a sort of instant vulnerability on which relationships could build. Case in point: the burnt-orange underpants.

═

In 2005, the year he turned ninety, he moved with his wife to Westminster Manor, a retirement home that draws a hefty number of former university professors and Austin luminaries. In a pair of five-story apartment buildings about three miles northwest of the University of Texas, Westminster holds within its cloisters a small university of its own: regular classes for its residents, who range in age from sixty-five to over a hundred; a lively dining hall with tables that different social groups claim. Some tables are more exclusive than others. ("We got invited to sit over there once," my grandfather told me. "They invited us. Us!") In the courtyard, squirrels trapeze from tree to tree, and several residents sit quietly on benches. During Christmas there are colored lights; during Halloween, occasional decorative pumpkins. You could trust the routines. You could expect coffee and donuts every Tuesday morning, a chocolate fountain every New Year's Day. Flyers for classes, lectures, or field trips paper the elevator walls each day. Sounds like college, right? Lively people eating and living together and trying at once to relax and to improve themselves.

Johnny has always thrived in this sort of setting. Within a few weeks, he was head of the New Members Welcoming Committee as well as "Pierre" in a play that one of the residents had written. The play featured a high school reunion where the main character, a former wallflower, arrived fresh from Paris with her heavily cologned beau, an international mystery man who made a stir among the provincial high school returnees. The play, held in an upstairs Westminster Manor ballroom, was a big hit, standing room only. It featured the residents playing roles reminiscent of their lives at their peak. Johnny, of course, played the Parisian beau, complete with impish smile, blue suit, cologne, and navy beret. Anytime another actor forgot a line, Johnny whispered a prompt, having memorized the entire play.

From infanthood to centenarianhood, Johnny McKetta has always done well in places where everyone knows everyone. He flourishes in fishbowls. He is the winningest person in any room. You cannot help wanting to be his friend. His love and admiration of people is the single force that has most shaped his hundred years. When John J. McKetta Jr. made the choice as a young man to leave his job as a coal miner and become a chemical engineer, nobody in his town had heard of such a profession. *Go back to digging coal*, well-meaning adults might have chided.

But instead he was inspired—and pulled up, and encouraged, and nurtured—and all the other words that deal with getting-help-with-dream-chasing—by a network of people who wanted this bright young man out of the coal mines. And later a different community who wanted him out of World War II. In fact, his whole life looks like a warning map of which dire situations to avoid. He avoided each and every one, narrowly. Each time there was a person, a guardian of sorts, who stood at the threshold and said, "Johnny, step back. There are bigger places for you to go."

When you talk to him about his life, these mentors surface as the keys to his success. There was Red, the boxing coach. There were his brother, his father, his mother, his older sister. There were Sunday School teachers and football coaches. Later there were department chairs and laboratory advisers. Throughout all of it, there was his wife, his numero uno person, whom he nicknamed on their second date "Pinky."

His students remember Johnny and Pinky for their epic romance, their generosity, and their hospitality, for they opened their lakeside home to generations of students. They attended student weddings, lending them money for honeymoons; they served as godparents to numerous friends' children. Students remember Johnny for his practical jokes, his sense of humor, his ability to make each person feel special. The university remembers him for his divine loyalty, from his burnt-orange underpants and burnt-orange car (often with University of Texas decals and occasionally a pair of white horns stuck on either side of the roof), to his coming into the office to meet with students daily even after retirement, to, at age eighty, adding up all of his paychecks from UT and offering the full amount ($984,000) as a gift to the department and a challenge for former students to match. When asked by an administrator why he didn't offer a full million, Johnny responded, "Why in the hell didn't you pay me more?" But in the end he offered a million, which his students matched and exceeded.[2] Department lore claims that half the students donated because John McKetta was the most inspirational person they had met in their lives, while the other half donated large amounts "so the son of a bitch would have to match them." The McKetta Challenge returned on a bigger scale fifteen years later: the university established the $25 million "Challenge for McKetta" campaign to rename the Department of Chemical Engineering for John J. McKetta Jr. on the occasion of his ninety-fifth birthday.[3] These are some, but not nearly all, of the efforts he has made to hoist the UT Austin Chemical Engineering Department into the top-five departments nationwide.[4]

Chemical engineers know him as one of the top in their field, once awarded the International Chemical Engineering Award in Venice, Italy. They know him also for his research that produced the "McKetta Method" for measuring the temperature of a gas or oil well, and they recognize him as a global authority on the thermodynamic properties of hydrocarbons. John McKetta has served as an energy adviser to Presidents Nixon, Ford, Carter, Reagan, and George H. W. Bush. He's also authored ninety-four books, including the sixty-nine-volume *Encyclopedia for Chemical Processing and Design*, a thirty-four-year project on which he collaborated with University of Texas students and chemical engineers around the world. He has taught more than six thousand students over a nearly seventy-year career, and he calls the ones who are still living on their birthdays every year. English was not even his first language, and he has made a career lecturing in it.

But all of these accomplishments would be merely paper without the great heart of the man behind them. This is a story of a man who loves people, life, and who, as one of his students observed, has "a phenomenal energy level";[5] a man who gives children half dollars that he calls Texas pennies; a man who makes friends wherever he goes and who singles out people for their own special contributions. His is a humble story that starts with a family of Ukrainian immigrants. His story begins in a coal mine.

ONE═COAL
Childhood

Johnny McKetta's childhood was marked by two certainties: family meant love, and work meant death. The stories of his family are not stories of conflict: they are stories of a small group, two adults and three children, struggling against outside forces—poverty, frequent coal-mining disasters, and a peripatetic lifestyle of moving towns every few months—while they cared for each other with a loyalty that was both fierce and practical.

On October 17, 1915, twenty-one-year-old Mary Gelet McKetta stood hanging out clothes she had just washed, having scrubbed out the soot by hand. The coal miners' wives faced endless housework and laundry; none of the houses had electricity. This was in the village of Wyano, Pennsylvania, named for the Youngstown and Ohio Steel Company (Y&O), which owned rights to mine ten thousand acres of coal and employed all of the men. Mary felt a labor pain and told her oldest son to call a neighbor. The neighbor appeared panicked at first, for she had never assisted at a birth before—but Mary herself had helped several women and knew what to do, and besides, this was her third child. He weighed ten and a half pounds. He was healthy. They named him John J. McKetta Jr., after his father. ("It all turned out okay," my grandfather said, "'cause now we have a beautiful one hundred seventy-five–pound baby boy at age ninety-nine and a half years of age.")[1]

The *New York Tribune* headlines of the day herald a few events of the First World War and some lore of the local: "Allies Help Serbs Defend Nish Railway: Bulgaria Blockaded"; "Tribune Poll Gives Suffrage Big Lead in New York City"; "Motor Train Crashes through Bridge—Buries Teachers in Water and Mud."[2] There is a small front-page story about a Rhode Island executive who became so impressed with poultry departments in county fairs that he erected a one hundred–foot chicken house in his garden on Coggesall Avenue. There is some news about Germany capturing ships. It was an unsettled time in history—though we say that about most times in history, this particular time still felt like the late Victorian era with the fading monarchical colonial system meeting the new industrial system. The old and the new were crashing against each other; a nervous energy hung in the air. Prohibition had not yet been ruled the law, but it was on the way. Small conflicts such as the 1916 Mexican border dispute were resolved using swords and sidearms, but soldiers fighting the Great War in Europe were using automatic guns and early efforts at airplanes for reconnaissance. Can you imagine—for the first time, airplanes! Technology was on the rise. The industrial middle class was on the rise. Everyone seemed on the rise except the coal miners.

The coal miners' lives were eternally the same. In this small town in western Pennsylvania, every family included a coal miner. They bought their goods from the company store, supplementing it with home gardens. When they got sick, they relied on home remedies for medicine. Their focus went to the health of the family and to the digging of coal. This region and others like it served a single purpose: to provide America with energy to run companies, fuel trains, cook food, and light and heat homes. Unlike the older coal-mining operations in the eastern part of the state, a region known for producing the harder, purer coal called anthracite, western Pennsylvania is home to layers of bituminous coal,

Johnny, age three, and his older sister, Anna Mae, in Wyano, Pennsylvania, 1918

which is softer, more tarlike, and considered lower quality than anthracite. What concerned the citizens of Wyano and other coal company towns were the logistics of the mines: their use of the old technique of "room-and-pillar mines," scraping away coal to make a room, holding its roof up with pillars of the remaining coal. Such rooms had no windows. And there was the need to worry about retreat mining, which collapsed these rooms to get the coal from the last remaining pillars. Most of the time the miners got out before the rooms collapsed, but there were often stories of men who didn't. It was deadly, dirty work. *Were the men okay?* Mary Gelet McKetta and others would have spent their days wondering. *Is the mine sound? Did I pack him enough food? Will my children be able to breathe through the dust?*

Her two older children had survived so far. John's birth meant that the family was complete. The oldest son, Charles, had been born in 1911 in a tent during a coal strike in Strikertown. The second child, a daughter named Anna Mae, arrived in 1913 in relative stability in the town of Wyano. Mary, who had married at age fourteen, took endless care of her family and home and never seemed to sit down. Her husband woke up at 4:43 every morning, Monday through Saturday, to mine for coal— but in the evenings he worked toward his dream of completing a correspondence course and becoming an electrician. The course was in English, and John Senior spoke only Ukrainian, so he began the course at age twenty and did not complete it until a decade later. The family John Junior was born into was surnamed McKetta, but that name was a mistake.

=

My grandfather's paternal line came from a sinusoidal wave alternating fortune and fortune's fall. The first generation that anybody knows about came from Korotchenko, a small, pretty village on the western border of Ukraine. In 1828, almost a century before John Junior came along, a boy with the name of Ivan Miketa was born. At age sixteen he pledged his love to Catherine Melnyk and then headed off to war with Franz Joseph's army. He was promptly captured and spent seven years eating gruel as a prisoner of war. Catherine, loyal woman, waited. But after seven years and no news, she decided to marry another man. On the eve of her marriage, Ivan showed up. This was in 1851. He was twenty-three years old, and Catherine did not recognize him. The army changes a person. So does seven years as a captured man. But at last she recognized him, she canceled her wedding, and they married each other.

This was the generation when fortune ran high: Ivan married his love and also received for his army service a grant of one hundred acres of Ukrainian land. This made Ivan a man of means. He and Catherine had only one son, Wassail Miketa, born in 1854. But what a disappointment their son was. He was spoiled and grew up a rascal, a dresslifter, an epic vodka drinker, and a moneysuck. After his parents died, Wassail sold off the land, acre by acre, to pay for his misadventures. He ended up with only ten acres. Still, somebody married him—Anna Machnyk, ten years younger.

Wassail and Anna had three sons, and the oldest was the senior John Miketa, born in 1889, the father of our hero, Johnny Junior. Wassail himself amounted to nothing. But his sons came along, and for them, only for them, would Wassail ever be part of a story. Fortune ran low in this generation. Wassail's three sons, John, Frank, and Steve, spent their days wandering around their dwindling land, shepherding sheep, cattle, pigs, and chickens. There was no school, no prospect of a job.

Even as a child, the senior John Miketa understood how fortune worked: it depended on the man. His father had inherited a fortune and lost it. John Senior would be a different type of man. He inherited nothing but would work to gain a fortune for his family.

In 1903, he learned of an opportunity that sounded like a dream come true: American steel mills were looking for coal miners to supply fuel and coke for their operations, so they were combing Europe for suitable men. The men would receive a job, free passage to America, and twenty-five dollars cash. America was late to the scene in discovering that coal was useful. It could be burned for heat. Only when humans got better at locating it were men forced into such dangerous depths to find it. Europe was way ahead in this particular game. The Romans had figured out elementary ways to dig coal by the second century AD,[3] and in the nearly two thousand years since, coal use had increased in Europe to the extent that smoky cities and lung damage were presenting a problem. But coal use in the United States was still on the rise.

As a fourteen-year-old in Ukraine, John Senior wrote to one of these American steel companies for work as a coal miner, pretending to be sixteen. He was accepted. He gave twenty dollars to his father and kept five dollars for himself. John knew he would have to send money back to his poor father, so on the boat ride to America he spent no money and fasted for three days. The very last night, he arrived in the ship's kitchen, wobbly and famished, and he croaked at the cook, "Is there anything I can eat?"

"Your ticket includes food," the ship's cook answered bluntly. And the young John spent the next twelve hours in the ship's kitchen, eating and eating and eating until the boat docked. This story sets a precedent for the life of his son: When there is scarcity, exercise extreme discipline and go without. When there is bounty, enjoy it.

When the ship docked in Baltimore and John was asked his name, he had no idea how to spell it. He pronounced Miketa as clearly as he could in his immigrant accent, and what the immigration officer wrote down was McKetta. The officer asked his middle name, a question to which John had no answer—so the officer wrote down a second J., just the initial itself. With his new name and his five dollars, Ukrainian immigrant John J. McKetta, age fourteen, was met by a representative of the Y&O Steel Company and then placed like freight on a train to Wyano. There he was met by another company representative and taken to a boardinghouse. He began work underground as a coal miner the very next day. It would take him four years of mining coal to save enough money to pay for his brother Frank's passage to America, and then two more years for the two brothers to save for their youngest brother, Steve, to join them. The Miketa—now McKetta—family's fortune was about to rise again, but slowly.

=

When John arrived in America, he was one of perhaps a hundred unmarried men in Wyano. There weren't any hotels or inns, but there were plenty of frugal families who were more than happy to rent out rooms in their home in exchange for extra income. This was the default rooming arrangement for most of the single male workers. The boardinghouse women worked hard, washing all of the miners' blackened clothes, preparing meals, and packing lunches for the equally hardworking men living under their roofs. John took a room and ate his breakfast and dinner as a boarder in the house of a family called Gelet, who played host to ten or eleven other miners. John didn't have much of a life outside work: he worked from before dawn until dinnertime six days a week, but he and the other miners had Sundays off. John spent his aboveground time at the Gelet home, and in the evenings after dinner he hired a school tutor for a penny to teach him a little English. They lay on the kitchen floor, where the stove gave them warmth and a coal oil lamp gave them light, and they practiced reading books. Soon enough, his brother Frank joined him as a boarder in the Gelet home. The two shared a room. It happened that the Gelet family had two daughters: Mary, born in 1895, and Julia, born 1897, just a few years younger than John and Frank McKetta. In 1909 John and Mary, the two eldest, fell in love, as did Frank and Julia.

The Gelet family also had roots in Ukraine. Anna and John Gelet, the Mr. and Mrs., shared a forbidden-love story: Anna had worked as a maid in John Gelet's childhood home in Ukraine, and the two felt a deep romantic pull toward each other. But John Gelet's parents had selected him a bride, and that bride was not their maid: so he married his betrothed, who died three years later, and then he went looking for Anna. She had gone to America, so he took a ship over to find her. Soon after, they were married with children.

Note a theme here: in a time when practicality often trumped matters of the heart, both sides of the family that produced Johnny Junior originate with couples who genuinely married for love. There were two McKetta-Gelet weddings, sister-brother and sister-brother, and then the babies started to come. From John J. McKetta Sr. and Mary Gelet came Charles, Anna Mae, and on that quiet morning in 1915 while Mary was out hanging laundry to dry, the hero of our story: John J. McKetta Jr.

His childhood was marked by the usual things: mischief, exploration, lessons. Johnny was a healthy kid with the usual smattering of childhood sicknesses: colic, smallpox, chicken pox, tonsillectomy, an ear fungus that caused some pain. Charles, Anna Mae, and Johnny looked alike and traveled as a pack. They spent time playing with their double cousins. The older siblings got in trouble when they concocted a money-making plan of sending little Johnny, age four, to sing songs at the street corner with a tin cup in his hand. A neighbor saw them and told their mother, and the activity ceased. In a town of under three hundred people, every adult policed and praised the actions of the town's children. So villages raise their own.

The McKetta kids were given free range: playing tag; shooting marbles; telling stories; walking in the woods; swimming in summertime in the reservoir, which each coal mining town had; and ice-skating on it in winter. The towns nestled into the Pennsylvania hills, and the children liked to sled down the hill onto the frozen reservoir. Kids played outside a lot, making up games and doing their chores. Johnny recalls, "Every morning it was my assignment to make sure coal was available where needed, ashes taken to the nearby dump, water buckets filled at a hand-pushed pump for the people in the area, potty buckets emptied and washed. In the spring I seeded the area where we grew our vegetables, pulled weeds, and mowed the lawn during summer with a hand-pushed mower."

It was a happy, community-based childhood—but always lurking be-

The network of double cousins: Johnny (top left); his brother, Charles (center), 1919

low were the stories of the coal mines. Children dreamt of the ground, like an ashen beast, opening its mouth to eat their fathers. When boys dug dirt trenches and hid from each other, they were always playing their fathers, tempting the ground. *Try swallowing me. Just try.* But the ground waited patiently—it would get them in its mouth when they were meatier, when they were men.

Johnny and his siblings grew up in an environment where their work, efforts, and cooperation were required. Their parents rarely rested. John Senior, whom the children called Pop, had to be in the mines at 5:00 a.m., and Mary rose with him to make his breakfast and box his lunch. She spent her days cleaning, sweeping, cooking, and sewing but would stop immediately to share time with her children. Neither parent had any formal schooling, and the family spoke Ukrainian at home. This changed the year Johnny started first grade. He tells a wonderful story about it:

In the fall of 1921, although I could not speak English at all, I went to first grade at school. We were told to take our seats (at least I saw that all the students were taking their seats after the teacher said something in English), and I happened to sit on the left of a young student who could draw. He was drawing steam shovels, and I was extremely impressed. The teacher asked some kind of question, and several of the students raised their hands, as did the artist sitting next to me. For that reason I also raised my hand. (I later found out that what she had asked was, "Who has been in the first grade before?") Thereupon, she marched eight of us to a room across the hall to what turned out to be second grade.

The second-grade teacher lined eight of us against the wall and handed us a little primer that had some very nice pictures in it. The first person in line was asked by the teacher to read, and she proceeded to read in English from the primer. The second did likewise, third likewise, and finally the teacher looked at me (I was in fourth position) and asked me something in English, which I did not understand. Fortunately, I had a cousin in the class who yelled at me, "chit-tai!," which means read. I told my cousin I did not know how to read, and she explained this to the teacher. The teacher then told me, with my cousin as interpreter, to go back to the first grade.

Instead, when I got into the hall between the two grades I ran out the back door and was through with my education. I did not go back to school for three days. I went to the woods, near the streams, or anywhere until three o'clock each day; then I would go home. Fortunately, my cousin told my mother that I was embarrassed because I could not speak English. That was the time when Pop made the decision that there would be no more speaking in Ukrainian between the parents and the children. My parents always spoke Ukrainian to each other from then on, but they always spoke in English to the children. This was quite difficult for Mother because she had trouble speaking English. I went to school the rest of the year at Wyano and must have done all right because I was promoted to the second grade at the end of the year.

It speaks to the strength of the family's pack mentality that the parents made such a sacrifice to drop their native language in front of their children. But that was the world young Johnny McKetta lived in: family helped family. We are all in this together, and we cannot let our kids fail. It is astonishing to think that if it hadn't been for Johnny's cousin ratting on him and his parents' support, he might not have known English, would not have been able to apply to and attend an American university, would not have become a chemical engineer—and so the slope slips.

So the McKetta adults learned English unsteadily, secondhand scraps their children brought home from elementary school. For the most part their community was made up of eastern European immigrants, none of whom spoke English or identified as "American." The three children answered at home to Ukrainian nicknames: Chalcho (little Charles), Hanya (remnant of Anna), and Ivanchko (little John). They were unquestionably loyal to each other, in part because the children grew up moving several times a year due to the nature of their father's work. At age thirty, John Senior, after digging coal for sixteen years, made a life change that inspired his youngest son forever after: he completed his correspondence course in electricity and became an electrician for the town of Wyano. The one-year course took him ten years to complete because it was in English, so he had to translate each word with his Ukrainian-English dictionary—but he did it and was able to quit the mines. West Penn Power Company hired him to work in an electric substation: his job was to electrify the coal-mining plants. His work lit up mines all over Pennsylvania. Johnny was four when his father finished the course. Before then, people used kerosene—"coal oil," as they called it—for their lamps; the only electricity in the town of 250 was in the company store and in the home of the coal-mine manager. Technology at the start of the century perched on the cusp of a massive and irrevocable shift, whose waves Johnny would spend his life experiencing and contributing to. He remembers the day in 1924 when their father connected their house to the company store, via electric wire: "Pop turned

John J. McKetta Sr.

on the switch and the light bulbs, one in each room, went on. We could read books at night, with the light bulb ten to fifteen feet away!" Johnny was in the third grade and proud to bring friends home to see the lights. Most homes did not have this luxury—five years later when the Depression hit, still fewer than ten Wyano houses had electricity.

Because of the scarcity of such skills, John Senior's work was in demand; he could convert the mines from steam-powered to electric. So the young family grew up portable, moving from coal-mining town to coal-mining town, Wyano to Franklin Township to Cambrook to Moxin to Brier Hill, moving about every six months and crisscrossing Pennsylvania for the early years of Johnny's life. One of his first memories, in fact, involves a moving truck taking away all their furniture.

Johnny spent his childhood in over a dozen towns in ten years, making friends anew in each one. He would take this skill with him his entire life. Johnny also grew up a witness to his father's example. By becoming an electrician, John Senior had implicitly stated, *I want to live a bigger life than this*, and then he had taken the laborious steps to do so. Indeed, he inspired his son to know that you can go beyond where you began: It's possible to get beyond poverty. It's possible to climb out.

John Senior was exceptional in his community. For most people, this was life and people didn't think to complain. These were the jobs, the houses, the food. So families accepted their fate. "With one exception," my grandfather recalls, "the coal-mining houses were quite comfortable." Each house contained four rooms: two bedrooms upstairs, and a kitchen and living room downstairs. In the "comfortable houses" they inhabited during the early 1920s and 1930s, Johnny and Charles shared a bed, with Anna Mae sleeping in a cot alongside them, while their parents shared the next room. The uncomfortable exception was a six-month stint in Franklin, Pennsylvania, when the family of five lived in a single room; Mary Gelet hung sheets in a resourceful effort to separate sections. One section contained a bedroom with one bed, where the parents slept with their heads at the headboard, and all three children slept at foot of the bed, stacked into parallel lines: Johnny at four years old, Anna Mae six, Charles eight. On the other side of the sheet were a kitchen, living area, and a small area with a chamber pot. There was a flushing toilet in the basement, so several times a day one of the children took the pot down four flights of stairs to the indoor toilet in the basement to be flushed. The only heat came from a kitchen stove fired with coal. There was no running water, but there was ample water from a pump in the basement, and the children carried water up the four flights for drinking, cooking, and bathing. All were stingy with the use of the water, which is a detail I love, a moment of conservation in action. Today we American parents can say "turn off the faucet!" until we lose our voices, but still our kids see only the spout from which water keeps coming. But in 1919, using up the water meant another trip down four flights of stairs, which nobody wanted to make.

John Senior's job remained the same from town to town; the children made friends, and Mary kept house. Converting coal mines to use electric power meant living in the shadow of the mines, often two hundred feet from coke ovens that spewed out black air from the combustion. It meant that the children breathed in the pollution and that the wives, like Mary, could not hang out their families' clean clothes to dry outdoors because they would end up covered in soot. Mary didn't complain; she recognized that their fortune, though small, still made them fortunate.

John and Mary raised their brood with old-country Ukrainian values that would help Johnny and his older siblings climb unfamiliar American ladders toward success. The parents instructed their children so many times it became like a mantra: "You won't ever be the richest people in the world in terms of rubles and kopecks; you will never be the tallest; but you three can be the most honest, fair, and nicest three children in the world if you continue as well as you are doing." For both Mary's and John's entire lives (his much longer than hers), they insisted to their children that they believed them to be the best children possible.

This advice and blessing stayed with the McKetta children for the rest of their lives. Charles, Anna Mae, and Johnny learned to be pleasant to everyone they met. The three nearly always passed the test of "do your friends' parents want to adopt you?," and their parents received compliments on the behavior of their children. They were, in Johnny's words, "the best friends of everyone in school and play."

The children learned to be kind to one another and to stand up for themselves: "Pop told me that most people will insist they are right when they are not and for us to admit when we were not sure. But if you are sure, then stick with your point because people may try to run over you. Most important, make sure you are right. Pop even encouraged us to defend ourselves when he thought he was right. Like, 'Did you eat that last piece of cake?' If I didn't, I would say so. He did not expect me to say 'Annie did,' but he believed me when I said 'I didn't.'" There was no rivalry between the brothers. Quite simply, Charles was the hero and Johnny was the cheering squad. Their parents made it clear to both brothers that their sister, Anna Mae, deserved only kind attention: in other words, no arguing or fighting with girls.

Throughout childhood, Johnny had opportunities to practice these values and set them in action, supported by his parents. Many of these opportunities took place in Brier Hill, where the family at last settled after their itinerant tour of coal towns because John Senior was offered a job as the town's chief electrician, a terrific honor and the highest position in town held by a non-American. Once, testing the boundaries of his childhood lessons about honesty, Johnny and a friend stole a dozen ears of corn from a neighboring farmer, and John Senior marched him back to apologize and pay for the corn. He remembers, "I was even more embarrassed because a girl I liked very much was Grace Higinbotham, the farmer's daughter." In small towns, our actions face us fast. The moral: be honest; don't be sneaky; behave yourself. As was often the case in Johnny's life, it took only a single time for a lesson to be learned. Many of his later stories build on the theme of honesty and transparency, a lesson that traces back to stealing corn. These stories he cherishes as pebbles along the way; he would learn from his mistakes, and he would go on to live an exemplary life. Johnny recalls, "Many times a little fib would get me out of trouble, but I kept remembering Mom and Pop's advice and told the facts."

In Brier Hill, the family joined a Catholic church. (They would have preferred Greek Orthodox, which was John Senior and Mary's religion, but they took what Brier Hill offered, which was Catholicism.) The priest, however, was nobody's idea of a good role model. People often spied him drunk around town. He also had a rotten temper, and one day he took this temper out on Johnny: "During catechism class the priest asked me a question, and when I had an answer that did not please him, he called me a bad name, reached over and grabbed me by the ear, and lifted me off my feet. While I was off my feet and facing the priest, I kicked him in his shin as hard as I could with my hob-nailed shoes." Johnny's parents noticed that he was acting quiet after church and asked him if anything was wrong. Reluctantly he told his father that he had kicked the priest. What happened next left him with a vital lesson about family loyalty:

Whereupon Pop said, "Come with me," and he grabbed me by the hand and said, "We are going to see the priest." I was so embarrassed because I felt that Pop was going to ask me to apologize to the priest as I had apologized just recently to Mr. Higinbotham for stealing his corn. When we got to the priest's house, Pop knocked on the door, and when the priest came to the door, Pop said, "If you ever put one hand on my son again, or on any child in this town, or any person that I know of, I'll come over here and punch you hard on the nose, and maybe even break that hand of yours. I don't want my son nor any person that I love to ever attend any of your functions again. Why don't you sober up and start behaving?" I was so proud of my father for having the faith and love in his son.

This story stands as a magnificent triumph for a child's sense of justice, as well as a reminder that authority figures are quite often in the wrong. This break with the church led to another experience that changed Johnny's life forever: at the new church the family began attending, Johnny was given his first chance to be a teacher.

He began teaching Sunday School. Mrs. Kelly, who had cofounded the church, noticed that Johnny was good with the small children and loved the stories from the Bible, so when he was about ten, she asked him to teach the younger kids. She gave him a Bible-story booklet to use as his teaching guide. He then did something that would go on to influence his teaching: first he read the booklet word for word until he memorized it, and then he went to his Bible and read the longer original versions, which he told to the class—in other words, he knew what he was to teach them, and he made sure to know a little bit more than what they were required to know. He recalls, "They became so wide-eyed, and I knew they were enjoying the stories and could feel they liked me because they thought I knew so much more than they did. That feeling never left me." He loved his students and felt at home in the role of teacher. These were the first seeds of John McKetta the educator, the best friend to all his students.

Johnny grew to be a community leader among the children in Brier Hill. He started a group called "Frontier Boys Club" that met in his home cellar. Its purpose was to mobilize local boys to help out older and poorer people. The Frontier Boys did good deeds, and a pleasant side effect was that they benefited from each other's good deeds: once Johnny saw a bakery truck turned over and hurried to help the driver. As thanks, the driver instructed him to fill his bicycle basket with as many cakes and baked goods as he could carry. These cakes supplemented both McKetta meals and Frontier Boys Club meetings for some time to come. Johnny became a paperboy and learned the name of every person in town, for he delivered newspapers to nearly all of the two hundred families who lived in Brier Hill. On wet, sleeting, or especially cold days, families on his paper route invited him in to have bacon and eggs at their table.

A mark of Johnny's open and people-focused nature is that when he makes a friend, he keeps that friend for a long time. Six decades after Johnny left Brier Hill, I learned that my high school chemistry teacher in Austin, Texas, Frank Mikan, was the grandson of one of the Brier Hill homemakers who invited Johnny into her home on cold mornings. Mr. Mikan recognized my name on his class roster because Johnny McKetta stayed in touch with the Mikan family for the next sixty years.

In 1929 the stock market crashed, and Johnny graduated from eighth grade. The Great Depression didn't harm his family the way it harmed wealthier, urban families. The McKetta family had always economized, eaten locally, and worn clothes that Mary made and patched. The exception to their homespun wear was that every two years, John Senior bought his oldest son, Charles, a new suit. An upwardly mobile man needed a good suit, Pop reasoned—a lesson to share with his sons. When Charles's clothes wore thin, Mary did what she always did: tailor them again and give them to Johnny. The year 1929 marked the closing of many of the local mines, the first suit of his own that Pop bought Johnny, and the year Johnny entered high school. Some people panicked about the economy, but John Senior and Mary had spent their entire lives accustomed to poverty. The Depression hit and they cheerfully kept on with their business. Their children did the same.

Johnny's life in rural Pennsylvania went forward with characteristic fun and motion. He started ninth grade and developed his first major crush on a girl named Mary Bair. When Johnny fell in love, he fell *hard*. He said of Mary, "I thought that it was the romance of the century." He even wrote her a poem, which she laughed at and showed her friends: "Mary had a little lamb, she also had a bear; I saw Mary's lamb but I never saw her bare." This poem is characteristic of the type of note he continues to write in his adult life: part convention, part mischief, always with love, and often with bad poetry. He and his two-year-younger double-cousin Frank became notable flirts around town. They had a trick they played: First Frank would walk up to a pretty girl and greet her: "Susan!" The girl would respond that her name was *not* Susan and he must have mistaken her for somebody else. Then Johnny would follow a minute later. "Susan! How are you?" Exasperated, the girl would repeat herself. But somehow the boys' jovial and playful natures always ended up persuading that particular "Susan" (and some of her friends) into joining them for a date. It was a form of sport: a refining of his ability to make people fall in love with him, or at the very least find him charming.

In high school Johnny also played football, which seeded him into a life of enthusiasm for all things athletic. His coach, Clyde Smith, was a "Boy Scout type of coach. We were not allowed to smoke, swear, or misbehave on the field, or at any time that we were associated with his team." Johnny played alongside one of his best friends since third grade, David Ficks (not surprisingly, the Ficks family became lifelong friends of the McKetta family). By the end of his freshman year Johnny was playing quarterback.

During football off-season, at the beginning of his sophomore year in 1931, Johnny decided to take up boxing. Five days a week he and a friend walked along the train tracks for three miles from Brier Hill to Fairchance, Pennsylvania, where Red Richardson ran the Pleasant Valley Boxing Club. Red had credentials: He was a flyweight champion in the 1920s before retiring as a coach. He was twelve years older than Johnny and served as one of many mentors in Johnny's life whose guidance and advice shaped him: "I loved him immediately. He wouldn't let me fight officially until he felt I could handle myself and follow his strict orders. He was a perfectionist and insisted that you protect your head and face and never get hit there because the brain is the most sensitive part of your body." Red took a special liking to Johnny, and on fight nights, usually once a month, Red picked Johnny up at home, took him to the fight, and delivered him back home afterward. Red called his boxers "his boys," which later Johnny would call all of his students, male and female.

For five years Johnny boxed, winning thirty-three out of thirty-four matches in the American Amateur Union Golden Gloves group. He claimed that his one lost match was with a boxer who had no business being in the ring, so he was preparing to forfeit the fight to spare the poor guy's face, when the guy punched him and knocked him out. Red Richardson taught my grandfather several lifelong lessons. One lesson was that his hands were classified as "lethal weapons" and he must use them with discretion—a lesson that saved Johnny and his six-foot-four,

ninety-five-pound, beloved and eminently bullyable cousin Frank from
a bully at high school. Johnny recalls:

> George Menser [the bully] met me in the hall and said, "I hear you think
> you are pretty tough and are a boxer. I'd like to have you come to the back
> of the building to see how tough you really are." I replied with a fact, which
> was, "George, I'd like to accommodate you, but as an active boxer my two
> hands are classed as lethal weapons and I could be arrested and serve time
> in jail if I ever hit someone with these hands. But . . . I would love to show
> you a few things I learned in the ring." He replied, "That doesn't scare me
> at all. Why not go to the back of the building with me?" I said that I would
> if we could have at least one witness. He called several students, and we
> four went to the back of the building. I said, "George, I would feel better
> if you would take the first swing at me." Without a word he threw a hard
> haymaker at my head. It was hard, but slow, and I was able to get under it
> easily. I countered with a very hard right uppercut to his solar plexus. He
> grabbed his abdomen and gasped for air for almost a full minute. He lay on
> the ground and tried to breathe. Finally he was able to get up but couldn't
> talk. I told him I was careful not to hit him in the face. I was also glad
> to have the two witnesses who could testify that he swung his fists at me
> first. . . . Incidentally from that day on George and I were on friendly terms
> and he never teased Frankie again.

During his senior year, Johnny's family moved once more to a different town, so his football coach, Clyde Smith, invited Johnny to live
with him and his wife. ("Was this unusual?" I asked. "To live with your
coach?" He responded, "Of course not. He was a wonderful friend. People help each other out.") But by midseason Johnny tore the ligaments
in his right knee and had to stop playing. So he moved to live again with
his family, beginning classes at a new high school.

Johnny adored high school. He was made for it, just as he was made
for life on a university campus and, much later, in a retirement home.
His days were made up of games, friendship, flirtations, sports, and tri-
umphs. He knew everybody and was very much in the center of things.
He seemed to be good at everything: during these years he picked up a
cornet at a secondhand store in Yukon, Pennsylvania, and taught himself to play, which resulted in his playing first trumpet for the Yukon

Johnny and brother Charles with their mother, Mary Gelet McKetta

Volunteer Band. Between the Frontier Boys Club, the football team, the Sunday School teaching, joining the dramatic society and volunteer band (Johnny loved the arts, but he loved sports more), falling in love, and the paper route in Brier Hill, a theme was emerging that would live on in Johnny's life: the importance of being part of something bigger than himself, a group to which he could fasten his loyalty.

His nuclear family was the first and tightest of these units. The encouragement and love he gave and received formed the basis for the rest of his life, shaping him into a person who trusted people and allowed himself to be permeable, vulnerable, to ask for help and to offer it.

If one were to characterize his childhood, then, it was both lucky and unlucky. Johnny remembers the love, the freedom, the friendship, the first sighting of an airplane (which terrified him!), the first encounter with his uncle's new car (which fascinated him: the headlights were lit by acetylene gas), the adventures with friends and cousins. But he remembers also the constant threat of the coal mines, which served as both monster and livelihood.

And the existence of this monster was about to change the landscape of his family forever.

INTERLUDE=

In 2010 West Virginia suffered what *New York Times* journalist Shaila Dewan calls "the worst American mining disaster in 25 years." Dewan interviews miners and dead miners' wives, and she concludes that "the explosion that killed at least 25 miners on Monday has done little to alter the steel-toed blend of pride, resignation and economics that defines a coal miner's life."[1] This occurred at the Upper Big Branch mine, cited for 204 violations over the previous two years. Rescuers did their best but ultimately abandoned their efforts due to "difficult conditions in the mine," which included lethal gases that their oxygen masks could not protect them against.[2]

We are talking about this at dinner at Westminster Manor, where my husband and I eat weekly Friday-night dinners with my grandparents. We call them Baba and Djiedo, our anglicized attempts at the Ukrainian words for "grandmother" and "grandfather." We eat early, usually 5:00 p.m. This night my husband and I are going afterward to an absinthe bar, so our conversation wavers between consternation at the mining accident and excitement at the luxury of absinthe, as my grandmother makes suggestions about which drinks we should try.

"There is one with frothed egg white in it," Pinky offers. "It is awfully good."

I have been reading the stories of this collapsed coal mine. The newspapers print interviews with the widows: widows who cautioned against this line of work, widows with two-week-old fatherless infants, widows who accept that it's the only way to make a living. The widows astonish me in their acceptance of what has happened to their husbands.

I cannot stop myself from reading about them.

And even while my loyalty is with the living, I cannot help thinking of the men. West Virginia borders western Pennsylvania, where my grandfather mined coal. These men could be the grandchildren of my grandfather's high school classmates. They could just as easily have been the grandchildren of my grandfather if my grandfather hadn't left.

We are a world apart, here at Westminster having our Friday-night dinner talking about absinthe. Here my grandparents are, *almost a century old*, surrounded by people who love them, with evidence all around them of a life well crafted: they survey it from where they sit at the head of a long table, at the end of a long life. Compare that to those poor young men.

TWO═GRAPHITE
Coal Mining

High school, for the young men of Brier Hill in 1933, was marked by a finite sense of festivity, much like a New Year's Eve party before the grave restraint of January 1 sets in. All the boys were expected to become coal miners. It was the fact, the single truth they knew about their lives. Most had no idea yet which young woman from their class they would marry or how many children they would have, but they all knew their work well. They had seen their fathers do it.

Johnny McKetta proved no exception. When he was a senior in high school, he had never heard of chemical engineering. He wanted to be a coal miner after graduation because that's what men did and what their fathers did. Sure, a miner died about every other day:[1] normally this was because the roof caved in, but there were also mine-car collisions, asphyxiation, drowning, explosions, and burns to worry about. But mining for coal was pretty much the only job option, and obviously people must work. College-educated teachers were one exception, but none of the coal miners' kids had any idea how to enact the miracle of becoming one of those. John Senior was another exception because of his expertise in electricity. But he had worked for sixteen years in the coal mines first. Nobody expected to get away with less.

Because of their parents' hard work and dutiful economizing, the McKetta family was able to move into a farmhouse during Johnny's final year of high school. This was his first experience living in a home that his family owned, and it was a notable triumph in his family's life as new Americans. For Johnny's entire life, his parents had saved 10 percent of their meager earnings each month, and they collaborated with Johnny's uncle Frank to put a mortgage on a 185-acre farm in Yukon for thirteen thousand dollars. The property was a dream for the McKettas. It came furnished with three homes, a lovely forest, a barn and silo, and an old coal mine that had closed at the end of World War I. This purchase of land also felt like a righting of a wrong: These McKetta brothers were born into a negative inheritance as sons of a father who squandered away their grandfather's 100 acres. Yet as adults they were able to gain 185 acres in a new country through their own hard work and discipline.

In 1932 the McKetta family made their move. The house was full of luxuries unknown to Johnny in his early childhood: it had electricity, a basement with a coal-fired furnace, running water, and a small (indoor!) bathroom with a toilet. They sublet to a farmer who, as part of the exchange, provided the family with milk, meat, chickens, and vegetables. One of Johnny's chores in the new house was to dig coal from the seam in the yard. It wasn't great coal (it had a high sulfur content), but it was enough to heat their furnace and sell some too for just under thirty cents per ton—and it gave Johnny a small taste of the work he would do after graduation.

What he remembers about the coal mine on their farm is detailed and grounded in Depression-era sensibilities: the coal was close to the surface, only five to ten feet deep. Most farmers in southwestern Pennsylvania had this vein running through their land, but because most towns were built on hills, it was too far down to effectively mine. Johnny and his family used picks and shovels. "It was easy," he says, "because we were breathing air." They didn't have to wear handkerchiefs to cover their mouths to prevent breathing the black dust of the deep, unaired mines. During the Depression, John Senior and his brother Frank formed a small coal company of their own, the McKetta Bros. & Sons Coal Company, which sold this second-rate coal to local people for cheap prices. Johnny recalls that over a third of their customers could not pay, but McKetta Brothers gave them the coal anyway. "People took care of other people who were destitute." Farmers shared their food if they could afford it. John Senior had coal and a truck, and he could afford to be generous with both.

Charles had already begun working in the coal mines. Johnny watched as his older brother began adult life, going underground with his lunch pail and miner's helmet Monday through Saturday, just as their pop had. Charles, being the type of person he was, made mining look exciting and glamorous, because he made everything look that way. Johnny also watched as Charles stepped up into adult life of a different sort. Johnny had flirted, had even had crushes and written an occasional bawdy love poem, but he had never invited a girl over to his house to meet his parents. But one weeknight Charles asked their mother if he could bring a friend to dinner. "Of course," was the answer. A few nights later, Johnny came home from boxing and saw, standing in their kitchen, a very pretty girl whom he assumed had to be a friend of his sister's.

It was Nellie Parris. Charles had met her at an after–football game party and fallen for her fast. Nellie's dad worked in another unincorporated coal-mining town called Adah, known for having the "largest river coal docks in the United States."[2] It was known for shipping coal more than for mining it. Adah stood twenty-five miles from the McKetta home in Yukon, and Nellie was the first person the McKetta kids ever knew who had two American-born parents. Mary McKetta served her best dish: stuffed cabbage—Ukrainian food—and sensing that this was an important introduction, she even made apple pie and homemade ice cream. And there sat Nellie. Johnny thought, "She is so beautiful. So American!"

Nellie asked for seconds, apologizing as she asked. Johnny thought she was magnificent. In their little town of immigrants, they had never known an American close-up. She dressed in such nice clothing; her hair was so smooth, so prettily fixed. And Charles was so proud of her.

Having her at the table elevated the whole family—it was one more way Charles was a hero. What Ukrainian guy could bring home to dinner a girl like that?

It was October. Johnny was just days away from turning seventeen. Nellie asked the McKetta family what they were doing for Christmas.

"Won't the mine owners give men the day off?" Nellie asked.

Charles and John Senior nodded.

"Won't you—do any gift exchanges?" Nellie wanted to know.

The five McKettas stared at the face of this beautiful American girl asking such an absurd question. Just the fact of her in the room was startling. Equally startling was the idea that there was money enough for meals like this one every night! Of course they did not exchange gifts. "Who had heard of that? Who had the money for such a thing?"

A few months later Charles and Nellie announced their engagement. They married soon after, and year and a half later they had a daughter and named her Mary Ann. Until they could save enough money for their own house, Nellie, Mary Ann, and Charles continued living with Charles's parents, so Johnny got to see his brother, his idol and best friend, every day. Both with coal mining and marriage, Charles provided his younger brother a lens for a certain kind of adulthood, one that blended responsibility, love, and exceptionally hard work—work that climbed infinitely toward some better, more promising American future.

═

It was an era in which seventeen-year-olds were called on to think responsibly about their future. In Johnny's high school graduation booklet, *Klass Klassics*, which acted as a yearbook in 1933, somebody wrote an editorial called "Education to the Student." The writer explained, "The importance of these years during which, perhaps the whole course of their life was moulded [sic], cannot be overestimated. They have, in a measure, determined whether they are going to be an asset or a liability in the business of life. . . . College education is not necessary to success and it is likewise not a guarantee: it is merely an advantage over those who do not have such training."[3]

Most of the graduating class would not go on to college. Education was a luxury. Immediate work was the norm. Still, *Klass Klassics* lent itself to goofy humor about the world as the graduates understood it. A

*Johnny graduates
from Brier Hill
High School, 1933.*

rascally question was attributed to Johnny: "Why telegraph when it is cheaper to telewoman?" He was the circulation manager for *Klass Klassics*; Anna Mae was an associate editor. Each student's photo was paired with a quotation: Johnny's, "He mixed reason with pleasure, and wisdom with truth"; Anna Mae's, "And cloud or stormy the night, The sky of her heart is always bright." *Klass Klassics* also had a column titled "Can You Imagine?" This section posited the unlikeliest of scenarios about its soon-to-be-graduates. Two items involved the McKetta children: "Can you imagine Anna McKetta being angry? Can you imagine John McKetta being a wall flower?" Johnny was also recognized as the class of 1933's "tough guy" and "bad boy."

Johnny graduated from high school, and the very next day he and the other seven graduating boys (out of a class of thirty-three) stood in line at first light, hoping for a job that day in the mines. Because of the Depression, most of the coal mines had shut down. Everybody wanted work. The pit boss gave preference to the older men with families.

The first day Johnny stepped into a metal cage that descended deep into the darkness belowground, there to stay for eight hours. In between loads of coal, he took a few bites of sandwich and drank sips of water. He was down 160 feet with no electricity, no fan. The mines were not aerated. At least the miners had partners. The first day eighteen-year-old Johnny went down into the mines, he was partnered with his brother, Charles, who taught him safety and care: "Before we started to dig coal, Charles would make sure the place was clean and everything was in its proper location. He insisted that you do this preliminary work before you would start digging coal because this would expedite matters later. This lesson stayed with me."

But on the first day Johnny went underground into the mines, there was a tragedy: A crash sounded and Charles said, "There's been a bad cave-in somewhere." They ran up the track to another digging spot to find that underneath the fallen rock lay one of Johnny's high school classmates, crushed. The classmate had been working alongside his father, who had died next to him. It took the company a day and a half to dig out their bodies. This first crash changed everything for Johnny. He began his first day in the mines believing that coal mining was a way to be like his heroes, his father and his brother. By the end of his first day, he had changed his mind. "I was the yellowest and most scared coal miner that ever existed. I hated it. But it was the best thing that's ever happened to me because I got away from it."

At the time, he didn't have other options. He waited in line every morning for the next two years, and when he was given work, he put a handkerchief over his face and dug, loading coal into the two-ton wagon, hanging his brass check with his miner's number on it to mark his work on the wagon's little hook. Some days he was assigned to work in areas that had suffered recent cave-ins, and those days he spent the majority of the day cleaning up the place and laying track for the coal wagon. There was no pay for this; pay was only for the coal loaded in the wagon and sent to the surface. On good days, he loaded several wagonloads, and

Johnny gratefully received twenty cents for each ton of coal. Over the next two years, until he was age twenty, he mined for coal whenever he could get the work, which was about half of the time. Sometimes Johnny McKetta was given work; sometimes he waited all day for nothing.

Intriguing characters peppered his memories of these years in the mines. Once he was partnered with a "Holy Roller," who spent an entire workday yelling out prayers for God to fill his wagon with coal. Another time he joined a coal strike led by John L. Lewis, the "King" of the United Mine Workers of America. Their striking resulted in hourly pay for cleanup work and a raise to twenty-five cents for each partner per ton of coal. Johnny dropped out of the coal miners' union soon after this triumph. He was lucky; he had a job. He dared not ask for more.

But he never stopped being afraid.

One night in the late winter of 1935, Johnny noticed an interestingly titled book in his brother's hands. Charles was sitting in the living room, finishing reading a book by the light of electricity—the idea still seemed surprising!—that the librarian at their old high school had given him: *Coal Carbonization* by Dr. Horace C. Porter.

"What's it about?" Johnny asked.

"How to make chemicals from coal—there's a profession called a chemical engineer who does it. Here." He handed the book to his younger brother. "Make sure to return it when you're done."

In that simple gesture, Charles would be passing on a blessing to his younger brother. The librarian's blessing to Charles was a hint in the form of a book: *Look! You are a smart boy. There are other options. You can still work in coal but not go into the mines.* Johnny read the book hungrily. There was another way, the book promised. There is work to be done in the sunlight, in open clean air. *Coal Carbonization* would be a turning point in Johnny's life. It wasn't lost on Johnny that the book, and the safe life it represented, was meant for his older brother. But Charles stayed in the mines.

The book opened up the possibility of another world outside the Pennsylvania coal mines. Making it happen would be a matter of going to college—and going to college meant first getting in and then getting a job to pay for it. Johnny did his research. He learned of fifty-five colleges in the United States with chemical engineering departments. That spring, he decided to write to every single one of them. Johnny used a pencil to write his letters to colleges—the irony being that even the graphite in pencils was a by-product of coal. He was using coal to get away from coal. At night, he kept the electric lights on until long after an early-morning-coal-miner's bedtime, and he wrote letter after letter after letter, over and over, putting graphite to paper in his neat hand, always the same words: *My name is John McKetta. I have a high school degree. I am a coal miner and I want to learn how to make chemicals from coal, as per Dr. Porter's discussion in Coal Carbonization. I have no money, so I'll need a job to pay for my education.* Letter after letter he sent out. The responses came back. Some colleges flat-out rejected him. Others said he could come, but they had no work for him. Then finally, the fifty-fifth college responded.

The response came from Burton Handy, president of Tri-State College in Angola, Indiana. The letter informed Johnny that Tri-State would be happy to have him join their Chemical Engineering Department and they could certainly get him a job working twenty hours a week at twenty cents per hour making concrete blocks and working to construct a building. Tri-State was not prestigious by any means. The school advertised in magazines such as *Popular Mechanics* that their "time tested, world famous accelerated B.S. Degree courses" could be completed in twenty-seven months.[4] But it was a college. For Johnny, it was a ticket out. He would leave the familiar coal-veined hills and try his fortune in the Midwest, where a person could have clean hands and get an education.

Johnny said good-bye to his friends and family, and he packed up and left Pennsylvania the following month. He didn't have much to pack—just his few suits, a few personal items. He left his coal clothes for another miner to use. But just before leaving, he packed his dirty coal miner's cap with the light. It might be able to serve him.

INTERLUDE=

"What do coal mines even look like?" I ask my grandfather one autumn day eighty years later. We are sitting at the plastic breakfast table in his retirement home in Austin, Texas, not far from the university.

He is amused that I want to know.

"Honey," he says. He coughs. "My doctors say this shortness of breath is from the coal."

It could be other things. It could be that for seventeen years he smoked (followed by seventeen years of dreaming every night about smoking, of being at the end of a long empty hallway and lighting up, making certain nobody would see). At that point in his life, his world was public; what he did, people saw, except in those tunnel dreams.

"Honey girl," he begins again. Between us on the table are a box of Kleenex, a hand-carved wooden cribbage board snaked into the number 29, several DVDs from 1950s sit-coms, his glasses, and a container of pens, pencils, and pink highlighters. Always open on the table is his calendar, which is scribbled over and filled with engagements in his small, crabbed handwriting. It is 2014. Now there is an oxygen tank next to my grandfather's chair: it appeared around his ninety-eighth birthday.

My grandfather answers, "Honey, coal mines exist at different levels below the surface of the earth. They are closed systems until a person enters. As you dig into the coal vein, you are in an atmosphere with no outside effects. There is no wind, no air, and you feel a dank, musty, dampish air surrounding you. It is damp because rainwater ultimately will seep through the surface and get into the mine. So you need a pump to pump water from the wells formed where you dug coal, and you need air blowers—fans, honey—to bring air and oxygen. The coal vein may be as thick as eight feet—in this kind of mine the miner stands on his feet and digs coal. Some veins are three to four feet thick, and miners would dig while lying on their backs in the shallow mines. Above the veins are solid rock slabs, which may crack and fall onto the miner. This is usually fatal, honey. In the Wyano mines we would lose one or two miners per month who were killed by falling rock."

He pauses to let me try to picture this.

Can you picture this?

It is hard for me. When I close my eyes and try, I see slabs of rock like bacon, the coal a glittering black, like treasure, beneath. I can feel the dampness, but I cannot picture the being-without-air. I can picture the falling rock. It is hard to imagine. But I force myself to go into the mines of my mind and come out breathless and hungry.

THREE═BLOOD
College

ere is the scene when Johnny arrived at Tri-State in the fall of 1935: He had hitchhiked from Pittsburgh, leaving at 7:00 a.m. He arrived in Angola by dinnertime, said good-bye to his third driver of that day, and stepped out of the car in the nicest of his suits. He carried a light suitcase whose heaviest item was the dirty old coal cap. When he walked onto the campus, it was like walking into a pasture of heaven: so much grass, so well cared for! Students (his age) walking in clean clothes to class, breathing clean air and knowing—expecting!—their futures to be aboveground. Buildings like cathedrals built of stone, with windows all the way up. In his dreams for the rest of his life, universities would rise like castles. This was clearly the end of the rainbow.

He entered the office of Burton Handy, the president. President Handy, a well-dressed man, a man of stature, a man like no man Johnny had ever met, looked up from his paperwork. He immediately put down his pen and ushered Johnny straight to the registrar, Dr. Raymond Roush, who called in Professor Gerald Moore, chair of the Chemical Engineering Department, and said to him, "This is the young coal miner I told you about. See if you could help him." These words would ring in Johnny's ears for the rest of his life. "See if you could help him."

Yes, my twenty-year-old grandfather thought, looking down at his pitiful but best-effort suit, his scrubbed but imperfectly clean hands. *Please help me. My God, I could use the help.*

Johnny was given a job working construction on a new campus building: twenty cents an hour for twenty hours a week—half of his earnings went to him, half to Tri-State to pay for his tuition. Certain colleges, including Tri-State, received these work funds from a government program called National Youth Association that helped young adults pay for college. Johnny was on the cement-block team, where he and other students made concrete blocks for use in building classrooms and dorms. "I couldn't believe it," he says. "I could work aboveground in front of God and make four dollars a week. This work felt so easy compared to digging coal that it was like taking a heavy stone off your broken foot."

Tri-State was happy to have Johnny. The college seemed to know at some deep level how happy Johnny was to be there. He was lightheadedly relieved with the extreme gratitude of a stray dog who has just been adopted: it was this life of comfort versus the pound. And he was going to work harder than they had ever seen any student work.

Like his father, starting a new job in a new land, he first needed to find a boardinghouse. This brought him to Mrs. Bert Nichols. "She was very old; she may have been thirty-five."[1] The price of a room was two dollars a week, but she offered him a room for free in exchange for helping around the house: cutting grass, painting the house, doing odd jobs. That took care of a place to live. As for meals, on his first day on campus, he passed a diner called Doc's Lunch in downtown Angola where a man was putting a "help needed" sign out front. Johnny recalls, "I asked the gentleman (his named turned out to be Doc Boyce) if he had a job for me. He said, 'I haven't had a single customer, this is my first day open, but yes come on in and have a cup of coffee and you will be my first dishwasher.' For the remaining time in school I washed dishes

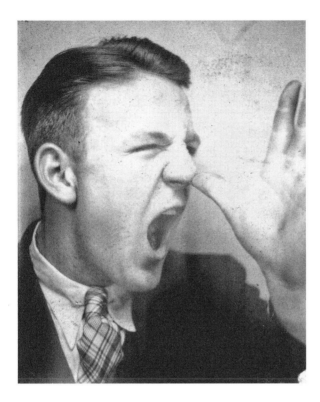

Goofing around

every day, helped Doc cook to relieve him, and served tables at Doc's Lunch." For this, Johnny received three meals a day for three hours of work a day.

Always resourceful, Johnny rooted around and found more work he could do: he cleaned a doctor's office every Saturday for fifty cents. He formed his own twelve-piece student band, Johnny Jay and the Kampus Kollegians, which played to audiences on Wednesday, Friday, and Saturday nights. Johnny himself played trumpet, and he paid each of his musicians two dollars per evening, which meant that he had four or five dollars per evening left over for himself. Though Johnny was always industrious, at least once he ran out of money. (Naturally—he was hardly out of his teens.) He wrote his dad a postcard: "No fun. No mon. Your son." His dad, in characteristic good humor, responded within the week. "Too bad. So sad! Your dad."

And the professors adored him. They understood that he had come a long way to be here. Several in particular took Johnny under their

Jumping in his best suit, 1935

Johnny Jay and the Kampus Kollegians

wings. One of these professors was Gerald Moore. "He knew that I was a coal miner and that I wanted to go into industry making chemicals from coal. Every time we got to a new topic, he'd say, 'Tomorrow study pages 17–65, and McKetta, we'll ask you to report on pages 55–58.' And it'd be on coal chemicals. He aimed those things at me. He was my professor and hero." In his wish to focus on school, Johnny retired from boxing in 1936, after a successful half-decade career. His coach, Red Richardson, advised him, "Johnny, do one thing for me. Never, ever change it. Don't ever shave in the morning until you have done your exercises." And as with all pieces of life wisdom passed on to him by men he admired, Johnny followed it all his life. For nearly seventy years, each morning he did a set of squats, sit-ups, push-ups. He stopped at age ninety-eight.

"Didn't that take a lot of willpower?" I asked him once. "Did you ever feel tempted to just skip a few days when you were on vacation?"

He shook his head. "Honey, you admired people and you tried to be like them."

While Johnny was rising fast toward a non-boxing, non-coal-mining future, the McKetta family back in Yukon was living a relatively stable life. John Senior still worked running the McKetta Coal Company with his brother Frank. Mary McKetta was working hard, keeping house, feeling proud that her children were beginning their own adult lives. Charles and Nellie were still happy as honeymooners, their daughter growing up nicely, and they were still saving money and living with John Senior and Mary. Anna Mae got married, moved out into an apartment with her husband, Merle Thomas, and began doing hair at the LaMona Beauty Salon. Life had never been easy for the McKetta family, but they had always been lucky enough to have each other, and that love struck sparks that kept them all hopeful.

But inevitably life in coal country would take more victims, and this time the death knell struck home. In February of his freshman year at college, Johnny's beloved people began to die. First he received a call on February 4 from his brother Charles, telling him that his mom was going into surgery. She had been having acute pains in her abdomen, and doctors advised a hysterectomy. Johnny came home for the surgery, which took place at the Uniontown Hospital on February 10, 1936. It was a hack job: his forty-one-year-old mother died on the operating table.

That wasn't all: under a week later, on February 14, Uncle Frank, his dad's brother and business partner, the father of his double cousins, was working on a steam shovel in their home mine. The gigantic steam shovel ("so big," my grandfather tells me, "it would fill a room") was supposed to dig away dirt so that miners could get at the coal—but this particular steam shovel had a problem with its engine. Somebody else had already taken it apart, and Uncle Frank McKetta was trying to fix the engine. But on the icy February day while he worked at it, he slipped on the ice and grabbed the motor to steady himself, and a piece of it shot out and hit him in the chest. Johnny, still at home to mourn his mother, was with his uncle when he died on the way to the hospital.

So among the items in the Uniontown newspaper on February 15, 1936, which covered the Lindbergh kidnapping trial, Roosevelt's reelection campaign, and a call for a medal for a young girl of eleven who sacrificed her life to save two boys from running into a train on a sled, there was a headline about Frank McKetta, titled "Crushed to Death beneath Shovel."[2]

Johnny stayed in Yukon for both his mother's and his uncle's funerals. The funerals were mere days apart in a small church in the center of town. In Yukon, a town of three hundred people, perhaps two hundred turned out for each funeral. Even people who did not die in accidents still died young—to live past one's fifties or sixties in a town with soot and bad air was rare. At his mother's funeral, the Yukon Volunteer Band (in which Johnny had formerly played) came to play a song. During a time when everything was falling apart, their presence and their music offered Johnny some consolation. But consolation went only so far.

The family reeled in despair—and they tried to move forward. On February 17, Johnny went back to Angola to resume his studies. He received regular news from his twenty-five-year-old brother in a letter, fragments of community news: "Source of income rather slow. . . . Everything around same as usual, Old man steps out 2 days at a time, he was out 2 days after Frank's Funeral, he told Uncle Chas to put a good word in for him with Aunt Julia, and you know what she said." This uncle Charles was the brother of the newly widowed Julia; was the new widower John Senior being sincere? Was he flirting? In the end, it did not matter.

Ten days later the worst of it happened: his brother, Charles, had gone back to work on the steam shovel that had killed their uncle. Charles saw that there was a steam leak in the back of it—he leaned in to tighten a bolt to seal the leak, but the bolt broke and Charles was burned by the steam pouring out. He died that afternoon in the hospital. Johnny was in shock.

All three, in one month. All three—his mother, his uncle, and his beloved big brother—in such ghastly ways. The death custom in these coal towns was to embalm the bodies and keep them in the house for viewing and services, but all three bodies were damaged beyond what could be preserved for friends and family to view, touch, and bid good-bye.

After Charles died, his widow, Nellie, and their three-year-old daughter moved back to Adah to live with her parents. Anna Mae returned to Yukon to stay a little while with her aunt, Frank's widow, to help and comfort her. John Senior, age forty-seven, stayed home alone, sonless, brotherless, and wifeless, in the big three-bedroom house that had at the beginning of the month housed four other McKettas. Johnny said later, "I didn't understand because I was brokenhearted. My mom was my very dear friend, and my idol was Charles—looking back I can't imagine how Pop felt."

Then in April of that same year, a fire started in the house where the whole family had lived. John Senior jumped out of a second-story window and broke both legs when he landed on concrete. "Thank God he was built well," Johnny said. The house burned down completely.

And the remarkable thing was not that Johnny and John Senior and Anna Mae went on, but that they did with such determination and—still!—love for life. All three were heart sore, and their sorrow lasted a long time. But they would go on to live well into their eighties and nineties, loving the world and its people and discovering ways to find beauty, meaning, and life after all those horrible, unnecessary February deaths.

═

Once I had a fortune cookie with this saying inside: A fool learns from his own mistakes; a wise man learns from other people's. My grandfather has always been extremely receptive to both the advice and the cautionary tales of other people. In the autobiography he wrote for his grandchildren, a number of stories are not about him but about others who made dumb errors: men who hopped into romances with women on trains and as a result were parted from their clothes and wallet, or those who tried to blackmail their professor—that sort of thing. Through these warnings costumed as hilarious stories, all his life Johnny learned from listening what to do and what not to do. He had seen whims derail good people. He knew choices mattered. He wanted a life of climbing, as his dad had climbed, only even higher and even farther away from the coal.

Johnny knew which track he wanted his life to go down, and he took extreme care to build the habits to make it possible and probable. He watched other men succeed and fail according to their scruples, their work ethics, their temperaments—all things that he could control. In this way he borrowed other experience to shape his own. But the pain of losing three close family members in a single month—that was his own, unborrowed. His own and his family's. And as much as any lesson he ever learned, this one haunted him: the idea that you had better love your family hard, faithfully, always, more than anything else—because you never know how long you'll get to keep them.

He went back to college in March and completed the year. He had a C+ average—not great but good enough for somebody who was also working fifty to sixty hours a week—and he began developing the habits that would sustain him lifelong. One was the exercise-in-the-morning habit suggested to him by Red Richardson. Each morning, he continued to do squats, crunches, lunges, wall sits, and triceps lifts for about forty-five minutes before he shaved. Then there was the early-rise habit. Like his father and all the coal miners in his childhood, he learned to go to bed early (which doubled in keeping him out of the types of trouble that his night-carousing friends fell into), and he learned to wake before everybody else and in those hours do his homework. His work ethic, formed early, never faltered. It is nothing short of remarkable, and hundreds of his students have in fact remarked on it. What drove him? What kept driving him day in and day out for an entire career and even after?

Anyone who knows his childhood knows the answer. What drove him was the intense burning desire to get away, as far away as possible, from coal.

And it seemed, from his first impressions, that a formula could be written. University is the opposite of coal mine: Aboveground/Belowground. Richly paid for enjoyable work/Poorly paid for terrible work.

Clean suits/Sooty dungarees. One of the safest professions/One of the deadliest professions. And so on. And yet the skills and discipline that helped him survive as a mediocre coal miner would help him become one of the world's best chemical engineers.

Much later, when he was a father and his middle son, Mike, wrote him a letter saying, "You and mom struggled so that I wouldn't have to—but I don't want to go straight into law school, into my life's work; I want to struggle and travel and learn first-hand how to survive,"[3] Johnny had zero empathy or interest. He thought of the coal mines, of the universities, and of the vast difference between the two. He called his son on the phone and said, asphyxiating his hopeful plans, "Don't even think about that, Mike. You've got a future all set out for you. Use it."

Johnny completed Tri-State in two and a half years. How? By working all the time. In addition to his schoolwork and his paid work, he joined the drama club and performed in one play every semester—which entailed three nights in Angola and then some traveling performances in surrounding towns. He did Shakespeare and Noel Coward, as well as a memorable stint as Bob Cratchit in *A Christmas Carol*. He loved his roommates and loved the other members of the engineering department, and with the habits he was developing and his natural way of engaging people and making them laugh, he got through college easily and with pleasure. People liked him and wanted to help him succeed.

When he was not working a job, he clung to his desk like a shipwreck survivor, learning all he could about the field he wished to enter. On the corner of his desk, he kept his dirty coal-mining cap, reminding him to work hard and save money so as never to have to work underground again. His patchwork of jobs, plus the coal-mining-cap-on-the-desk reminder, enabled him to graduate in August 1937 with a degree in chemical engineering from Tri-State and $310 in his pocket.

INTERLUDE===

A woman at Westminster came up to say hello during one of our Friday-night dinners. Johnny and Pinky greeted her warmly. They greeted the man next to her, who didn't look very happy. He was young by Westminster standards, and he complained about something minor, perhaps the food.

Johnny nodded very sympathetically while reaching into the breast pocket of his jacket, as if reaching for a handkerchief. But what he pulled out instead was a tiny card that read: "Your story is the saddest I have ever heard. Please accept this card as a token of my most sincere sympathy."

The man frowned at it and then unexpectedly began to laugh.

I had seen my grandfather hand out these cards before, once to a Vietnam War veteran with one thumb missing whose story was actually quite sad. He gave these cards out the way he gave out half dollars to children. He had a different set of homemade cards that read, "I can only please one person per day. Today is not your day. Tomorrow's not looking good either." He was like the fairy in a nursery tale, bestowing gold on the good characters and frogs and snakes on the mean ones. But we all understood the message. With the card, my grandfather was saying, *Don't dwell on your complaints, son. Be happy, young man.*

FOUR⚌MERCURY

Industry + Graduate School

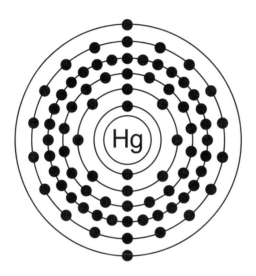

When Johnny neared graduation from Tri-State in the summer of 1937 and still didn't have a job, Professor Moore, his mentor in the Chemical Engineering Department, made some calls and set up an interview for him at Michigan Alkali in Wyandotte. Soon after the interview, Johnny received a letter from its president:

Aug 18, 1937

I received your letter and the stamps which you inclosed [*sic*].

We feel that anyone who has done as much for himself as you have so far should be worth giving an opportunity to, and although we have nothing definite, we will give you a chance to show what you can do in our Engineering Department. You will be expected to fill in and do whatever type of work they have available.

We suggest that you start to work on September 1. Your beginning salary will be $125 a month.

Please let me know if this is satisfactory.

Very truly yours, W. W. Knight, Jr.[1]

Michigan Alkali hired him for a job recovering benzene compounds from its coal-mining plant, and he remained forever grateful to Professor Moore for securing him the chance to interview. Like many of Johnny's friends and heroes, Professor Moore stuck with him for life.[2] Johnny gathered his few belongings—including the coal-miner's cap—and moved across the country to start a new life in Michigan.

As far as companies go, Michigan Alkali (now part of BASF) was an older company by the time Johnny arrived. Established in 1893 and built on a seam of salt in the earth alongside the Detroit River, the processing company used its own salt supply, combined it with limestone, and made soda ash for industrial glass production. The company used the chloralkali process—the electrolysis of brine (its salt and water from the Detroit River) to produce chlorine and sodium hydroxide (in other words, lye, or caustic soda, which made up an entire division of the company's work). This was an energy-intensive process; it had room for improvement. Also, the timing was right for the company to expand: the world suddenly demanded chlorine to produce plastic. This would need to be done more efficiently, and Johnny soon proved to be the man for the job.

There were a few things Johnny knew for certain going into his first post-college job. First, he didn't parse out whether the job had come from luck or skill or strings Professor Moore had pulled: he knew he was lucky to have a job—especially since only eight students in his class did, and since (of those eight) his was the second-highest-paying job. He knew to be grateful. He knew that luck and skill and strings all mattered: this he would remember, and he would remember it especially when mentoring his own students.

Also, he saw clearly that the future of energy would be in petroleum and natural gas, not coal; this meant that he would need to follow the oil and gas, which would eventually require him to leave Michigan. He explained, "Most reactions take place in liquid or gas phases. Coal is solid; you have to dig it out, crush it, and then treat it to become liq-

*One of his charac-
teristic silly poses,
1938*

uid or gas and then react that product to get the chemical you want. It
takes lots of energy to liquefy, or gasify, and it is costly. At that time natural gas was being burned as waste or sold at extremely low prices. Making money on your investment is the name of the game." He could enjoy working in industry now, but he would have to go back to graduate
school. And enjoy it he did.

Johnny loved working in industry. He was one of only six trained engineers in a company of fifty-five hundred workers. His specialization
made him valuable, and working there he joined one more family—

like football, like his hometown, his family, like his bands and theater groups—where he got to feel like a vital part of a much bigger whole. This position always felt good to him and served him well. He was and still is at age one hundred a social animal, a good and loyal participating member. He liked to have both significance and belonging, which twenty-first-century child psychologists not surprisingly now recognize as the dual needs of all humans.[3] Johnny recalls working on exciting projects and enjoying "the greatest cooperation from every individual that I met, whether he was the chief engineer, general manager, or the newest man on the line who was shoveling dirt at the calcium chloride plant."

His skill and work ethic were easy for anyone to see. It didn't take long for him to be promoted. In under two years, by mid-1939, he became assistant superintendent of the Caustic Soda Division—now making a dream salary of $450 per month! Michigan Alkali was a huge company with more than five thousand workers. And he was this upstart crow from nowhere-town Pennsylvania who had one thing that marked him as different from all the rest: his college degree as an engineer. It was a strange thing to have such a pedigree after having nothing. Unlike money or family members, his BS in chemical engineering was his to keep. It couldn't die; it couldn't be lost. Nobody could take it away.

At the time it hired him, Michigan Alkali had been using antiquated methods and all of its equipment was old. Johnny said, "It was a gold mine!!!! Just a heaven for a chemical engineer to straighten out. After one day I got the plant producing purer chemicals (such as benzene and toluene) at much higher efficiency, and at the end of the month they made three times more profit than ever before. So, naturally, the management encouraged us five engineers to look at other spots that could be improved and more profitable. I had the top management freedom to work at any process. None of the owners of the company were technical (all had business degrees), and us five engineers became twelve after the first year. Now about thirty percent of the company employees are technically trained."

Professionally, Johnny habitually excelled not so much at making things but at improving them. He could take old systems and make them more efficient, more organized. Like his father before him lighting up the mines with the new electricity, Johnny would become famous by taking what was understood by a few and making it useful to many. In his twenties, he was given incredible opportunities to apply his knowledge of the new science to some old established industries; he made them useful for a new era, and he would help keep them from going extinct. He took opportunities when they came—his success at Michigan Alkali was a burgeoning mixture of his own abilities and the times in which he lived. He saw what was coming, and he used his skills to help his company and himself rise.

Early in his days in the Caustic Soda Division, he met a man named Bill Cashmore, who drove a truck for the company. Johnny felt drawn to Bill because he reminded him in many ways of his brother, Charles— but Bill did one thing constantly that Charles would never have done: he complained about his wife. The most horrible things! Day after day after day. And then one day Bill Cashmore invited Johnny over for dinner. *And meet the shrew?* Johnny thought. He went reluctantly, expecting the worst—but a lovely woman opened the door and introduced herself as Ethel Cashmore. Johnny recalls that she acted like a decent person throughout the meal, but "because I had heard Bill talk about her, [I knew that] she was no good. But I had to admit that she was a mighty good actress because if I had not known her reputation, I would have fallen head over heels for her. The whole evening was just delightful, as was the dinner and all the conversation. At the end of the dinner I knew that I had been had!" It appears that Johnny's reputation as a flirt had preceded him—either that or his reputation for appreciating a good practical joke.

Bill Cashmore would matter in Johnny's life in more ways than one. He was the type of friend who provided a safe testing ground for new ideas, and this intrigued Johnny. The practical joke and first meeting with Ethel proved that Bill offered a model for Johnny both in terms of playing practical jokes in professional settings and having a happily-ever-after marriage with a great woman. Several years later when Johnny fell in love with the woman he would marry, their first date was to the Cashmores for the weekend.

Also, Bill was scrappy and willing to try new things. What resulted was that the friendship between Johnny and Bill's family blossomed into a business. Johnny was always willing to do extra work—more work meant more skills and more money, which translated into more distance between him and the coal mines—and he had the idea that they could make, bottle, and sell sodium hypochlorite (bleach). Here is why this idea made sense: Sodium hypochlorite is produced by mixing two by-products of the chloralkali process (chlorine and caustic soda) and then diluting them with water. Since Johnny and Bill had a ready supply from their work at Michigan Alkali, it just took some initiative and know-how to make a profitable moonlighting gig from the waste chemicals of their day jobs.

Bill liked the idea and brought his son Bill Jr. into the business. They marketed their product as "Sno-glo" and placed it in stores all over the area, selling it for twenty-five cents per gallon, half the price of most bleaches on the market. They made small batches, sold every ounce they made, and were very happy with their income, about two hundred dollars per month. Johnny recalls, "We set up an operating shop in Bill's garage where every night we could chlorinate the caustic soda (lye) and drink rum and Coca-Cola." The company outlasted Johnny, who moved on after a few years. The company itself lasted until Bill Jr. went off to World War II.

The war would change things for many men—what it did for Johnny was crystallize his value in the American economy. By the beginning of the US entry into World War II, Johnny was a valuable chemical engineer. His work could make a difference. His work at Michigan Alkali was the foundation in that it gave him confidence in his own ability to work among colleagues in his chosen field. And it taught him to trust his ability to excel: He told his colleagues that he would be leaving in 1940 to go to graduate school, and his letters of recommendation are shimmering. They range from, "He displays great interest in problems which are assigned to him and is quite resourceful. He was also well liked by those with whom he came into contact," from the Technical Division head at Michigan Alkali, to "He has won the friendship and respect of all who have come in contact with him in his work," from the company's superintendent, to "He has had as high as $980.00 credit and has always paid as agreed. I recommend him highly for any credit dealing," from his local credit union.[4] Unanimously people loved and trusted him. People liked to work with him.

Johnny knew by that point what his future would entail. He would teach, and he would continue his research. He would do all of it with the coal-mining cap on his desk, the memento mori that would remind him of the deathly underground. If he worked hard enough, he would never in his life have to face the coal mines again. His dream career would require a PhD, so he began visiting schools. He chose the University of Michigan for its reputation with petrochemicals and for its illustrious professors, including Dr. George Granger Brown, whose students called him "Great God" Brown. Johnny was beginning to see the possibilities of a life at a university, a life doing international energy work and being a friend to students. He would teach in castlelike buildings and spend his days walking across heavenly swaths of grass. Perhaps one day his students would joke about him as being "Great God" McKetta. But something interrupted him just before he was to start graduate school.

Chemical engineering was a small world, and his work leaked out as news. "During 1939–40 I was doing some experimental work on a gas scrubber using an alkaline liquid to remove sulfur products from the gas. The unit that I was using was an old dust collector that had been manufactured by the Claude B. Schneible Company. This was the vane type of water scrubber with natural circulation and it worked extremely well for our purpose." Claude Schneible, the company head, learned about Johnny's work and attempted to hire him to design a ceramic scrubber able to withstand corrosion. Johnny initially said no. His future lay on a college campus, he felt certain. Some part of him had known this ever since setting foot on the green lawns of Tri-State. He had imagined and planned for his future as a university professor and researcher, and he might linger for a little while but would not stay long in any environment that kept him from directly meeting his goals.

But the Schneible Company did not give up easily. It was a new company, founded in 1935, known for its production of air-pollution-control equipment. The company saw the value of Johnny's work in terms of cost and kept approaching Johnny with better and better offers. At last he and the Schneible Company worked out a compromise: Johnny would work as technical director for the company in Chicago for one year, during which he would earn $450 a month and have all his expenses— travel, lodging, food, even dry-cleaning—paid for. This year he wrote many small reports on blue paper: some were on removing hydrogen sulfide and sulfur dioxide from a gas or airstream. Both are highly toxic:

hydrogen sulfide with its trademark rotten-egg smell occurs naturally in petroleum and natural gas and is flammable and toxic; sulfur dioxide, also found in the combustion products of fossil fuels, is one of six criteria pollutants regulated by the Environmental Protection Agency (after the Clean Air Act was passed) for its harm to the respiratory system and its contribution to acid rain. Both of these pollutants could be contained and made less harmful by placing a good scrubber inside a factory smokestack. So basically Johnny was doing an air purification job. He would improve what already existed (the scrubber was a finned plate that pushed clean water through a tower filled with gas—it left the gas clean by scrubbing out unwanted chemicals). To do this, he took the scrubber to some local toolmakers and had them make the same thing out of ceramic. This would make it less expensive and hardier, able to withstand more heat and acidity. He would test and test and test it in the laboratory until it got the job done.

This one-year contract might have been insignificant except for the lesson it imprinted: big companies were willing to pay for his expertise. Johnny realized that he could accept these offers one at a time, while still dedicating his life to a university. He could learn to dart like quicksilver from goal marker to goal marker, making sure not to miss opportunities. Later in his life, he would use these opportunities to shape himself into the international energy force, and friend to all, that he would become. While he worked, he saved forty-two hundred dollars toward graduate school. Even though Schneible asked him at the end of that year to stay longer, Johnny kept his promise to himself and began graduate school in 1942.

In Michigan after a one-year hiatus, Johnny settled easily into the routine of academic life. Ann Arbor at that time was a small university town with a population of thirty thousand, over a third of its citizens students. Over the 1940s the student body would change from being mostly liberal arts to more science and technology oriented, in great part because of the university's role in training the military during the war. It was still a quiet town, and to Johnny it soon felt like home. He did research on gas and oil wells. He showed promise. His professors adored him. "Great God" Brown wrote him a letter to tell him that he has passed his master's degree tests and would be moving on to candidacy for his PhD: "My dear Mr. McKetta: The staff extends its congratulations to you to becoming an applicant for the Doctorate Degree by successfully passing the first section of the preliminary exams. We are very proud to advise that your total grade of 92.08 percent in these examinations is the highest grade ever achieved in this department."[5]

Johnny moved from his old home in Michigan during his industry days and found a room in a boardinghouse across the street from the chemical engineering building, 533 Church Street. The other seven roomers became his lifelong friends. And with the exception of sleep and some meals, he lived in the Chemical Engineering Department, where he quickly found a role model in Donald Laverne Katz. He looked up to Dr. Katz as he had once looked up to his high school coaches: ethically, professionally, and personally. Katz supervised Johnny's work on hydrocarbon-water systems at elevated pressures and temperatures. Together they developed a method, called the Katz-McKetta Method, which was essentially a "set of tables relating to underground temperature and pressure in gas and oil wells that reveal the composition of the surrounding terrain." This ability to assess the earth and its components, to see how they could be useful for energy and production, would become a lifelong interest and area of expertise for Johnny; it would pave the way for his usefulness to Texas and its rapidly developing oil and gas boom.

During graduate school, Johnny lived what we think of now as an "ordinary" college existence. He witnessed mischief and youth behaving badly, in a decidedly undergraduate way. Just as he and his cousin had picked up girls and gotten into fights, he and his roommates created and participated in story-worthy escapades. There was the time when one of the roommates, a dental student, needed to fill a gold inlay in order to pass dental school. Johnny allowed him to drill a tiny hole into one of his teeth so that he could fill it. It takes a good friend to voluntarily undergo tooth drilling. Then there was the time that one of the roomers had a clingy girlfriend who gave Johnny a shock in the middle of the night:

In late 1942 the roomer in the adjoining room next to mine was Henry Holst. Henry had a girlfriend who loved him dearly and would hound him at all hours by visiting the house, phoning, et cetera. Let's call her Gloria. One night as I lay sleeping (I've always gone to bed relatively early in the evening) I dreamt that there was a man on a horse with a big lance rushing through my room. I then dreamt that a classmate, Ed Merz, came to me and said, "Johnny, I have a date downstairs. Can we sit in your car?" I told him that he could. Then, my next dream was that a nude woman was sitting on the chair where I kept my clock, right next to my bed. As I awoke startled, I looked and there sure enough was a nude woman, Gloria, crying and asking me, "Where is Henry Holst?" It seemed she came to visit Henry, removed all her clothes and lay in his bed waiting for him. I jumped up and asked the important question, "Where is my alarm clock?" She got up and sure enough she had been sitting on my alarm clock. I told her to get her clothes on and leave the house right away; otherwise I would call the police, because I did not want to embarrass Mrs. Kearney, who was a lovely landlady. Gloria did so, and as I escorted her out the front door I noticed some movement in my car. When I went over to look in the car there was Ed Merz and his date in the backseat doing what should be done in the backseat. So I wasn't dreaming after all. Therefore I ran upstairs to look for the knight on the horse with his lance. I never did find him.

I love this story for the details of Johnny's life at the time. Of course he went to bed and woke up early—those are coal-mining hours. Also his memory of waking up to a nude woman and asking instead about his alarm clock hearkens back to the eternal divide of the struggling worker, positioning temptations of flesh versus the clock. Which one wins? Duty, of course. In addition to the healthy dose of roommate dramatics, Johnny—as usual—found his way into some extra jobs. He worked as a sorority house cook at Gamma Phi Beta, which doubled in securing him three meals a day and keeping him surrounded by young women.

Beginning in 1943, he taught several courses of the Naval Reserve Officers and of the Army Specialized Training Program, which rushed soldiers through a bachelor's degree program in eighteen months, sending them, degrees in hand, to earn commissions in the military. "Great God" Brown sanctioned this teaching opportunity as a way to help keep Johnny from being drafted. His draft designation was 1-A, meaning "available; fit for general military service." Also, he was twenty-six years old, one year older than the maximum age for the draft that swept away 95 percent of Michigan's male students.

During the war years, Johnny worked ten hours a week on the separation of uranium isotopes (separating Uranium 235 from 238) under Dr. Ed Baker. "I didn't even know what uranium was because we never took it up even in advanced chemistry class. But we had to swear we would never tell anyone what we were doing." This work on uranium separation soon led to the production of the atom bomb, so in a covert way, Johnny's research contributed to the Manhattan Project and developing the first nuclear weapons.

Each career has its moral quandaries, and Johnny observed that this was one of his. Albert Einstein himself urged the government to try to produce the atom bomb before Germany did. Certain physicists must have had knowledge of the possibility, but Johnny wasn't a part of that community. His training was specialized in a different way. He could do the work, but he didn't understand its full possibilities. He must have known he was doing valuable wartime work, at least by virtue of the demand for secrecy; but like many men who do not go to fight during wars, he probably felt some guilt. Most of the men he knew, both friends and students, were drafted; his cousin Frank served in the military, later returning to an impressive career as a Pennsylvania law enforcement officer (and ultimately chief of the Federal Protective Service—it is a point worth making that the McKetta immigrant generation raised both of these sons to rise above the typical coal miner's life). So while the war ravaged Europe and killed so many men, Johnny's work on this weapon excused him and kept him alive. After 1943, when the draft age was raised to thirty, Dr. Baker had to write to the government excusing Johnny from military service based on his secret uranium work. It would eventually be his wife, in fact, who realized the connection between Johnny's laboratory work and the bomb: "One day Pinky brought me a paper at breakfast that said 'U.S. Uses Atom Bomb on Japan.' That was the first time it dawned upon me that I was working on one little phase of the nuclear bomb."

The whole time he was doing research and taking classes in school, the work ethic part was easy for him: his amazement that *this was work* never left him, and he treated graduate school as an important job. He worked days and nights. He made friends with all his colleagues. He made practically a second career in being his friends' best man in their weddings (fourteen times, he says, and only one divorce). He worked more. While all around the world war raged, Johnny took very seriously the fact that his studies and his professors had kept him alive

Postcard of the Little Shop, the café where Johnny and Pinky first met

June 21, 1955

Surprise Honey! — here's where it all started. Charley and I ate leench here today. It's the same. Gee, travelling thru town gives me spine tingles. As we drive thru some very fond memories come back. And you know what? — — you are a part of each and everyone of them. thank you for meeting me here in May, 1949. I love you, mucho mucho,

Johnny

The back of the Little Shop postcard sent from Johnny to Pinky in 1955: "Here's where it all started."

twice: once from the coal mines, now from the war. And into the night he worked.

One night, around 10:00 p.m., on May 5, 1943, he was all set to run an experiment but found that his mercury pump wouldn't work. This set him back. But what can a chemical engineer do? Stay in the laboratory all night and curse at the broken pump, or go outside into the rain-soaked spring evening and have a cup of coffee and come up with a new plan?

He took the second option. And his broken pump and unplanned stop at the Little Shop in downtown Ann Arbor would constitute a second interruption between Johnny and his immaculately planned future. A brilliant interruption. An interruption that would change his entire life. I've heard him say, "Some men are eyes men. Some are breasts men. I am a smile man. And the most beautiful smile I've ever seen walked into that diner on May 5, 1943."

It was Helen Elisabeth Smith, twenty-three years old. She was with a friend who knew Johnny. He sat with them. All the while he felt something about this woman. She Was It. They talked for forty-five minutes—about the draft, the war, cars, experiments. Who cared, really, what they talked about, for all Johnny wanted was to keep the talking going so that he could drive this woman home. He had his 1940 LaSalle parked right outside, it was raining, so far he had been charming, he thought, and so he hoped.

After nearly an hour, the women needed to go home. Gallantly, Johnny offered to drive them. The women peered out at the rain and accepted. He dropped off the friend first. Then from here the versions of the story differ. In one version Johnny proposed to Helen that very night, roughly an hour and a half after they first met. In another, he simply asked if he might call her. Either way, he had placed a stone marking the head of his interest. She would have understood.

INTERLUDE=

Many McKettas are in town to celebrate a family birthday. We are placing dishes on the table for McKetta Brunch, a family Sunday affair notable for its 8:15 a.m. start time, which no reasonable person would categorize as "brunch." We are all awake and coffee is flowing and we are telling jokes and making wordplay. Randy, the youngest of Johnny and Pinky's sons and a chemical engineer like his father, is listening to his dad talk about somebody in their field. Mike, the middle son, first nods his head reverently, then makes a joke about the initials *Ch.E.* Charley, the oldest son, says that anything with the letters *C*, *H*, and *E* in it has got to be a good thing.

My grandmother sits quietly, listening, near the head of the table where my grandfather sits. She is the best of us with words, though she speaks the fewest. There is no pause for breath before she responds: "Cheat. Ache. Lecher. Catastrophe."

FIVE═HONEY

Love + Marriage

Unlike Johnny, Helen Elisabeth Smith grew up in a comfortably middle-class lifestyle in Kalamazoo, Michigan—a city slightly bigger at the time than Ann Arbor. Kalamazoo was known for Gibson guitars, paper mills, and the number-one hit song "I've Got a Gal in Kalamazoo," a song Johnny undoubtedly sang to his bride-to-be during their courtship. Helen was born in 1920 to Anne Ewing and Robert Andrew Smith, the little sister to Robert Jr. Like Johnny she was the family's youngest. It could be said that the Smiths were one generation of American success ahead of the McKettas, for both of Helen's parents were born in Pennsylvania—a different part of coal country, but coal country all the same. Perhaps this shared background led in part to Johnny and Pinky's interest in each other. She would have heard from her parents the stories about coal; he actually lived it.

Here the similarities ended. The Smiths were Republicans, Presbyterians, and college graduates. Robert Smith came from Pennsylvania, the son of a jack-of-all-trades father who practiced law, manned a drugstore, and served his parish as a Presbyterian minister. Anne Ewing came from a socially pedigreed lineage: her parents, Ertinsa Shaver and William Ewing, had lived in the Shaver Mansion in Mount Union and had helped with the Temperance movement; her ancestors had been directly involved in securing American independence, which qualified her as a bona fide Daughter of the American Revolution. It is often said that smart men marry up.

Helen's dad worked in the automobile industry—he sold cars, owned a service station, and worked for Oldsmobile—while her mom started a successful advertising business and at one time listed her career as "city hostess." Having both parents working outside the home left Helen and Robert in a welcome state of freedom and independence. When the Depression hit and her father needed new work, he moved to Lansing, Michigan, while her mother stayed in Kalamazoo, and it was clear that, although she spoke neutrally of both, her heart stayed with her father. Whenever Helen had the choice, she favored Oldsmobile cars. Whenever we as her grandchildren asked about her mother, her only response was, "Mother was a businesswoman." In a self-analysis written for a college psychology class, she observed: "Mother is rather easily disturbed and excited, and I always found it much less wearing to exhibit little initiative, and to be scolded for not doing anything, than it was to do things on my own and be scolded for not doing them right. As a child, I was always a little afraid of my mother."

The Depression gutted the Smith family, stripping away their security of having the whole family live in one place. Helen recalled feeling homesick while she was living with her mother and her dad was away. She noted in her self-analysis that for quite some time "home as a unity for us hasn't existed." Interestingly, because of their relative affluence, the two-parent income of the Smith house, the Depression hit them harder than it hit the poorer McKettas, for whom poverty was no surprise. The Smiths managed to hold on to their house, even without the whole family in it, during the 1930s, but by 1940 Anne Ewing Smith was registered as "head of household" in a rented home.

Helen Elisabeth Smith was one of those people who never had the chance to enjoy her real name: in childhood she was called "Honey," and as soon as she grew up, moved out, and met my grandfather, he nicknamed her "Pinky." When she became a grandmother, we called her Baba. (But I was named after her, so at least her middle name gets some good use today!) At the same time, she was also one of those people who take life in a sort of humorous and realistic stride. If somebody had pointed this out, she would probably have said "yes," accepting it, and then made a quiet joke. She rarely expected things to turn out perfectly; she rarely complained. All her life she had a polite smile and mischievous eyes and a deadpan sense of humor. She seemed, overall, grateful for her life—but in a quiet, calmest-of-calm way. She rarely participated in argument, but she was also not a pushover. She observed of herself: "I really care little one way or another as to what my friends or the country wants or achieves, but I do know where I stand if I am forced to show an interest."

She was a ravenous reader and preferred reading to interacting with most people. She wrote of her adolescence: "The boys whom I had known for years stopped calling me by my nickname of 'Honey,' I began to form a few close friends among the girls, and I began to be irreverently flip to my parents and acquaintances, while at the same time I began to feel emotional about Tchaikovsky's 'None but the Lonely Heart.'" She felt unprepared for adolescence, and she did not confide much in her mother or her friends: "I didn't even know why or how a baby came until I was over sixteen years old, and that knowledge came from reading a magazine article about how a mother should tell her inquisitive five-year-old where he came from. Apparently I was eleven years behind the times."[1]

And she kept notebooks: meticulous ones. While a student at Kalamazoo High School, she developed a teenage crush-from-afar on the American singer/actor/heartthrob Nelson Eddy. Helen kept an entire notebook of carefully clipped and pasted Nelson Eddy articles, dates and sources written in her careful script—it turns out she, like Johnny, was a natural archivist. In an article from *Photoplay* (September 1936), written by Howard Sharpe, the young Eddy is described as telling his mother that he wants to work instead of going to school—that he could study at home. He had been reading too many Alger novels, his mother said when he made his proposal, but still she said yes. So he began at fourteen an apprenticeship at a plumbing fixture store owned by his uncle—and then moved on to newspaper reporting, studying all the while. A self-made man, a hunk at that, chronicled by the one-day first lady of chemical engineering. Were there seeds sown of loving a self-made man? Somebody who knew life closely by age fourteen, who had risen up through independent spirit and hard work? Johnny himself was also in a band, had stage presence, and was in many ways self-taught (though when asked about his successes, he is always quick to credit his teachers). His life contained tremendous self-made meaning; he was also charming and had a sweet, impish smile.

Soon before meeting Johnny, Helen had graduated from Western Michigan Teachers College. She kept her college essays. She wrote in 1938, in an essay called "In Esteem of Essayists," "To judge by the majority of great artists, it is true that genius seems to thrive in the midst of adversity. Charles Lamb and William Hazlitt are two very convincing proofs of this unoriginal theory." She was eighteen: she knew her voice, knew the limits of her originality, knew how to craft finely wrought essays using words like "misanthrope." Also she took an interest thematically in people who rose above their misfortunes. This is my thesis, anyway, about what she initially saw in Johnny. He saw wife material in the instant.

In college Helen wrote in an essay about Keats: "[His] earliest poems show a boy in love with words." You could substitute boy with girl and say the same thing about Helen Elisabeth Smith. She adored literature: words were her thing. She wrote an essay describing the work of Edna St. Vincent Millay that was so persuasive that her professor wrote in his comments, "By careful attention to some of the points in [Miss Smith's] paper, I found that some of my ideas about Millay had to be reconstructed."

Like Keats, Helen adored words, but she had reservations about the compulsions of school. In an essay titled "Science and Religion" for a class on nineteenth-century prose, she wrote in her introduction: "When such men as Huxley, Jeans, Eddington, and Kant have utilized years in thought and research on the relations of science upon religious thinking, it is rather a humorous fallacy for a college sophomore, with practically no experience, knowledge of science, philosophy or religion, to attempt an explanation of the implications of science upon modern religious thought. Under the circumstances, the best I can do is to cross

Pinky's high school senior photo

my fingers and explain my understanding of the subject as I have assimilated it, to some extent from readings of Huxley, W. R. Inge, J. C. Ransom, and J. A. Thomson, and mainly from my own convictions." Unlike Johnny, for whom education was a lifeline to do great things, a beanstalk taking him up, up, up, for Helen a life spent reading was enough. College was a formality, a waiting ground before the inevitable marriage, children, and other myriad distractions from reading.

Her awareness of her own mortality shaped her youth; unlike Johnny, who saw his beloveds die, even sat with them while they were dying, Helen's awareness of mortality was more poetic; it came from her reading. "During my teens I was Pagliacci, I was a poetess, I was unique. No one who said the days of childhood were the happiest days knew what they were talking about. It must have been at this time I decided not to be a teacher or a librarian—there wasn't much use in planning for the future when I was sure that I would never live to be twenty."

Before meeting Johnny, she had had crushes—but "the difficulty was that the boys, on closer acquaintance, didn't exhibit the wonderful qualities I had seen in them at a distance." She played safe: "Rather than show my awkwardness on the dance floor, I said I didn't like to dance. That's still my excuse. Rather than have dates with the boys who asked me, I stayed home and read. Mother was rather expert at golf and bridge; I refused to try to learn either game, even when free golf lessons were offered me. My best friend was an expert piano player; I stopped playing my piano at all. Fortunately, I could easily bring home an all 'A' report card, or I might have quit school, too." She stuck with the activities that were unthreatening. She skipped her senior prom. In college, she turned down invitations to join sororities and said no to dates with interested men—avoiding "relationships which would make any demands on me."

Toward the end of college, she worked full-time as an information clerk in the Records Office at Western Michigan Teachers College. It was easy for her to balance this work and her schoolwork, but she had fallen in love for the first time and was reckoning with romance's impact on her formerly controlled life. "I wasn't prepared to fall in love; but now I have done so and find it demanding, unavoidable, and pleasant." Note that pleasant comes third. Again and again we see in Helen a portrait of a self-contained woman, more virgin goddess than vulnerable one. It was in this college first love that she realized for the first time "that what I really want out of life is to spend it in sympathy and understanding with some one individual." Luckily Johnny would benefit from the timing of meeting her: her first love, which did not last long, left her open and ready for what would become her great love.

There are different versions of their courtship. One version says that he called her and proposed every day for six weeks until she said yes. Another version, which Johnny cites in his autobiography, goes that for a month after meeting her he got busy with his PhD preliminary exams, and he finally called her on June 6 to invite her for a weekend in Detroit with the Cashmores. She said yes to the Detroit weekend—but secretly purchased a return railroad ticket in case the date went south. She wore a pink blouse for the drive to Detroit, solidifying in Johnny's mind her obvious nickname: Pinky. They all had a grand time, the best weekend-long double date ever, with good meals, laughter, and evening storytelling bringing together Bill and Ethel and Johnny and Pinky.

From there on, the versions are all the same: he called her daily asking her hand in marriage, and after five months of giving him a flat

Pinky laughing at the Cashmores' house in Detroit on their first date weekend

The wedding day! (and Johnny's twenty-eighth birthday), October 17, 1943

no, she at last agreed. Their wedding took place on October 17, 1943, the day of Johnny's twenty-eighth birthday. She was twenty-three. She wore a blue dress and a veiled hat with an enormous rose on the front. In the wedding photo, a close-up of their faces, her dark curls frame her face, and she smiles frankly, directly. He has his hair parted neatly and squints in the sun at the camera; he cannot believe his luck. He wore a borrowed suit from one of his classmates (which fifty years later the lender sent back to Johnny in tatters and said, "You throw it out; you were married in it"). Johnny remembers the wedding on the tips of their toes, literally, because they couldn't find their footing when the preacher kept instructing them to step this way or that. "I was so excited that I was marrying my dream girl." It was a tiny wedding near the boarding-house where Johnny lived. The other boarders congratulated them and wished them well on their honeymoon.

A few things happened on their frugal honeymoon, a trip to Union-town, Pennsylvania, to stay with Johnny's sister, Anna Mae, that forced them into the position of seeing each other in a new light faster than usual. One was that the boat ride from Detroit to Cleveland over Lake Erie left Johnny stuck in the bunk with seasickness. So picture Helen Elisabeth Smith, now entering into a new era as Pinky McKetta, waiting in her black honeymoon negligee while her husband spent the night throwing up in the bathroom—what he later called "a very disappointing honeymoon night" for Pinky. Then, first thing in the morning, she woke to see him on the floor, contorted and out of breath. "Are you okay, Johnny?" she asked. He did not look okay.

"Yes, honey," he gasped. "I am doing my morning exercises."

The rest of the honeymoon had some small notable episodes. They were hitchhiking, and the first driver who picked them up took them to a bar for drinks and got them "crocked," and then the next driver immediately after that was a priest who put them out of the car after a few blocks because they reeked of booze. Johnny's sister and her family took in the newlyweds and introduced them around town, roasting and toasting them. After three days of that, Johnny and Pinky took a Grey-hound bus to Niagara Falls for two nights, and from there they took a bus back home. They both felt ecstatic. They were beginning a new life and their honeymoon would last forever, and they were so young and a whole life of adventures spread before them like a deep pink sunrise.

INTERLUDE=

Westminster Manor, 2010, the usual Friday night. My husband and I arrive in the lobby at 4:55 p.m., say hello to the people at the front desk, and take the stairs, two at a time, to the second-floor suite where my grandparents live. Both are seated at their cribbage table, dressed for dinner. My grandmother wears a pale green suit and a turtle necklace. She is quiet and elegant, as always. My grandfather is beaming, fidgeting, and tapping his feet in his orange-and-white shoes. This Friday night marks the end of two years of the weekly dinners my husband and I have shared with my grandparents: my husband and I are leaving Texas to start our own family across the country.

Over dinner, Pinky asks if I am looking forward to nesting. The tone of her voice is fading, but her questions are still good. She looks at me, and I realize that this dinner may be one of the last meals I share with my grandmother; I will see her again in the autumn for Johnny's ninety-fifth birthday party.

In January she will go into hospice care the same cold clear day that my daughter will be born. (My grandmother and my daughter will share the same love of words, the same curls.)

My grandparents ask questions about our new house, our new city, whether we have friends there already. We tell them about the small white house with green trim where we lived together before we were married and where we will live again.

"Wait!" My grandfather interrupts us abruptly. "You shared a house before you were married?"

Pinky places a hand gently on his arm. "I'll explain everything later," she says.

SIX═CHALK
A Young Professor in Texas

$$Ca^{2+}$$

$$^-O \diagdown \diagup O^-$$

$$\|$$

$$O$$

A fter the honeymoon they moved into a small apartment together at 418 Hill Street. Johnny said good-bye to Mrs. Kearney, and Pinky let her apartment go.

They began practicing marriage. They devised the systems that would bridge them toward (they hoped) stability, wealth, health, healthy children, and an overall good time. He continued as a teaching fellow employed by the University of Michigan. She continued her job as information clerk in the Records Office at Western College, earning fifty dollars a month, while he earned just fifteen. They combined their earnings and budgeted to the penny. They put aside 10 percent of their small combined income for savings, just as his parents had. They were poor and had grand plans, and they were "deliriously happy." They talked about their future and planned to be a family as close-knit and openly affectionate as the McKettas had been during Johnny's childhood. The Smiths, Johnny remembers, were "bright, highly moral, and would talk to you if you started the conversation. They had love within themselves and shared it, but you did not know it until later." But Pinky wanted to be the matriarch of a more openly loving family, one that kissed and hugged and talked about everything. She told Johnny this and he understood and agreed.

They struggled initially, as many newly marrieds do, to find activities they both enjoyed. After failed attempts to introduce each other to their favorite forms of entertainment, they made a pact that Johnny would never have to go to an opera or concert (too boring) and Pinky would never have to go to a boxing or wrestling match (too bloody). And they found something that was free that they both enjoyed: playing cards. Both came to the marriage knowing how to play cribbage, a card game that involves putting tiny pegs in a board to chart each player's progress and points. Johnny could not recall a single meal at home that wasn't followed by a game of cribbage. "Pinky was so smart, and such a good player, and several times when we were traveling she would pull a deck of cards out of her hand bag and we would play cribbage. I would guess our overall average of winnings were sixty-five percent for Baba and thirty-five percent for me." Their habit of playing cribbage between breakfast and work would last their entire lives.

They settled quickly into a routine in Ann Arbor. Between 1943 and 1946 (when Johnny graduated), most days they woke at six, finished breakfast (and cribbage) by eight, at which point Pinky went to work and Johnny went to class and labs until five. They had dinner at six, and Johnny returned to the labs until 9:30 p.m., Monday through Saturday—the harder he worked, the faster he would get through school, and the sooner they would begin earning money. He said of their long days apart, "It seems dull for most, but for us absence made the heart grow fonder." Sunday—the same day the coal mines closed—was their day to be together. Sundays they went to church, had lunch, walked in an arboretum or a park, visited a friend, went on a drive, had dinner, and then played cribbage until bedtime. Their love and trust in each other deepened. Pinky told him one of these Sundays, "We share our souls." That became a catchphrase for them. When they were apart in a crowd and would catch each other's eye, one of them would mouth "SOS."

The newlyweds in 1945

Even with their divergent days and their frugality, they would always remember Kalamazoo as a place of great romance. Twelve years after they met, Johnny was back in Michigan and sent his wife a photo of the Little Shop with a note on the back: "Travelling thru town gives me spine tingles. As we drive thru, some very fond memories come back and you know what?—you are a part of each and everyone of them. Thank you for meeting me here in May, 1943. I love you, mucho, mucho, Johnny."[1]

Their ways of complementing each other charmed their friends. Back in college, Pinky had written in her class notebook about humor: "Smile is of intellect; laugh is of belly. Should be as much enjoyment in the kind of wit you smile at as the kind of wit you laugh at." In their early years of marriage she and Johnny were forming into an entity that would be funny, entertaining, likable. Her forte was clearly wit; at her words people would smile. Johnny's strength was in antics and stories that would make people belly laugh. Together they entertained each other. They worked.

One morning in September 1944 Pinky seemed quieter than usual over breakfast. At last she told Johnny, "I have bad news for you." She had missed her period and was pregnant and apologized that she hadn't told him earlier. Johnny's response: "I jumped from my breakfast seat and five feet toward the ceiling screaming, 'We're gonna have a baby!!!!! Oh, honey, what good news you've given me this moment. I am so happy for us.' She began to smile and cry and she said 'SOS' softly. Then she said, 'If the baby is a girl, I would like to name her Mary Anne for your mother and my mother. If the child is a boy, of course we will name him after you.'"

The pregnancy went well—Johnny took an extra job at the university so they would have a little extra money, and both Pinky and Johnny felt thrilled and excited for the birth. At the birth, men were not allowed into the hospital room, so while Pinky labored for nineteen hours in the spring of 1945, Johnny was supposed to sit in the waiting room, but instead of sitting, he discovered a tiny window between the waiting room and delivery room and spent most of the nineteen hours standing with his feet on the door knob while he tried to peek into the room. Finally, a boy was born. Finally, Johnny was allowed into the room. Pinky looked up, happy and fatigued, and said, "I know we talked about naming him after you, but I know how you idolized your older brother, and I hope we can name this first one Charles William, and I promise the second son will be named after you." And—this fact astonishes me—they played a game of cribbage while the newborn baby slept.

Things changed, of course. Among other changes, Pinky stopped working and Johnny spent more time at home on weekends, and he planned to stop working late evenings once he graduated. Charley was a smiling, happy, quiet baby, and the young family was in the particular form of paradise that comes when you've made something together that you both really like. They were proud of their creation. They wanted more.

=

In 1946 Johnny graduated with a PhD from Michigan. He won awards for his work, including the Allied Chemical Award for Outstanding

Engineering Student. His references shimmered. The Katz-McKetta Method that he helped devise was being put to use in places like Texas, where gas and oil wells were plentiful and needing to be assessed. His method and his expertise would follow him, like the tail of a bright comet, during the next phase of his life in academia.

Finding a job was easy. He went where instructors were in demand and oil wells were plentiful. He recalls:

> Because of the war years there were very few graduate students available and in 1946 I was one of the very few PhD Chemical Engineering Graduates in the entire country. As a result I had many, many offers from industries and universities. MIT, Wisconsin, Caltech, and many others had offered me jobs. I knew by then that I wanted to go into teaching and that I wanted to go somewhere where I could do research in the petrochemical or petroleum area. This brought the decision down to Oklahoma, Texas, or Louisiana. I chose the University of Texas and that was again an extremely good choice. The salary was $3,400 per year, which was $283 per month. Pretty good for a guy who was making $450 a month with a BS degree before he left industry to get a PhD. But fortunately the choice was a great one, and I've been very very happy here with the faculty, staff, all the students and everything else. Pinky and I found out this was such a lovely place to raise our family.

They drove down and moved in the summer to a small house near the university. Neither John nor Pinky was prepared for the heat. Austin, Texas, in 1946, population 115,000, was still a quiet town with an abundance of trees. Its Chemical Engineering Department and Johnny were exactly the same age. The department was founded in September 1915—he was born across the country one month later. It first began offering classes the year my grandfather turned two. Fittingly, the department and the man for whom the department was ultimately named would grow and age together.

The University of Texas Chemical Engineering Department's early records list only three chemical engineering majors in the 1915–16 school year: none of the three graduated, which suggests they went off to fight in World War I and never came home. All aspiring chemical engineers were required to learn German. The German made sense because the United States then depended on Germany for its chemical industry expertise. But in the early 1900s, the great state of Texas was an unspoiled garden of natural resources. Its Gulf Coast had abundant sulfur and petroleum, oil and minerals. The central part of the state had seemingly endless pine trees for lumber and for pulp; and in East Texas several oil wells had recently gushed, making men and women rich from the "black gold." The first of these, a field called Spindletop located near Beaumont, blew in 1901 and ushered in the biggest oil boom the world had ever seen, producing eight hundred thousand barrels in nine days.[2] These natural resources could make a lot of energy. Suddenly all eyes were on Texas.

Naturally, somebody needed to figure out what to do with all these raw materials. All of a sudden these resources mattered, as did the scientists who could convert them in huge quantities for humans to use. Texas pine tree pulp was becoming Kraft paper. Sulfur from the coast was being used for a whole host of purposes, including gunpowder, fertilizers, disinfectants, and the vulcanization of rubber. Natural gas could produce helium, which might one day be useful to make machines that could fly. In 1914, the year Johnny was conceived and World War I began, Texas had twelve oil refineries operating. The cat was out of the bag. The oil was out of the ground. This was not the first time a petroleum rush had happened on US soil—the first successful oil well was discovered in western Pennsylvania in 1859—but the wells in Texas were productive and receiving a great deal of attention. The nation's largest state (this was before Alaska became a state) was turning out to be good for something besides agriculture. In other words, American chemical engineering was an infant industry on the rise.

Before the political and social churning that produced World War I, America had depended on Germany for chemical imports—but with the world at war, depending on Germany was out of the question. It was clear that America's chemical industry needed to come into its own fast. So the department began in 1915: the scrappy lovechild of the more established Chemistry and Engineering Departments. Chemistry sorted out the funding, and Engineering set the curriculum. Students would learn an engineer's mastery of handling machinery, a chemist's mastery of processing and manufacturing. Dr. Eugene P. Schoch, a chemistry professor, founded the department after a childhood friend showed up in his office carrying a bag of dirt. The friend had come to ask why the dirt in his small Texas town had stopped yielding crops. This was

Dr. Schoch's eureka moment. He realized that the University of Texas needed a department whose focus would be "applying chemistry to the use of Texas raw materials to advance the economic well being of the state and its citizens."[3] Its basis was quite practical: *We have this; let's make it into that! And let's hope it makes some money.* Put in a crude way, chemical engineering was a trash-to-treasure endeavor. Things that most reasonable people would consider waste (oyster shells from the bay, for example) could be turned into chemicals that would make the modern world run. Texas, it turned out, had a lot of "trash."

Despite its bounty of lime, cement, cottonseed oil, sulfur, and acid plants, Texas was mostly about oil: the demand in the United States was for gasoline. Early-century refineries heated huge drums of oil over fires, burning off the "coke" so that the oil would purify.[4] Oil was also discovered on land that the University of Texas owned—Santa Rita in 1920, which ushered in the Permian Basin oil field—which guaranteed the university's financial security early in the century. The department was, to a great extent, a systems maker. In the days before it, any fool with a backyard bit of oil could become an oilman, but with a bit of education, chemical engineers could unify nationwide to set out basic operations for any chemical process—in other words, chemical processing systems that could be done on a huge industrial scale.

The chemical engineers were practical, and they were hardworking. They were also, mostly, goofballs. They inherited from the chemists a joking culture. Even as far back as 1911, when the Chemistry Department used little "shacks" for laboratories, there was a university parade to initiate a new shack, but instead of champagne one of the chemistry students broke a bottle of a bubbly, foul-smelling liquid.[5] These people had access to the potions and understood how they worked, when they would cause trouble and when not. Nobody else could experiment with things that burned and exploded. It was the start of the Chemical Engineering Department culture of the jokers.

The pioneering faculty members, most of all its energetic founder, Dr. Schoch, got to build the department from the ground up. His class notes became the department's "textbook." The very nature of the department's genesis required its members to be constantly inventive. Texas industry, growing beyond anyone's wildest dreams, needed all the chemical engineers the department could provide. By 1920, the department had the marks of a success, and it expanded into a one-year master's program, a research program that could manufacture graduate students who in turn could manufacture more resources.[6] Using his love of people and his love of chemical processes, Schoch stood as a matchmaker, linking students and Texas industry and becoming a hero to both. Johnny's role in the department could, decades later, be described the same way.

A decade before Johnny arrived, Schoch hired his former teaching assistant, Bill Cunningham, to be a full-time professor. These two Texas men set the stage for the kind of professor, scientist, and community man Johnny would become. While Schoch was a mentor in terms of relationships with industry and vision for the department, Cunningham was a friend to all students, a mentor of the heart: the man who always kept a drawer full of ten-, twenty-, and fifty-dollar bills available for students who needed to borrow money and who invited students to dinner at his house for barbecued homegrown rabbit, Texas-style pinto beans cooked with salt pork, light bread with honey, and ice cream and homemade cake (both made by his wife, Mary, with honey, as sugar was rationed).[7] Cunningham also began the *Chemical Engineering Newsletter* to keep students in touch with their home department. This was an early effort at alumni friendship, and it set the foundation for what Johnny would later continue by calling his students and hosting graduate lunches. My point here is that "self-made men" are myths: a man like Johnny is made up from the material of his mentors. Johnny trained himself to learn from them, to be great like them, to rise to meet their energy.

When Johnny entered the chemical engineering profession as a young assistant professor in 1946, he stepped onto a parabola that was on the rise. The industry had been called "Depression-proof" because it flourished in the 1930s while the rest of the nation flopped. Chemical engineers could always find work, and at the time when Johnny joined the university the four big American chemical companies—Union Carbide, Shell, Dow, and Humble (later Exxon)—all were working fast to research petrochemicals and to open new plants in Texas, a state that also appeared Depression-proof.[8] The Depression, if anything, added to the field's expansion, for it constantly sought more efficient processes and better ways to save energy and reuse waste. New processes were being invented, such as hydrogenation, catalytic cracking, isomerization, cy-clization, polymerization, and alkylation. Johnny entered an industry that seemed invincible, an industry that was rising into Schoch's predic-tion of "an era of chemical manufacturing which is likely to assume un-dreamed of dimensions."[9]

The university itself, instead of a weedy Texas shantytown, in 1946 looked more like a park with landscaped walkways and modern build-ings. When Johnny first walked on campus, the small unpainted (oc-casionally exploding) chemistry shacks had been replaced by a state-of-the-art chemistry building with a huge five- by fifteen-foot stone-top table in the middle of the laboratory room and a half-ton crane span-ning the room. This room was referred to as "The Big Lab," and some professional organizations even used it: The Bureau of Industrial Chem-istry used it to test the alcohol content of Texas beers and wine. The bu-reau tested a bit from each bottle and left the rest for the engineers to drink. Students could enroll in a road-trip class called "Inspection Trip" where they got to visit chemical plants on the Gulf Coast, driving by the night flares of natural gas,[10] like giant tiki torches, that lit up the road-side between Corpus Christi and Beaumont.[11] These guys were privi-leged. All doors were flung open to them. The students had a grand old time, because who wouldn't?

The chemical engineering students were made aware of their value. Like Johnny up in Michigan, many of these students whose research was considered "essential" (as most Ch.E. research was) were given de-ferment from World War II. Instead of serving in uniform, these men spent the war staying up late in their labs, figuring out how to make syn-thetic rubber from acetylene and doing all sorts of experiments on the grateful government's dime. The war effort needed chemical engineers badly, for it takes a lot of petroleum products, chemicals, and equip-ment to wage a war. The war sealed the deal on Texas being crowned king of petroleum. The value of its chemical plants rose from $4 mil-lion in 1939 to $235 million in 1947, making the Texas Gulf Coast the largest petroleum refining area in the world.[12] Not surprisingly, oil and chemicals were considered the best stock market investments, and high school boys who excelled in math and chemistry (girls did not get this push until later in the century) were steered toward college majors in the chemical engineering field. Each new wave of graduates became the next leaders in the wildly growing industry. They became solid, methodical solvers of the nation's chemical problems, and they put their brainpower toward solving potential problems that might one day exist. Engineers seemed to be weaving the future while the world watched. If there were ever a place poised to generate energy, Texas was it.

It is easy to see why the University of Texas hired Johnny. He was innovative, scrappy, bighearted, and could run an experiment like nobody's business, working tirelessly and keeping at it until he got the results he needed. He could explain things clearly. He could make and keep friends. He had experience in industry and knew a lot about hydrocarbons, and he was quickly learning more. So, PhD in hand, seven years of well-paid industry work in his pocket, John J. McKetta Jr. joined the faculty in September 1946 as assistant professor. He was assigned five courses, three lectures that met in the morning and two laboratory courses that met in the afternoon, and the rest of the time he was free to study and begin his own research programs. He recalls that "the chemical engineering faculty wisely insisted that there be no lunch courses, so we all (four faculty and five staff members) brought our lunch and met in a study room and ate and talked and planned and dreamed about our research."

Johnny was a man of his times, and his teaching philosophy was simple: he wanted to be close to his students and treat them as equals, and he wanted to answer every question—just as the professors he admired did. He felt good when he could do these things. In September 1946, his first month of teaching, the department enrollment had ballooned from a reasonable 196 students to 447 students, nearly all veterans home from the war and entitled to an education through the GI Bill.[13] Because there were so many students, the classrooms reached capacity, so UT erected a village of temporary wooden buildings. The GI Bill signaled a new era in the American college with a "chicken-in-every-pot" approach to education. The old exclusivity was giving way to a mass scale—not coincidentally the same transition that all businesses, including the chemical industry, experienced in the first half of the century. University culture was tipping: it was still old academia with professors in suits taking long lunches—they were the men; the students were the boys. Yet it was shifting too, and different sorts of men were entering: men in their twenties, men with wives and children, men who looked

In characteristic form, he wrote on each student's chest his name, and on himself he wrote, "BELT!"

their professors in the eye as only men, after all. It was an equalizer in the long history of education.

To their professors, these students on the GI Bill seemed anything but entitled. They were respectful and hardworking and family dedicated and peace seeking. Among his forty students, Johnny was the third youngest—but this didn't worry him. Johnny still remembers them as the best students he ever taught: "They had worked and fought so hard, and they came to class wanting so badly to learn." He kept his class in military order and required students to stand up to answer questions. He made an exception for one student, an ex-marine who at six feet eight inches towered over everyone else and was allowed to answer questions from his seat. This was part of his teaching method too, knowing when to strategically bend his own rules.

Dr. McKetta ran a tight ship, and he respected his students. He respected their experiences and their desires to go to school. These young men had faced death as he had. The sudden and almost simultaneous deaths in his own family had confirmed his commitment to a life different from what he could find in Pennsylvania's coal country. These veterans had fought in the war that Johnny had avoided by staying in school and doing the best research he could. He felt it his duty to teach these men to work in the industry, to use the skills he had learned. He worked to educate them and raise them into professionals. In 1946, the world demanded what chemical engineers could make. Plastics and new materials were on the rise, and engineers were doing work with polymers. ("Palmers?" I asked my grandfather. "Polymers," he repeated, spelling the word out. Then he explained that a polymer was not a monomer, but a mixture of monomers chemically joined to form materials like plastic, a fact that I clearly never learned in my literature studies.) Johnny taught with love and discipline: on the first day he told them his rules about what was expected and what excuses he would and would not accept. In forty-four years of teaching, he estimated that only about ten students quit his class—though five he sent away. Three wished to become doctors, so he sent them to the Biology Department (and two of these eventually became Johnny's own medical doctors!). One became a Broadway actor instead of a chemical engineer, and the fifth, Walter Blaney—among his favorites of all time—wanted to be a magician. Johnny saw his job as helping students reach their dreams, not somebody else's dreams for them—so he marched young Blaney to the Psychology Department, and many years later "Zany Blaney" would be named America's Outstanding Magician. Overall, Johnny worked hard to retain his students—on occasion when a student dropped out of school for personal or financial reasons, Johnny was known to track down the student and say, "We want you back and we will find you a job that will enable you to keep up your studies." He did this gladly, just as Johnny's own professors once arranged such jobs for him.[14]

As a young professor, Johnny loved systems, graphs, and charts—this is a man for whom spreadsheets were invented. So he went into his classrooms, a man with a plan, and his plan didn't change much. For example, he forbade note taking in class because he wanted students to pay attention to the lecture; however, at the end of each class he handed each student a copy of his typed lecture notes. He explained, "I would write on paper everything that I wished to cover that lecture. Then I would make copies of these notes. As I lectured, each student was expected to watch everything I said or wrote on the blackboard. The student was not permitted to have a pencil, nor paper, in his hand while I lectured and placed items on the blackboard. I wanted full attention. At end of period I would give each student a copy of everything I said, developed, and discussed. My notes were much better than they could take while I was lecturing. They took these copies, and many kept them throughout their career because my notes contained more than any textbook."

Johnny had learned in industry the importance of thinking on one's feet, so he developed his own form of quiz. He trafficked in two types: a standard ten-minute quiz at the start of every class to make sure that his students had understood their homework assignments. And his more memorable fifty-second quizzes, designed to teach students to think on their feet and to understand the scale of the world they would go on to work in. When I asked for an example of these quizzes, he looked around his living room at Westminster. Then he looked out the window. "I might ask them how many bricks it required to build Westminster."

Silence.

He broke it down: "They'd then have to figure that Westminster is five stories high, and each story is, say, thirteen feet, and then each story has two rooms on either side, so thirty feet across. Then they'd have to figure the size of a standard brick. I was happy with ballpark answers." Nearly every one of his former students remembers these fifty-second quizzes. How many Ping-Pong balls could fit in the classroom? How many drugstores does the United States have? How much water in Lake Austin?

His quizzes may have been ballpark, but his sense of time was hard as steel. His classes started on time every day because he locked the classroom door the second the bell rang. He promised his students that if he were ever late, they would be allowed the day off. "I was late to class only once," he says, "and even then I swear I had my left foot in the door when the 8:00 a.m. bell rang. But still, because it was the agreement, the students knew that they were allowed the day off. So they picked me up and carried me down the street to Scholz Garten. It meant that I had to let my 9:00 a.m. students out of class too—I couldn't have taught after that beer session." His calling-students-on-their-birthdays tradition had its seeds in his strictness about attendance. "You must come to class every day," he explained to his students, "but if on the first day of class you write down your birthday on a piece of paper and hand it to me, I'll grant you absence on that day only."

More than that, Johnny was genuinely interested in his students. One of his students recalled, "He always asks where we were from. Tells you how your town looks from the sky, because he's flown over it. He made sure to know something about everyone. In his eyes, you were special." Not only that, but he always brought everything back to application, not just memorization: "His classes were hands-on, down to earth, with real-life problems."[15] His students remember being able to talk with him about anything in their lives, any problem. Johnny cared about their lives and wanted to stay in touch. That was part of the birthday-call impetus: Johnny recalls, "I was anxious to learn what they were doing after they left me, so I called them on their birthdays to let them know I was interested in them, their family, and how things were going." Over the years this tradition continued, and it still continues today—each morning when he wakes, Johnny consults his spreadsheet of student birthdays. Then he waits until it's a reasonable hour and begins his calls. This yearly touching base is one of many ways he paved the way for his students to feel like one big family. He began saying early in his teaching career and he still believes, "A student you befriend is a friend forever."

Johnny also at times misbehaved. When a student fell asleep in class, he threw his chalk at him. Who throws chalk after grade school? Would he pull their pigtails next? It was effective. People stayed awake. They laughed. They listened. He also used his students for accountability: after years of boxing he watched his weight carefully, and if he ever grew too heavy and needed to diet, he wrote his daily weight on the corner of the chalkboard so that his students could bear witness as he worked to meet his goal. Johnny also knew when he was bested. Once he threw his car keys at a snoozing student, for he didn't want to give up his only piece of chalk, and the student woke and kept the keys until the next day, meaning that Johnny had to beg a ride home with another professor. Johnny adored the student's gumption in keeping the keys. He could dish it out, and he could also take it.

Students loved him. They learned, they rose to his expectations, they respected his rules, and they flourished. Among the first class of students Johnny taught were James Haun, who later became a member of the Food Industry Advisory Committee of the US Department of Energy; Fred Harmon, who gained accolades for his pioneering work in the aerospace industry; and Henry Groppe, who started a firm that fore-

casted oil prices and market conditions. The chemical engineering students were becoming giants in their fields, and their good work fed the
university that had initially fed them. Johnny's fast rise at the University of Texas happened partly because he worked in a field whose wave
was cresting, and partly because he loved his work, was good at it, and
was willing to work hard. In this and other ways the man and the century met. In fall of 1947, after only one year, John J. McKetta, our once-
upon-a-time coal miner, actor, trumpet player, and mischievous youngest son, was promoted to associate professor.

INTERLUDE=

I e-mail my grandfather in the early, early morning. I inherited from my father, who inherited from my grandfather, who presumably inherited from all the men all the way back, a love of the early morning, four or five o'clock, before the world awakens. *Madrugada*, they call it in Portuguese. *Ranok*, apparently, in Ukrainian. These are coal-mining hours. Reasonable people don't wake then. I ask my grandfather what it was about teaching that inspired that passion. Was it helping others grow? The learning in a group setting? Something else entirely? As a teacher myself I am curious.

He writes back before anyone else in my house is awake.

"Dear Liz: I think it was Freud who said each of us has ego (some very little, some extreme) and an innate wish to be liked by others."

He then retells the story of teaching Sunday School to children and how good it felt to be listened to and liked.

He continues: "Always, throughout my career, I prepared deeply before class so the class would know I knew even a little more than they did. So in such a case you can see I was highly egotistical. The important thing was that I never tried to fool them or trick them and I could feel they appreciated me. . . . They are like my own children even though some were my age. I compared my life with the coal mining days and always felt I was the luckiest teacher alive."

SEVEN═PETROLEUM
Research + The Laboratory

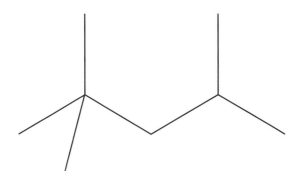

I t was like a dream, Johnny later said of coming to the University of Texas. He was an academic in the 1940s, an era when professors wore suits and had lunches together and balanced their research and teaching in an almost equal measure. Johnny never once stopped comparing his university work to his airless coal-mining days, and each day he reminded himself of his luck on his walk to class. He was earning enough to support a family, and added to that was an offer by Humble Oil to spend the summer months making one thousand dollars per month doing research in his lab in Austin and then flying to Baytown, Texas, on weekends in Humble's private company plane to make reports. His work as a teacher and as a working scientist were marrying beautifully. At last he felt secure in the work he could do throughout his life.

For Johnny had arrived at the University of Texas with the right skills at the right time. Because of the energy and expertise being dumped into the field of chemical processing, as well as antitrust laws being waived so that companies could pool their knowledge and produce results more speedily, nearly every major chemical company would soon have a facility along the Texas Gulf Coast and Johnny's work on petroleum was gaining traction. He was creating knowledge that companies could use. His research, as was the case at Michigan Alkali, was becoming well known. Here's how the department introduced him: "McKetta soon established an extensive research program to develop phase-equilibrium data on hydrocarbons and related systems at pressures ranging from high vacuum to 15,000 psi. The work covered determination of vapor-liquid equilibria, compressibility characteristics, and other thermodynamic properties of both pure hydrocarbons and mixtures, as well as the solubilities of water, carbon dioxide, and other gases in these systems over broad ranges of temperature and pressure. Both the petroleum refining and chemical industry found such data valuable design aids as processes became more sophisticated with operation at high pressures and temperatures common."[1]

The implications of Johnny's work were vast, especially in the aftermath of World War II. *Petroleum Refiner* articles in the months after Pearl Harbor show that the industry had been planning a massive undertaking for the war effort, with an eye toward how those products and the level of production could transition into peacetime applications. Extracting and refining fuel for airplanes, ships, trucks, and tanks for the United States and its allies was job one. However, Japan had cut off the vast majority of the rubber supply, so a great concern was finding a way to create synthetic rubber for tires and for bulletproofing airplane fuel tanks—a project that would require petroleum. Also, light hydrocarbon products such as toluene would be needed for explosives and could be used widely in peacetime as solvents. The tone of many editorials at this time is that the nation's industry must maintain its war production footing to maintain peace through strength and then transition into the consumer economy driven by automobiles and household goods. Johnny's work had great relevance, as it applied to finding and extracting petroleum to fuel the military and industry, as well as to refining the hydrocarbons that were crucial to the war effort.

Johnny's university laboratory was the site of a terrific amount of useful information. His experiments, worked on by his graduate students, built on his own PhD work and yielded important results. For the first time, he figured out a system, an accurate method, for determining the temperature profile of a flowing oil well or gas well. This McKetta Method meant that anytime a well was discovered—underwater, in the Texas dirt—his equation could be put to use. This put his research on the map for Texas industry, which remained in a feeding frenzy over oil wells. From this laboratory, day and night, came methods and systems, answers and correlations that industry could use, furthering the department's original aim to generate practical knowledge to benefit Texas industries. He published his results in over four hundred technical articles. And the results were newly enabled processes in learning just about anything you would ever want to know about an oil well. Industry gobbled it up, putting it all to use.

In addition to predicting the well's temperature, oil drilling companies could use Johnny's methods to determine the chemical composition of materials in a well—in other words, since petroleum can be made up of more than a hundred different elements and compounds (methane, ethane, etc.), it's useful for an engineer to know what chemicals he or she is working with. Also, engineers used Johnny's method to gauge the size of a petroleum well. (The trick? Take measurements a week apart and compare them.) One of his most used methods—published early in his career—is for figuring out the water content of natural gases at high pressure and high temperature (he specifies: "up to twenty thousand pounds per square inch and up to five hundred degrees Fahrenheit"). He also put these high-pressure thermodynamic principles to use to figure out the friction loss of fluid flowing in a pipe that has been contaminated by mud or another nonsoluble substance. Texas industry felt like it had won the lottery with Johnny McKetta. His research still forms a foundation for much of our knowledge about these things. Later, his findings would help make offshore drilling a safe possibility. Though still in its early stages (the first drilling "out of sight of land" took place off the coast of Louisiana in 1947), Johnny's research on pressures and temperatures would be very important as this more demanding form of drilling became more common.

His research—four hundred technical articles are *a lot*—put Johnny on the map. By 1950, he was recognized as the world's expert in high-pressure research, a distinction that he took at first very humbly, but

As a young professor, receiving the 1959 Publication Award from the South Texas section of the American Institute of Chemical Engineers

eventually he said, "started believing it a little." People designing refineries and chemical plants, anyone doing hydrocarbon extractions from the earth, depended on these properties to make correct calculations. They were essentially the facts on which chemical engineers could build and make things. His data became the trustworthy basis for equations that are still being fed into computers for use today.

Based on his expertise, he was conscripted by board presidents to serve on their boards and lecture to their companies. In Johnny's words, "Most boards had heard of my ability in areas of chemical processing, design of chemical plants, efficiency of operation, high-pressure behavior of fluids, my reputation as energy expert. In fact I turned down about half of the requests because I never served on more than ten boards any particular year. I insisted that I would not be asked to be a politician but I would express what I truly believed best for the situation in question." But he said yes to the lectures.

In his early days as a professor, his research grew in demand for a different reason: lawsuits. Lawyers began to call to hire him as an expert witness. In his laboratory, Johnny and his students worked daily on high-pressure hydrocarbons. How did they burn? What made them explode? This research led many people in the community to know him as an expert on explosions. Johnny and his students used their research to help the community, doing research for lawyers. One day in 1949 Nussbaum, a barbecue restaurant on Sixth Street, exploded, killing three people. Jay Brown, an attorney, contacted Johnny and asked him to investigate. He added, "I have a new lawyer working for me named Frank Erwin, and he'll do anything. If he doesn't do anything you ask, let me know."

Johnny and his students took samples of the soil near the stove. Ordinary Texas soil has 200–800 parts per billion (ppb) of hydrocarbon. Anything over 1,000 ppb indicates a gas leak. Frank Erwin took all the samples, and sure enough, the soil sample had 1,200–1,500 ppb of hydrocarbon. The lawyers took this evidence to court. My grandfather added, "Frank Erwin did everything I wanted." This last line was ominous, knowing what came later. But the expert witness work pushed Johnny's work further into places that were relevant outside the laboratory and the university walls. It was also very superhero: Problem in San Marcos? Call Johnny! He tells of many of these stories in his autobiography, *My First 80 Years*. His expertise served at times to protect the big company, at other times to protect the individual. Humble Oil especially counted on him for his research involving Texas gas and oil cases. One of his lawsuits involved determining whether some leased land in Katy, Texas, had an oil well on it—Johnny proved that it did. A bigger case involved a three-thousand-gallon oil spill in San Marcos: Johnny was responsible for proving that the water supply was not contaminated with oil. He tested twenty-five wells around the area and was able to prove the water (astonishingly!) clean. In another case, he determined whether there was copyright fraud between two large chemical corporations (there was not). Other of the lawsuits he was involved in were more personal: a man died in his bath at home—was the gas heater at fault?

His students participated in all of these lawsuits, helping gather and test samples. During all of these experiences, his children observed their dad, just as Johnny had observed and learned from his own dad's successes and hard work. Johnny's second son, Mike, would hear stories around the dinner table of life as an expert witness, and he would determine that lawsuits were interesting stuff and become an attorney. The oldest son, Charley, was interested in the conservation aspects and became a forest economist. The youngest, Randy, would follow his father into chemical engineering and earn a degree from the University of Texas.

During all of this time of growth and building, Johnny kept putting his energy into the work and the people he loved, letting the fruits of his labors grow, each fruit creating more labor for the days that would follow. His loyalty to his institutions and family, and even more so to himself and his aspirations, form a structure through his adult years. Holding on. Staying put. Letting it all unfold. This is a hard thing to get one's mind around—earning that thing you have worked so hard for and holding on to the gratitude, maintaining focus, day after day. That's serious labor. So often we forget; we get used to things. But Johnny was remarkable in this way. There was a meditative quality to his work, his early mornings, his exercises, his interactions with people. Each bit of work he did took him one step further from the coal mines.

=

In the projects Johnny spearheaded, you can see his elation and joy with his life. Department members claim that "his influence kept the common academic disease of over-seriousness from ever gaining a foothold in the Chemical Engineering Department at UT."[2] This influence certainly was becoming visible in his first year there. In early 1947, some pretty hilarious tricks began. Since the early 1940s, the department had annual picnics for their students and families, usually held in some public green spot such as the sunken gardens in Austin's Zilker Park. One year, some students (aided clandestinely by Johnny) pulled a prank in which they brought in a female friend of one of the students to dress in furs and act drunk and leer at all the professors and their wives, embarrassing everybody. This was a prefeminist time: many tricks like this wouldn't hold today—nor would public drunkenness (male or female) be such a source of shame. Yet at the time, it was a moment of playing with a taboo, seeing what would happen and how people would respond if it were brought a little too close to home. Humor was the particular way he used to get closer to people and to navigate his world.

Another legendary prank took place at his first Chemical Engineering Department "Power Show." This was a yearly performance of feats of engineering, a way for the department to share its skills, people, and ways of working with the greater community. Educators have always known that students do their best work when they feel a "real-world" stake in the process. In the case of the Power Show, the young engineers had to get their projects in good enough shape to be seen by outsiders: their parents, other Texans, and even people who traveled from far away. Most of the features were fairly serious engineering projects. But in 1947, two exhibits bore the mark of having Johnny's mischievous sanction: one was "The Chemical Cow," which he describes in his autobiography:

> This exhibit covered one end of the room and showed grass entering into a large glass reactor, and then many types of glassware led to the finish line where milk was coming out of a tube. The students told the visitors that this was a "mechanical cow" and we made milk directly from grass without going through the cow. The secret, of course, was that on the floor above we had gallons of milk slowly being dripped down through a mess of tubes ending up at the extreme sampling end. We had one gentleman from Egypt and also one rancher from West Texas who both wanted the patent rights so they could put this onto the market.

The other humorous exhibit was called "The Alcoholic Breath Detector." A student sat at a booth with two carafes of water: one tap water, the other saturated with lime. People came by to take the "test" by blowing through a straw into a sample of water: if the water stayed clear, it meant the person was sober; if it went cloudy, it supposedly indicated alcohol. It was a joke: the tap water always stayed clear, and the lime water always went cloudy when touched by carbon dioxide. So the student in charge of the carafes gave most people tap water but selected a few guests to receive the joke. One guest was a preacher who raised hell when he saw the cloudy water but ultimately whispered to the tester, "You see our sins will always catch up with us. I did have one small drink before dinner." Such was the climate of the department. It was a place where science could be made funny, and people who didn't laugh became the butt of the jokes.

And his family life continued to grow: in 1947 Pinky got pregnant with their second child. Johnny and Pinky spent some of the pregnancy apart—she was in Michigan with her mother and toddler Charley, reading as many detective novels as her time would permit and keeping away from the Texas heat. Her letters to him during those months are playful, flirtatious, and deeply funny: She calls Johnny "dearest Poppy," and in one letter she regales him with a humorous tale from a prenatal doctor's examination, including a detail of the doctor getting distracted by her charm bracelet and pausing the examination to look at it. She begins the letter, "Had most instructive visit to Dr. Birch's office this afternoon, and am on a ration of iron pills, thyroid, Vitamin D, and embarrassing exercises." She signed this and all letters with "love" in all caps: "LOVE, Pinky."[3] You can see her humor, her appeal as a young wife and mother. It paints a picture of her going through one of the three human experiences that shape us all: birth, love, and death. And you can see her excitement at sharing it all with her husband.

The second son, born in May 1948, was by all accounts a hellion. He cried constantly, pestered his older brother, and never slept when he should. He was named for his father, John J. McKetta III. He was born with a fuzzy wash of red hair. Pinky's mother, down in Texas helping out for two weeks after the birth, insisted on calling John III Mike, for, as she said, "any red-haired little boy in Ireland is always called either Pat or Mike." Johnny and Pinky disregarded this nonsense and continued calling him John, but three weeks after she returned home to Michigan, Pinky's mother died, and while mourning Grandmother Smith, they called the boy Mike in her honor. As nicknames do, this one stuck.

The McKettas now lived in a little house at 3317 Perry Lane. It was a sweet house for a young family. Johnny and Charley spent several weekends planting trees in the front yard and pouring a cement ring around the young trees to shield them from weeds (causing them to grow predictably huge, as they are today). In the backyard Pinky planted a garden with carrots and cabbage. Beyond the backyard was the infinite expanse of Camp Mabry, the headquarters of the Texas Military Forces. Camp Mabry pastured horses in those days, and the horses craned their necks over the fence to nibble on Pinky's carrots. Once a horse nibbled at toddler Mike's carrot-orange hair.

Two years later Robert Andrew (Randy) arrived, named after Pinky's father. Repeating the history of the original three McKetta boys coming across the ocean to become Americans, Johnny and Pinky now had their own three McKetta boys. And these boys saw their father working hard.

While Pinky tended their growing brood, Johnny's schedule looked something like this: He woke at 5:00 a.m. and worked at his desk at home. Often Mike would wake soon after and join him, sitting quietly near the desk and sucking on his thumb. Charley would wake next, and eventually Pinky and baby Randy. They would have breakfast as a family, followed by a game of cribbage, and then Johnny would go to work and not come back until 5:00 or 6:00 p.m. He did this every day but Sunday—Sunday was the day for doing chores around the house, fixing leaks, mowing grass, and then taking a family drive somewhere. During the summer his work increased: he was making three hundred dollars a month at the university, and he could make a great deal more consulting. So for two months each summer he worked as a consultant for Humble or Dow or General Foods, and then for a single month—August—he belonged to his family. During August, the family began taking camping trips, sleeping in tents and eventually buying a sixteen-foot trailer to sleep in. This was the beginning of their identity as travelers. Over the years, they visited all forty-eight continental states. He worked hard to earn this time off; his parents had worked hard but found ways to make family time a priority, and he felt determined to do the same.

In planning these trips, the family talked quite openly about money, how it could be spent (on travel, for one thing) and how to save it. They kept putting away 10 percent each month. Johnny and Pinky discussed money with their children and invented novel ways to motivate them to help with chores: haircuts were done at home, and the first boy who got in line for a haircut received a quarter, the second a dime; then the third received a nickel and had to sweep the floor. Also, when Johnny invested in a Sears Roebuck riding lawnmower (the first in Austin, he claims), the sons desperately wanted to ride it, so—Tom Sawyer–style—he charged them ten cents a go to do the work of riding it and mowing his quarter-acre lawn. Eventually the boys caught on and lost interest, so he resorted to paying them instead. He also promised them one hundred dollars on their seventeenth birthday if they didn't smoke until then. (A family joke: Randy, age five, looked dismayed and said, "Why didn't you tell me last week!")

The university grew around him and with him. The petrochemical industry continued to grow too. Aided by the new National Science Foundation Act, graduate students were able to receive generous funding for their scientific research, which they conducted at the UT labs, supervised by Johnny and his colleagues. Most students still lived near campus, so their lives unfolded in the campus churches, at ballroom dances and music nights, at nearby restaurants and football games. It was a small world to those who lived in it, and even student mischief was easy to contain. The department history makes note of a "panty-raid craze" in which frat boys yelled up at sorority houses not for the old-fashioned handkerchief to come down but for somebody's knickers. Police stopped this.[4] Johnny's first generation of students had already entered the profession and become leaders and industry engineers, and many of the department's earlier graduates were reaching retirement age and becoming consultants to national companies, and those national companies were building chemical plants all over the world.

In 1950 Johnny was made chairman of the department. He joked that he called his dad and was so proud of himself, until he learned that he was asked only because nobody else wanted to do it. In a sort of logical continuation of his teacher habit of throwing chalk in the classroom, as chairman he continued to do ridiculous and childlike things, such as hiding under his desk when a faculty member came into his office with the vice president of General Motors. Johnny later explained that he hid because that particular professor had a habit of coming into his office to ask for funds from the department to match offers of funds from companies, so Johnny as chairman was making a joke about money. He didn't expect the General Motors visitor, and as stories go, this one kept coming back to bite Johnny in the backside at formal introductions for the next thirty years. His steely personal discipline and clear-eyed vision about the field, tempered by his goofiness and his genuine ways of showing love, made him a perfect chairman. It turned out to be the kind of peer leadership role that he shone in—people responded to him, inspired by his devotion to the department and his faith in individuals. Many of the faculty members he hired as chairman, and later as dean, remained at the university for over forty years, shaping the department into what it became. As a leader, Johnny held the bar high, and the people around him reached for it.

It was clear from his childhood onward that collaborative environments were where he thrived. He loved being part of a team, for example, the tight-knit and constantly moving McKettas, or his love of football and boxing and Shakespearean acting. He liked being part of something greater than himself, just as he liked himself being singled out for his contributions. Part of Johnny's innate understanding of how a team worked meant that he understood specialization and outsourcing. During his first term as chairman, he began initiating new systems that would shape the department for years to come. He introduced the idea of hiring a grader from the English Department for the young engineers' lab reports. Believing that his job was to build better systems, he saw quite sensibly that a writing expert would be more effective than an engineering expert in teaching students to write well. Like many of the systems he implemented, this one continues. But beneath the systems, he always saw the people, and he never failed to see his students for their full humanity.

The students were balancing a full life: not only their homework but also their marriages and their babysitting co-ops. These young men were not just names on a roll: in them Johnny saw himself, his brother, his father, all trying hard to make their lives better. They were all climbers. They looked up into the sky and saw a beanstalk, and they put all their energy into the climb. This act of constant climbing was something Johnny knew well.

All of these forces collided to make Johnny into a professor who could do the research, who indeed would become known worldwide for his research, but whose heart always and ultimately lay with the students. Many professors left the university for the chemical industry, with its more impressive pay and more illustrious job titles. But Johnny intended to keep his home in the place where people were constantly improving themselves through education. It was his way, somehow, of keeping his finger on an earlier version of himself.

INTERLUDE=

"What is triple-point?" I ask my grandfather while we are sitting at Westminster after Sunday brunch. I know this is something he is famous for. "Can you explain it to me? Or is it something I should just look up on my own?"

"No, honey, you can't." He takes from his front pocket a pen and a small pad of paper and draws a little graph. "See, this is L1—liquid. On this line, it's fixed. There are three phases that a substance can be . . ."

I interrupt to make sure I understand: "What kind of substance?"

"Anything, baby doll. Water, mercury, anything. It can be solid, liquid, or gas. And triple-point means the one temperature where all three coexist. Where something is solid, liquid, and gas."

He looks at me. I know I look blank. In my efforts to understand what a chemical engineer's laboratory looks like, I had observed the labs in the chemical engineering building that bears my grandfather's name. I peered through the windows of the laboratories, at heavy steel machines that look like microwave ovens. At one point I stood in the basement in front of a lively cartoon poster titled "Laboratory Mishaps." "Can you find the 65 dangerous situations here?" the lettering asks. It looked like most of the mistakes involve exploding things or setting things on fire.

My grandfather tries nobly to explain it to me again. "Honey, people want to know if you have two substances and you want to separate them. I'd take two pure substances and mix them fifty-fifty."

He puts down his pen and gives a little laugh. "My specialty was in triple-point and I can't even explain it!"

I apologize. I say, "I wish I had done better in chemistry classes and could understand it better."

My grandfather laughs a big, generous laugh. "Honey, I wish I understood it better."

EIGHT═PAPER
What Started the Encyclopedia

Even while teaching was his first love, in 1952 Johnny was offered the position of editorial director of *Petroleum Refiner Magazine* by Gulf Publishing Company. This was a great invitation to join a world-renowned magazine in the petroleum engineering field. At first he declined, but when they promised him nearly triple his professor's salary and twenty-five thousand dollars' worth of company stock, he accepted and for two years tried it out. He informed the department, who hustled to replace him as chairman and switch his courses to other professors, and Johnny and his family moved to Houston in August, the hottest month in one of the hottest states. Houston, which is close to the Gulf of Mexico, is more humid than Austin. Imagine Pinky, her Michigan blood still getting accustomed to this new climate, moving houses with three small boys. Johnny's feeling was clear: his heart remained with teaching, but he knew better than to turn down such an opportunity. He recalls, "This was an international magazine, and I would have contact with the leaders of the petroleum industry throughout the world, and it would be of great help to my profession."

The two years living in Houston were short but game changing for Johnny's career. The three McKetta sons had an easy time adjusting to a new city. Pinky supervised them, suffering a significant sadness in 1953 when her beloved father died six years after her mother. Both her parents had died young, before age sixty-five, an age that Pinky would come to see (falsely) as a cutoff point for her own life. With this loss, the McKetta family, as Johnny's family had done in his childhood, provided support and comfort for each other. It was hard for Pinky to be so far away from her father at the end of his life, as he was the parent for whom she felt most homesick. But the family was in Houston to support Johnny's career, and support him they did. This focus helped them move through the grief and through Pinky's private personal reckoning at being parentless.

As an editor Johnny was effective: He rebranded the magazine, increased advertising (much of which focused on the idea of "efficiency"), changed the magazine's name to *Hydrocarbon Processing Industry*, and increased its circulation on a major scale. He took all the ads off the cover and opening pages ("I hate to read a magazine that's all ads for first the ten pages," he said)—and to balance costs he increased total advertisement pages by over 50 percent. He broadened the readership beyond industry and academia to include technicians and managers. He introduced a letters section in the interest of creating a dialogue between these parties (many of the early letters congratulated him on gaining the position, showing the esteem in which he was held). He implemented reader suggestions quickly, taking the best ideas from the readership and creating a sense of community. For example, one letter to the editor suggested that the magazine publish the authors' mailing addresses with the "Science and Technology" abstracts so that readers could request copies directly. (In the past, the magazine had at times run out of reprints of an article.) Johnny jumped on this idea, showing that he could make quick changes to put others' ideas into action. It is clear that Johnny's decisions as editor stemmed from his values of sharing knowledge widely and crossing borders of academia, industry, and individuals.[1]

Put briefly, he made the magazine more relevant for a great deal more people. He even presented two sides of the debate on the question of unionizing technical workers. He expanded the staff by creating new, specialized editor positions. He also changed the tone by using more accessible language, in the editorials and the section titles, such as "Who Writes for Us?," and gave detailed depictions of the financial picture of the chemical engineering industry. An early editorial called "How We Do Our Business" lays out his process for creating each issue, emphasizing that he himself read everything. Johnny's editorship opened up chemical engineering expertise to a mass audience—in a sense, it seemed a way for him to "pay forward" what he had gained by reading the book on coal oil when he was a coal miner.

Johnny was also making more money as editor, which meant that the family's summer camping adventures could broaden. The summer of 1953, when Johnny had been at Gulf Publishing for most of a year, the McKetta family took their annual cross-country drive and camping trip. On this particular trip, the boys were all old enough to hold their own. They were also old enough to get into trouble. This trip was especially hard on Randy, who at four was a gentle boy with a strong sense of his own honor. Once he got into trouble for wandering away from the family during a trip to Vancouver—his parents found him in a drugstore nearby, and after Johnny bawled him out for breaking the "stay-together" rule, Randy showed his dad that he had hung back to get him a "Fawver's Day" card.

There was also the case of the pears. On a camping trip, the family woke to see that somebody had taken a bite out of the pear on the top of the fruit bowl on their picnic table. The bite indicated two relatively large front teeth, and the whole family looked at Randy. "I didn't do it!" he said. "Yeah right," his family responded. Randy insisted and it became a bigger and bigger deal—until Pinky spied a chipmunk jump up and take another bite out of the pear, at last proving Randy innocent. It was on this trip too that the family set up a new McKetta Rule: The boys could order anything they wanted to eat, but if they didn't finish their food, they had to pay for their entire meal. This resulted at first in the three boys ordering a single hamburger to share.

Johnny continued to work at Gulf one more year, and his advances to the field by disseminating information through the magazine were significant. The University of Michigan awarded him a Distinguished Alumnus Award, and Gulf Publishing arranged for him to serve on its board of directors. The owner, Ray Dudley, called Johnny "the brains of the whole outfit." After two years he was ready to return to teaching. Ray Dudley cried when Johnny gave notice.

But Johnny agreed to continue to serve on the board (which he did for fifty years, until 2003). His work at the magazine would eventually serve his home department: it brought these new friendships with petroleum industry leaders back to the University of Texas. He now saw how information could be disseminated and have practical consequences. If engineers could have access to good information about chemical engineering, imagine what advances could happen. Without his experience working in the editorial department at Gulf, his famous encyclopedias would never have been born.

When Johnny left Gulf Publishing, he and Ray Dudley agreed that Johnny would come to Houston one or two days each week to supervise the magazine as editorial director of the entire company. He continued this arrangement until 1965, even after Ray Dudley died and his widow, Frederica, became president of the company. Johnny left only after Frederica died and Gulf Publishing passed into other hands. During those years, Johnny taught on Monday and Tuesday, then took a Tuesday night train to Houston to spend Wednesday advising the magazine. Then he took the train back and taught his Thursday and Friday classes. For his weekly work, he at first earned three hundred dollars a day, and later five hundred dollars, to continue acting as "the brains of the whole outfit." An avid record keeper all his life, Johnny remembers the numbers. Perhaps they dignify him as an earner, as he saw his father—or perhaps it was a way to track his progress. Either way, his continuing relationship with Gulf Publishing became another way he designed his life to be "and," not "or." Whatever the options were, he wanted to do both: he could do both.

The McKetta family moved home to Austin. Back at the University of Texas in the fall of 1954, Johnny was earning less than when he worked for Gulf Publishing, but he didn't care—he was just glad to be back in the classroom, where he belonged. He had returned to the place where he would continue being a powerhouse intellectually—known

Celebrating Mr. Dudley's birthday, circa 1953

nationally for his work—and yet remain, at heart, a goofball and an actor in front of his students. He would do things like wear fake teeth to class. He continued throwing chalk. He continued to write his fluctuating weight on the chalkboard every morning so he could stay accountable to his students. His nephew, Merle Thomas, at that time a student at UT majoring in math, chemistry, and physics, remembers walking across the forty-acre campus and having people call out, "You wouldn't *believe* what your uncle did today in class!" Johnny generated the sort of epic stories that made people remember him. He was on his way to becoming a "great god" of his own making, as all of his mentors and professors had been in his eyes. The next years brought a second and third term as chairman, more collaborations with students, and a deepening of his administrative role in the university he loved.

Having been vice president and editorial director of the world's largest publisher of petroleum product magazines (Gulf Publishing put out six magazines, all with worldwide circulation), Johnny stood in a unique position in publishing. In short, he was briefly the king of a very small but lucrative industry. Petroleum processing was revolutionizing the modern world—and it was known that Johnny could lead its communications branch. He could collect the experts and give them a means to transmit their information to engineers around the world. This autumn of 1954, he busied himself with his usual duties at UT, but something was different. He could command bigger projects. He wanted to stay at the university his whole life and knew that he could do so but also have a life outside academia, serving as a link between the university and the world.

He came back to Austin with a desire to keep publishing, but on a much larger scale. His own numerous publications continued to reach many people in his field. The Gulf Publishing magazines reached the whole world. Johnny knew that there were thousands of good journal articles about making chemicals from hydrocarbons, and from this information a chemical engineer could learn how to do just about anything. Johnny also knew that there were many good chemistry books, but most of them dealt with theory, not actual application of chemical process to the design of chemical plants. What was needed, he saw, was a way to bring this vast information down to earth. He needed a single easy way, a complete compilation or system, to consolidate all this great information in a single searchable database. He envisioned a set of books that designers of chemical plants, or chemical engineers with any goal in mind, could use as a one-stop shop for all the known information in the field. Nearly fifty years before Wikipedia came along, Johnny decided to make a central place where all engineers would look first for answers to their practical questions. Nobody wanted to thumb through a hundred magazines to get a question answered. He invited a department colleague, Dr. Kenneth Kobe, to partner with him on his idea.

Johnny set his wakeup alarm for 4:00 a.m. instead of 5:00, which gave him three hours for encyclopedia-related tasks. He combed through all of the literature in his field, distilling it into an outline for a ten-volume series of books about chemicals from petroleum, titling it *Advances in Petroleum Chemistry and Refining*. Sadly, Kobe died before volume 1 was published, so Johnny finished the series alone. It took him ten years, which was astonishingly fast, considering all his other duties. This early series was the first inkling that such a publishing endeavor could be done. Without it, there would never have been his giant feat of the sixty-nine-volume chemical engineering encyclopedia, the project that made him a household name to chemical engineers worldwide.

His first ten-volume series proved useful. It was translated into twelve languages and made the publisher a lot of money, and it placed Johnny even more prominently on the map of capability in chemical publishing. But Johnny saw that it was not enough: "I noticed so many omissions published in this first series and saw that there was no encyclopedia available about this fantastic industry. Nothing like that was in existence. I suggested to the publisher, Marcel Dekker, Inc., of New York City, that I was interested in doing this job, and Dekker jumped at it."

The goal would be this: an encyclopedia of books from *A* to *Z* on how to design chemical plants and how to choose reactants—every step from start to finish. It needed to be a quick reference that would summarize an enormous body of information. It would be like the ten-volume series but much, much more complete. My grandfather described the premise to me in terms of coffee, which during our conversation we were drinking:

> Suppose I was a food student and learned, "To make coffee, one should mix ground coffee with water and heat before serving." The practical cook needs to know to use one (three-fourths, one-half) or certain amounts of teaspoons of coffee grounds per cup of water. We would have a chart showing this info and then tell them to put the mixture of eight teaspoons of ground coffee into a metal or glass container. Stir very well and then heat to boiling. Then pour the coffee (careful, it is very hot and may burn your fingers) into one or more cups for use by the drinker. Some believe that adding sugar and/or cream will enhance the taste. Yes, it sounds facetious, but you'd be surprised how many people do not know basic details of many topics. We go into detail on pressure, temperature, reactants, compositions to get certain desired products whether they may be plastics or food. We must advise them whether the feed, intermediate products, or final products are poisonous, inflammable, explosive.

In other words, an entire field's knowledge would have to be contained in these books. The encyclopedia would take a compendium of all that existed in the chemical engineering journals and put the information into one place. Any chemical engineer would be able to use and understand its information. The encyclopedia would have to be perfect.

For Johnny, this challenge was a chance to put all of his skills as a connector and an organizer to the greatest imaginable use. It was a chance for him to create a database of all his friends in the field, including colleagues and former students, and to organize and motivate them to compile their expertise into an encyclopedia entry and put it to use for chemical engineers worldwide. Encyclopedia making was a job that would require broad knowledge of an entire field with an ability to trust the experts on the specifics. Such an encyclopedia was a feat for someone who loved, in equal parts, chemical engineering and people.

It was clear to everyone that Johnny was the man for the job. It was the kind of feat, people later said, that only Johnny McKetta could have made possible. He mobilized students. He called on the people he knew. He wrote to new people and asked them to contribute. He began with a template and a list of experts:

> I selected about 250 experts in design throughout the world and sent them an alphabetical list of hundreds of chemicals, from acetic acid through xylene. I sent them a copy of one chemical process, acetic acid, written like I wished it to be of greatest help to the designer and to be used as an example for future authors who might help us. Within two years my board of experts approved a list of about fourteen chemicals chosen. . . . Many of my experts were willing to write the section of their expertise, and others sent me lists of names of expert designers who should be contacted. What was so unbelievable was that not one request to experts around the world was turned down.

For example, Tracy Hall, a chemical engineer from Provo, Utah, who had been charged with making synthetic diamonds. He solved the problem by putting 3.5 million pounds of pressure on pure carbon, which earned him a patent. Johnny met him at a conference, and they became fast friends. When Johnny was looking for an expert to write the encyclopedia section for synthetic diamonds, he asked Tracy Hall. He also looked inside his own department. Don Paul, a UT professor specializing in polymers,[2] wrote the section on ABS (acrylonitrile butadiene styrene) plastics—a tough, cheap, heat-resistant plastic used both as protection for fragile things and, more familiarly, to make LEGOs.

This was the genesis of Johnny's *Encyclopedia of Chemical Process and Design*. It would take until 1976 for *Volume 1: Abrasives to Acrylonitrile* to be published. Just getting that first volume to the public took Johnny nearly ten years of work. Over thirty-four years, he would supervise the creation and publication of sixty-eight more volumes. He would work on it for the remainder of his professional life, every single morning (before doing his exercises, which he still did every day before shaving). The final volume was published when he was in his mid-eighties. He never changed the technical content of the entries, for he was dealing with the world authority in that field. He only edited for better English. He remembers the work, overseeing all entries for his magnum opus, as being "fun, easy, and exciting for me."

When he began working in earnest on the encyclopedia, he had to drop other responsibilities, so he phased out his laboratory research and did no research after age fifty-five. His new focus was on disseminating information to the masses, both to fellow chemical engineers in the written form of his encyclopedia and to American citizens and policy makers in the spoken form of his lectures. He did this with tremendous energy.

When he accepted the job at Gulf Publishing and took his university hiatus, could he have known that something this big would come of the publishing job? Maybe. He knew that experience builds on experience, that a person needs to do great things in order to cultivate the ability to do more great things. The job of consolidating all of the expert literature in the entire field of petrochemical processing, all the scholarly articles and magazine pieces, and pulling them together into a single giant encyclopedia, was, in his estimation, the second-greatest professional job he had ever done—the first was always teaching.

These years his days held fast to a routine: early-morning encyclopedia work while his family slept. Then exercise, shave, shower, dress. He made time for a quick breakfast and a cribbage game with Baba, a morning chat with his sons. Then to the university. He liked to teach in the mornings, usually two classes in a row: 8:00 and 9:00 a.m., or 9:00 and 10:00 a.m. He always wanted to keep up with as many courses as he could. He maintained his systems and habits. And always his habits were about moving farther each day from being belowground. If you skip a day, you might squander this opportunity and have to go back to digging coal. *No way, sir. Not happening.* It seems there are two ways to approach life and work. The first is the "enough" way. What is the exact goal, and what is the minimum I must do to reach it? The second, and this was Johnny's way, is the "how much can I do?" way. How high is the sky? Shoot for the moon and you might reach a star. So with his coal-mining hat on his desk, he worked with absolute blind obedience to his systems and his promises to himself.

Surely he chafed at times at the routines he performed daily to pull himself up. A man is not a machine, so he must have gotten tired at points, thought, "I'll just take today off." But he didn't. He never complained, never seemed at war with himself the way so many of us are. Perhaps he held hard to his discipline, for it reminded him who he was. And his answer for how he did it always remained the same: "I compared my life with the coal-mining days and always felt I was the luckiest teacher alive." It kept him faithful to his choices and what they required. And like any good system Johnny designed, it worked. Harvard happiness researcher Daniel Gilbert has proven again and again that happiness is not about having limitless choices. Happiness is about choosing one thing and sticking by it.[3] Johnny still looks back on every one of his choices and says, yes, that is the right one. All his former choices trail behind him, standing (in his eyes) as evidence for his life's rightness. It is a matter of self-trust and having a good memory for the things that have worked.

On a personal level, the encyclopedia would be the thing that pulled Johnny and Pinky into affluence, making it possible to pay for their sons' college, purchase several tracts of land as investment property, and travel. Volume 68 came out just before the century turned: *Z-Factor (Gas Compressibility) Errors to Zone Refining*, and Volume 69: *Supplement 1*, in 2001, just three months after the twin towers fell. He began the smaller ten-volume series with Kobe in the mid-1950s, and then began the sixty-nine-volume encyclopedia itself around 1964. Numerous changes occurred worldwide in the thirty-four years between the first volume and the last. The encyclopedia proved a constant for engineers throughout these changing times. As one review describes it, "Written by engineers for engineers (with over 150 International Editorial Advisory Board members), this highly lauded resource provides up-to-the-minute information on the chemical processes, methods, practices, products, and standards in the chemical, and related, industries."[4] The encyclopedia proved a phenomenal success. Sales were twenty-five times higher than the publishers predicted, and because the series was being written as the world was transitioning from paper to computers, the series today is all online. It is updated regularly by new editors, but the original volumes remain attributed to John J. McKetta Jr.

And of course, the creation of the encyclopedia relates to the idea of using energy well. Chemical engineers had ideas and wanted to put them to practical use. It would not have been a good use of their time to spend hundreds of hours digging up articles in journal archives. For Johnny not only studied energy as a field but also was intuitively fascinated by energy on a human scale: what it means to gain it, save it, spend it. This made him an expert on systems, for a good system is merely a way to save energy in doing a thing over and over again. A good system prevents the wasting of energy. His encyclopedia was a way of systematizing, saving energy—those articles existed and any chemical engineer could find them—but in putting them all together, Johnny devised a simple way for all chemical engineers to have all of the information all of the time. It allowed them to conserve their energy for their work that most mattered.

═

But when the encyclopedia was still only a glimmer in Johnny's eye, and he was just beginning to shift his expertise from laboratory to paper, his personal life changed dramatically. In October 1955, nearly a year after the family had returned to Austin, Johnny and Pinky had their final child, a daughter. This proved complicated. Pinky had wanted several children, and she had wanted—very much—a daughter. They had a girl's name picked out even before Charley was born. When Mary Anne finally arrived, Pinky was thirty-five; Johnny, forty. Mary Anne grew up at first like a normal child, but then at age one, she failed to learn to crawl or do any of the baby babbling that the three older sons had done. Pinky and Johnny began taking her to doctors. They tried not to panic. They learned at last that she was severely mentally disabled, with an IQ that would never be higher than 5 or 10, and that she would never grow up as her brothers had.

These years must have been terrible. Johnny recalls of Pinky at the time, "It was a big hurt for her. And she would not show it to you, or to me, because she didn't want to bother us with her problems." I know that Pinky appeared unruffled, but toward the end of her life she admit-

ted closing herself inside a closet while the boys were at school and muf-
fling her mouth so that she could scream. Johnny, in a gracelessly des-
perate moment, asked his three sons if they had ever hit Mary Anne in
the head to make her this way. "No!" the sons said, but they remembered
the question. The family took care of their girl the best they could, taking her to doctors all around the state and country. "We went to Houston, we went to Temple, anywhere that had any good mental health fa-
cilities, we went. It got to the point where we knew she wouldn't get
any better. There were many private schools, but closest to us, and the
one that fit us best, was the State School. The decision was so hard for
Pinky."

It was with startling grace that the family accepted Mary Anne's con-
dition. By the time Mary Anne was five years old, her parents found
her a lifelong home in the Austin State School,[5] a lovely green campus with sunlit buildings and skillfully trained workers. Johnny and
Pinky would begin a Saturday tradition of visiting her there, followed
by a family breakfast without her at the Frisco, a nearby diner famous
for its root beer floats and plates piled high with onion rings. Having
a sister like Mary Anne meant a tectonic shift in the lives of all the
McKettas. It meant that Pinky, who couldn't *not* help, would volunteer at her daughter's institutional home for the rest of her life. At a
time when most mothers with school-age children might start enjoying some hard-earned free time, Pinky started going to the State School
for hours nearly every day. The school gratefully accepted her help and
put her volunteer efforts to use. She helped raise a half-million dollars
to build an indoor swimming pool, she initiated a "swimathon" fund-
raiser, and she helped establish a house where residents' families could
stay on campus while visiting. She even commissioned a statue of two
children standing next to a life-sized horse, which was placed at the entrance to one of the main buildings: you can see it still today. Years later,
in the late 1980s, Governor Bill Clements named her an "Outstanding
Volunteer for the State of Texas."

For the three McKetta boys, having a special-needs sister taught
them a new kind of patience. And it meant that Johnny would be forced
to continue to believe, at a deep level, that things could still be perfect
without being *perfect*. That without coal mining, he never would have
become the great professor he was becoming. And without his tight-knit

childhood relationships, the losses of his mother, uncle, and brother would not have affected him as deeply as they did, tearing a hole out of his loving tribe. He could see that Mary Anne, though not the daughter they had expected, would teach the rest of the family a type of closeness, tolerance, acceptance, that would keep them bound tightly together. He would feel tremendously proud twenty years later, when—unprompted by him or Pinky—all three of his adult sons took their brides-to-be to meet their Mary Anne.

Frisco Saturdays became one part of this family acceptance. It became a smoother, a salvation-by-procedure kind of ritual. Every week they would visit Mary Anne, talking to her, hugging her, playing her a cassette tape of songs that had her name in it (including "White Christmas," for it includes the line: "May your days be *merry an'* bright"). Their new routine was necessary, but it never stopped being sad. They then went to the Frisco, whose cheerful waitresses became their friends over many years of Saturdays, and there they spent time together and enjoyed pies, root beer floats, burgers, fries, and onion rings: comfort food of a certain sort, and after these visits the whole family needed comforting. And then, through these habits, it gradually became okay. Like any of Johnny's other habits, this one lasted him a long time: until Pinky's and Mary Anne's deaths in 2011, the daughter dying six months after her mother.

But mostly on a day-to-day basis, family was Pinky's realm, while work was Johnny's. She did the making of meals, the bathing of children, the marking of birthdays. He went to work, and nothing stopped him. His reputation kept growing, and he kept making new friends and making time for old friends. Students bonded through the experience of being in the particular trenches of his classroom: witnessing his weight tracking, getting chalk thrown at them, being allowed to skip class on their birthday but never, ever allowed to be late, learning to think fast through the quizzes, and knowing that in this professor and in the department there was seed material for friendship for life. His students entered the workforce, prepared by his classes, and as UT engineering alumni they began finding each other. Johnny kept up with them all. His reputation solidified as the "outside" professor,[6] the one who knew people in industry and kept up relationships and would always be happy to help find a student a job, always happy to travel to see his student and help in any way. "His network was phenomenal—he knew everyone," one student remembers.[7] If a student or colleague needed something, Johnny could get the right people on the phone in a matter of minutes. And each of these people responded because Johnny had invested a deep and personal love in them, making them feel valued, special, and part of his pack.

What is most noteworthy about Johnny's early days at the University of Texas has everything to do with charisma: his ability to smile, listen, joke, share, and make everybody feel like his complete and absolute and only "you." He won everybody over in this way. And the thing that amazes: it is sincere. He loves everybody as much as he professes to. People wonder at his energy, but the truth is that to hold it all back, not showing his immense enthusiasm, would tax him. But through his extreme gratitude, his awareness of himself as a peasant from the lowlands flung into position as a prince in a forty-acre castle, never stops waking him up, giving his face little slaps. I don't think a day goes by when he does not mark the comparison between this world and that. His secret is that every day he remembers climbing the beanstalk.

But his charisma runs deeper than just his gratitude. His job, even since childhood Sunday School, is as a teacher. That is the single thing he does best. When he looks at the wonder of the world of universities, of chemical engineering, of men who make encyclopedias, of the world outside Wyano, Pennsylvania, he inspires us to keep looking at it too. To say, yes, truly, this is amazing. Not perfect, maybe not what we expected, but still something to be proud of. He teaches people to look up and see how good it all is.

INTERLUDE=

For as long as I've known him, my grandfather has collected coins. I suppose it's a hobby, a pastime that makes him happy, but he takes his hobby as seriously as any work. He hand-wraps half dollars in coin paper and hands them out to people with a label that reads, "If you save these pennies, you'll never be broke."

When I turned thirty, my grandfather gave me a box of rolls of "Texas pennies" from my birth year, 1979. I unrolled each one, unsure what to do with so many half dollars. My husband and I spent an evening building a pyramid from them, and it was over a foot high. Too practical then, too worried about whether I was spending or saving safely, I dismantled the pyramid and took them to the bank from which they had come and turned them into grocery money. Even now I don't know if that was the right decision. I think of his hands turning over each half dollar, his then ninety-four-year-old eyes squinting at the date. I wasted his work by spending them.

But I am not a coin collector nor really an anything collector. And better to set them free like birds, to let them live and feed this girl I was, this granddaughter to whom he gave them as a source of joy. Then something happened a year after the pyramid that changed how I felt about it. My grandfather—age ninety-five—made a *tour de grandchildren* across the United States, inviting my dad as his companion. I had just moved to the Rocky Mountain West and had a new baby daughter, and during the visit we took my grandfather on a road trip.

"Did you collect coins when you were a child?" I asked him as we drove to Idaho City, a gold-mining town with diners that remained unchanged since its peak in the 1860s, houses with decades' worth of items cobwebbing in the windows, and a beautiful sunlit cemetery of very old graves.

"Honey!" my grandfather answered, with a chiding tone in his voice as if I had asked an incredibly foolish question. "If we had come by a coin back then, you bet we would have spent it."

NINE═LIMESTONE

Administration + The House on the Lake

$$Ca^{2+}$$

O
nce their income was steady and their family had grown to its full size, in 1956 Johnny and Pinky bought a swath of land on Lake Austin, three lots for a total of three waterside acres. On this land there were old cottonwood trees and a concrete bank where gentle waves swatted the land and the occasional water moccasin slithered serenely by. There, turtles popped out their heads and aggressive swans raised their cygnets. It was all grass at first: a perfect place for chemical engineers to have their department picnic. The land lay at the base of high limestone cliffs. It was on a nameless road a short drive from Mount Bonnell, the lookout point up a curvy set of hills that juts out sharply above the lake. This purchase was a homesteading act, not unlike what his father and brother did when buying their Pennsylvania farm with its huge acreage and inferior coal vein.

This land quickly became the site of the department picnics, which took place annually in April. Students dubbed it the "Place on the Lake," and Johnny and Pinky loved playing host. Even before they built a house there, the land offered a spacious and festive spot for engineers to play. Students volunteered to go out and cut the grass (mostly foot-high weeds), and then the picnic was always a great time. Pinky made huge batches of Mississippi mud pie, her signature dessert, and all the engineers brought their families and set up barbecue grills and kegs of beer. Often somebody brought a boat for rides out onto the clean, beautiful lake. Johnny always rode his tractor around the lawn, smiling and laughing and giving rides to the children of his students. Department members recall a wild rumpus that included volleyball, people swimming across the lake and back, and a dizzying game called a "bat race" where four students spun in a circle around a baseball bat and then tried to relay race to the other side of the grass.[1]

Always a man who took seriously both scientific labor and manual labor, Johnny used his newly purchased tractor mower (a step up from his old 1950s riding mower) during non-picnic times to mow not only his lawn but the lawns belonging to his neighbors on the lake. Misunderstandings always linger in his mind, and what happened next was one of the great neighborly misunderstandings of their life on Lake Austin: Johnny received a call during dinner (faux pas number one) from a neighbor who was quite annoyed. The neighbor demanded, "Say, you haven't been down to cut my grass for a month and it's quite a mess. I'm having a picnic this weekend, and I want you to come down here and cut the grass this week." Johnny kept up the illusion and responded, "Mr. Cowsert, I'm very sorry, but I'll be out of town all week and will not get back until Friday noon. I'll try to come down and cut your one acre on Friday noon." He answered, "See that you do." Johnny recounts the story: "Well, the next Friday after I came home, I changed clothes and ran down to the lake lot and started up the tractor and drove over to the Cowserts' place. There was Mr. Cowsert groveling in the grass in front of his drive. He said, 'I didn't know you were a doctor; I didn't know you were a professor; I thought my wife had been paying you to cut my grass; I didn't know you were doing it for nothing; how much can I pay you to make up for this horrible blunder?' I replied, 'Mr. Cowsert, you can't afford me. Now please get up and get out of my road so I can go ahead and cut your acre.'"

After several years, Johnny and Pinky hired an architect, Bill Coleman, to design and build them a midcentury modern house on the three acres. Coleman and Pinky had numerous conversations about the house. It would be built of stone to look natural. It would appear low to the ground but be three stories, with two boys' bedrooms on the second story and a basement that opened into a channel where they would keep a small boat. And the house took on a life of its own, becoming a landmark for the students who spent time there: a sunken living room and connected elevated dining room gave a place for conversation and mingling. Windows along the lakeside brought in a constant awareness of the water. A fireplace built into a stone wall anchored the living room; it had metal sculpted birds above it. You could probably climb the wall if you were allowed (we weren't). There was even a billiards room, complete with burnt-orange felt pool table.

The making of the house began a new era for the McKetta family. Establishing a large permanent residence in Austin gave Johnny the opportunity to cram it with as much burnt-orange of UT's football team as possible. He commissioned an orange bridge to rise across the channel. There were also enough bathrooms for him to persuade Pinky that at least one of them needed an orange toilet seat, and there was closet space to hold his burgeoning collection of orange suits. In the lake, there were always many turtles: an animal that Pinky, who was naturally shy and appreciated the metaphor of a shell, felt akin to. In honor of the turtles in the lake, Pinky brought in tiny turtle statues, bars of turtle-shaped soap, oversized turtle paintings. When the local US postmaster contacted the three families with houses on the still-unnamed street and told them that it was time to think up a name, immediately the other two residents suggested naming it after themselves. Pinky solved the problem. "How about Tortuga Calle, named for the hundreds of turtles living in the lake?" The postmaster nixed the Spanish word "calle," and the homeowners all agreed instead on naming the road Tortuga Trail. So the house grew around them, full of turtles and the color orange, and the infant neighborhood grew up around those three original houses.

The house at Tortuga Trail also became a way for Johnny and Pinky to help students. Remembering his own difficulties as an undergrad paying his way through school, and hearing Pinky once say that she needed help taking care of that big house, Johnny began advertising

With Pinky at the channel of their Tortuga Trail house—"the Place on the Lake."
He wears an orange suit and stands in front of an orange-painted spiral staircase.
To the left (out of photo) is the burnt-orange bridge across the channel.

odd jobs for students around his house for $2.50 an hour: mowing the lawn, helping patch the roof, washing windows, clearing out the channel of duckweed. One of his students, Jim Harris, remembers getting picked up by Johnny every Saturday morning for a day of work at Tortuga Trail:

> Every few years they lowered Lake Austin to kill the duckweed. They had that canal that led under their house where they parked their boat, and it accumulated silt between lake lowerings. One Saturday we were going to clean out that canal. This was in fall of seventy-seven. There was a lot of muck in the canal, and Johnny got down in there with me, and we started at the lake end of the canal and worked toward the other end, putting muck into a wheelbarrow. It was the hardest work I'd ever done in my life, and Johnny worked with me for the first ninety minutes. Then he had a meeting so he left me. I finished the rest of that canal by myself. I was so tired afterward that I went home and slept eighteen hours. I was probably twenty-five. He was in his early sixties.[2]

Some of these students lived with the McKettas for short stints, house sitting when they were away for their August vacation. Johnny recalls, "My kids [students] needed money. When you learn somebody is having trouble and might leave school, I call them in and try to help. By that time, I knew how happy those guys would be who couldn't pay their way and had somebody to help. The students were very close to my three sons, very brotherly."

As a professor, Johnny was becoming legendary: his students working in industry had already become nostalgic for the days when their favorite professor threw chalk at them and said things like, "This student successfully concealed his intelligence from the entire Chemical Engineering Faculty," or, if an issue didn't matter, "You're worried about the nit on the nut of the gnat." These students were making strides in the engineering world and running into other McKetta alums who shared the experience of fifty-second quizzes and had gotten jobs in part because McKetta taught them to think on their feet. He knew what qualities industry required, and he made sure to impart these qualities to his students. And these students wanted to return to mentor and help pull up future engineers.

And engineers were still doing very well in the serene 1950s and early 1960s. Looking back on this era, an article in *Chemical Engineering News* observed that "the inflated job market of the 1960s for chemistry and engineering graduates may have been a unique phenomenon of that decade and may not return for a number of years."[3] Nearly all engineering graduates got hired for good jobs, as US design firms were being hired to build petrochemical plants all over the world. Gulf Oil, a Texas company, had recently invented the supertanker, which made petroleum more portable and led to imported oil costing less than drilling on US soil.[4] In short, America and the world were still demanding the processes and products chemical engineers could make. Johnny was aware of his good fortune to be in this particular field at this particular time—and he kept training students to shine in this environment. His teaching didn't stale, and he shifted his teachings to reflect what the engineering world needed. "I made sure to leave my students every day with the feeling that what I taught them was something they had to have." Part of this preparation involved grooming: his students remember his insistence that if they ever went into any industry with a beard, they would last a mere twenty-four hours. A bigger part of this preparation was to offer an idea of a solution to every problem.

His fifty-second quizzes, which he continued from his first year of teaching onward through the decades, were a vital part of this solution-based plan. "We're making this out of salt; let's make it out of sodium bicarbonate. And if the boss says, ooh, this sounds very good, then you can say, 'It sounds like a good clean thing, but it will cost about 1.7 cents per ton more if you make it from bicarbonate. So you'd lose some money.'" Every day brought a new question, a new opportunity to teach students to think on their feet. He might say, "Yesterday my wife and I went to the waterfalls and they were just beautiful and we took the elevator down to the generator room. And it says thirty-one thousand megawatts." So he would ask his students to figure out the total amount of water, the height, the fact that there's no energy from anything except the waterfall. His students continued graduating into good jobs, and years later many of these students would retire into second careers as chemical consultants. They were shaping the industry that he was rearing them to join.

His teaching prepared the students, but he knew that he needed to continue finding ways to prepare the industry to see his students as vital links to their future. During one of the lunches the professors shared between their classes and laboratories, Johnny in his second term as chairman suggested, "Why don't we talk to some of our ex-students who are leaders in their fields and try to bring them once a month to campus to find out what are they doing, what should we be doing differently?" The faculty saw the benefits of this connection between students and industry. The department created a program called the "Chemical Engineering Foundation." The foundation began in 1955, composed of distinguished professional engineers from the biggest companies in the engineering world. One was Tex Cook, president of General Foods. These representatives would fly their company planes every so often into Austin at no expense to the university to meet with students. Some of these representatives were ex-students. And each company donated eighteen hundred dollars per month to the School of Engineering, all of which was used on students and equipment—things the state would not fund. When I comment on this generosity, my grandfather points out, "Industry had no choice but to help, for their livelihood depended on growth, and the best place to get growth and information is from your own school where you know the people."

The presidents of these companies were enormously receptive, and their excitement at being connected back to the University of Texas resulted in the beginning of Johnny's role as what his colleague Tom Edgar described as the UT Chemical Engineering "outside professor." He became the primary recruiter for these relationships, for in his hands every relationship became a friendship. One meeting Johnny especially remembers is with Monty Spate, the head of Shell Oil, who said he would like to join the Engineering Foundation: "I've got a check right here on my desk. I'll give it to you but I won't mail it." Johnny hopped on a plane that afternoon to New York City, and that night the executive flew him back home on the Shell private plane. Another notable meeting for the Chemical Engineering Foundation took place with Ernest Cockrell, owner of Cockrell Oil Company. Johnny recalls, "I went to Houston the night before and spent the night at the Rice Hotel. The next morning I had breakfast, paid my bill, and walked out the door to go to the Cockrell office in the Southwestern building. As I walked into his office, I still had the cloth napkin, which I used at breakfast, tucked into my belt. Thank goodness the secretary pointed it out before Ernie Cockrell saw it." When the two men met, Ernest jumped up and put his arm around Johnny, thanking him profusely. "Dr. McKetta," he said, "I've been out of school for nineteen years and no one has ever called me. I want to thank you because I am so interested in petroleum engineering." This first meeting was in 1956. Ernest went on to help UT engineers immensely, eventually resulting in having the entire School of Engineering named after him.

After the Chemical Engineering Foundation's early successes, the chair of the Mechanical Engineering Department created a similar program, and soon it extended to the whole School of Engineering. Now all engineering colleges in the United States have these foundations, with the aim of connecting students and industry as well as funding relevant student research. There were other support options for research, such as the National Science Foundation. But these local and personal connections, combined with the money to make new advances, would not have been possible without this idea that Johnny and his colleagues pushed through.

He was growing busier each day, so in 1957 he hired a departmental secretary, Ruth Crawford, who remained "his right arm," as he called her, for thirty years. Ruth later went with Johnny to the vice chancellor's office, then returned with him to the Chemical Engineering Department afterward. She later said of their work together, "You always knew exactly where you stood with Dr. McKetta—because he didn't hold anything back. But I like that in people. Sort of bossy." She also remembers a shoeless, long-haired student sitting for a long time by her desk. "I'm waiting for Dr. McKetta," he said. When Johnny arrived, he immediately told the student, "Don't come to my class again with no shoes."

"But Jesus didn't wear shoes," the student protested.

Johnny replied, "You're not Jesus."[5]

Having Ruth by his side allowed Johnny to scale up his work. He could leverage his best skills and trust her to do the rest, just as he trusted Pinky to take care of the affairs of the home. His personal life mirrored and supported his teaching; in both realms he had a responsible partner to take care of details while his life and his department grew.

But even while the department grew, things never got too serious—

Johnny as chairman made sure to nourish the engineers' joking culture. Once time in 1956, Johnny and Bill Cunningham lost a bet about who would win a football game, A&M or UT. So they settled their bet with their dollars wrapped up inside two bricks, postage to be paid by the recipient—who luckily had a sense of humor and thought it was a great joke. A year later they bet again, and this time Johnny won; he received his one dollar welded inside two steel plates. And students played jokes on him. Once they took his car, a red Triumph convertible of which he was deeply proud, and lifted it onto the curb on its axles so it couldn't be driven. Then the students peeked out of the department windows to see his response. Another time students wrote his name on the ballot for Miss Engineer 1957. The *Daily Texan* noted that the runner-up with the most votes was "neither a girl nor a student. He was Dr. John J. McKetta, Chairman of the Department of Chemical Engineering."[6] Johnny's response to these jokes was always to laugh, admit defeat, ask for help if needed, and move on. He once was asked to write a letter recommending one of his dear friends and colleagues, Carl Gatlin, for a position with the Texas State Board of Registration for Professional Engineers. He sent Carl a copy of the letter.[7]

Gentlemen:

You asked me to ha, ha, ha, ha, ha, ha, ha, ha, ha (please excuse me but I just can't stop laughing), but you requested me to oh, ho, ho, ho, ho (I'm sorry but I've never heard anything so funny), you wanted to know if Carl Gatlin, ha, ha, ha, ha, ha, ha, ha, ha, ha, ha, hee, hee, hee, ho (oh my sides are killing me), but your letter said that Carl Gatlin was applying for oh, ho, ho, ho, ho.

Surely you must be kidding or you must be talking about another Carl Gatlin.

Yours most seriously,

John J. McKetta

Glorious Leader

This, of course, was another of his practical jokes—he invested time in writing two letters, one proper letter highly recommending Carl and then the joke one just to get his friend's heart racing.

Through both humor and discipline, the foundations of both his home life and his work life were deepening and becoming more solid. What he remembers from his family life during these years are the faux pas, the failings of the perfect training he and Pinky worked to instill in their children: the time when a community priest came to dinner and the McKetta sons' attempts at saying grace fell flat. Randy's was, "Father, Son, Holy Ghost, who starts first gets the most"; and Mike, who tried to remedy the situation, only worsened it with: "God is good, God is Great, and we thank him for Den Eight." Or the rainy afternoon when Mike, age eight, was offered a ride home from the principal of his elementary school and declined on the grounds that he couldn't ride with strangers. Or the time when Charley nearly sent a visiting New Yorker into a conniption fit when he offered her his pet horned toad to hold. The McKetta backyard always had "critters": from horned toads to tarantulas to stray dogs and cats, which Pinky always gave "one bowl of milk," often leading to an animal becoming a pet.

Johnny also remembers Pinky, always quick with words, always speaking the truth with a wry sense of humor. Johnny recounts a story when Charley asked a typical oldest-son question: "Mommy, who do you love more, Daddy or me?" Pinky replied in her sweet, gentle, understanding way, "Charley, look at it this way. Someday you will grow up, meet some lovely girl, get married, and leave Mother. And there's one thing that we all know—Daddy will never grow up."

═══

But growing up he was. The 1960s were shaping up to be a big decade for Johnny precisely because they precipitated a wave of change in the engineering world—and Johnny knew how to ride waves. For example, the Russians, whom the United States had ignored as rivals in the technological sphere, to our great surprise sent a satellite into space before we did, in 1957. It was a classic tortoise beating the hare story, and it left the United States wondering, "What did we do wrong in the sciences?" This affected engineering, of course. The energy shortage crisis was still about a decade away—but the forces shaping it had begun to gather, and Johnny was watching closely. Americans who were paying attention had questions about energy, too. Johnny turned forty-five in 1960. He was able to speak to people's questions about these changing times, and he did it in such a way that both inspired people and made them feel secure. The beginning of his career as public speaker took off in 1962 when a major request was made of him: to serve as the president of the American Institute of Chemical Engineers (AIChE). He said yes, further rooting himself into the bedrock of the engineering world. He kept to his habits, his early-morning encyclopedia work and his exercises, and he stepped forward into being, in a wholly new way, a public and watched figure.

AIChE, founded in 1908 for chemical engineers to share knowledge, establish standards, and aid advancement of their field, had had many presidents in the fifty-four years since its creation. Johnny took his position as president a step further. He decided that he would become the first president to visit every single local chapter of the organization and speak to them about the state of energy. Building on his nationwide friendships from his stint at Gulf Publishing, it was easy enough to visit these eighty-nine sections in eighty-nine cities in one year. After all, he had friends in nearly every city. He had a thickly loyal department, so the other faculty members, especially Dr. Howard Rase, whom Johnny had hired, took care of his daily chairman duties, and the department continued to flourish. To make all the travel work, Johnny scheduled his classes on Tuesdays and Thursdays, enabling weekend travel. On occasion, if he had to miss a class for a trip to, say, visit the king of Saudi Arabia, he simply asked his students to do a makeup class Saturday, *and his students agreed*. His colleagues acknowledged that only Johnny could get away with that.

At each of the local chapters of AIChE, he became famous for a particular type of speech. He stressed the importance of procuring energy from more places, such as offshore and deep-sea drilling. He insisted that engineers communicate to the government to stop trying to restrict the work of engineers but rather to place more regulations on how American people used energy. He talked with pride about the importance of the work the chemical engineers were doing. He left people asking hard questions and thinking about the immense tasks ahead, but he also left the engineers feeling that they had a friend in their president. And truly, they did. That was part of his magic.

The word got out that he was both an energy expert and a great speaker. Like a prize debutante, he waited in Texas while the invitations poured

Goofing around in a costume during his AIChE presidency

in. He was invited by the United Nations Scientific Group, UNESCO, to lead a group of professors to Baghdad to determine if its engineering college was worth its salt, and specifically worth the $17.5 million it had requested to help the program grow. The professors' consensus: it wasn't, but even after my grandfather wrote the letter advising "give them no funds," UNESCO gave them $15 million—typical bureaucratic ineffi- ciency. This trip unsettles Johnny still, for it was clear to all of the pro- fessors that the Iraqis hated having to ask the United States for money— there was great animosity in the way they spoke about the United States, but Iraq felt there was no other choice. He says, "I knew they didn't like Americans; I just did not think they hated all of us." But he didn't let that affect his judgment as much as the fact that, as soon as they got off the plane, "we could feel that nobody at the university gave a damn about science and engineering."

Throughout his travels in this decade he kept deepening his founda- tion as the "outside professor," letting people know about the depart- ment, bringing in national attention, and traveling. In the engineers' own version of the space race toward greatness, Johnny acted in many ways as a shuttle between the university and the outside world.

I realize I am caught between metaphors—was he a satellite or a debutante? My debutante metaphor falls apart here, for his dance card was never full. Not once. He kept making time for more things. He kept saying yes to just one more dance, one more opportunity to share his skills and expertise. There was a cost. There is always a cost. In the case of these travel years, he saw his family only in fits and starts. During 1962, when he was president of AIChE, he traveled 190 days, which amounted to forty-three weekends—over half the year. Everyone at the Austin airport knew him. His sons were in and around their teens by then, so he wasn't missing their childhood and they most likely weren't particularly missing him. But think of how a marriage risks fracture when one person spends over 50 percent of nights away from the marital roost. Somehow they made it work. One evening Johnny had finished a talk in Cleveland and had to be in Los Angeles the next afternoon. He rerouted his flight through Austin and called Pinky and asked if she could meet him at the airport for a layover lunch the next day. Her reply? "You'd better wear a yellow flower in your lapel so I will recognize you when you get off the plane." They met for a two-hour lunch, and then westward he flew.

Then the year following his AIChE presidency, a second major request was made of Johnny: the University of Texas appointed him dean of the School of Engineering, which included chemical, electrical, mechanical, civil, and aerospace engineering. Johnny was a natural, easy choice for the deanship: an hour of small talk and decision making on a hot day in July, and the representatives from each area of the School of Engineering unanimously agreed on John J. McKetta Jr. He held this position from 1963 to 1969. The position, much like his presidency of the previous year, depended on a leader who could move a crowd, who could guide and motivate and connect. It was as a dean that Johnny was able to truly marry his skills as inside professor (steeped in his loyalty to the university) and outside professor (connected to engineers worldwide). The same year he was made dean he was also given the Most Distinguished Service Award from AIChE—he would receive their Founder's Award eight years later. And what would come in the decade between was a wholly different type of service. As a professor, Johnny

At a party with Pinky in 1965

served his students. As dean, Johnny was responsible for serving the whole university and engineering community. Naturally he did it with an eye for how both could better serve the students.

And he did it in great part because of Pinky—for not only did she take care of home details so he could work, but at public events, when occasionally Johnny (who held himself to the highest standards), got upset at somebody for acting in a way that disappointed him, Pinky acted as a tempering agent. By placing a hand on his arm and saying, "Don't worry about that, Johnny. It will be okay," she quieted his nerves so he could return to the task at hand. Johnny would be remembered as a firm and good-natured leader—but much of his ability to maintain a good nature in stressful situations came from her.

John McKetta's deanship was marked overall by a single word: yes. He said yes to growth, yes to fund-raising, yes to the new initiatives his colleagues proposed. It helped that the era was a comparatively wealthy one for the economy, the state, the industry, and the university itself—and Johnny used the available funds to move forward. He had internalized the lesson that when there is bounty, put it to good use and use it to create foundations for the possibly leaner years ahead. When he recounts his years as dean, he remembers working at a heady fast pace, starting new programs and handing them off to his colleagues to keep them going. "A dean's job is to keep things growing," he said. "Somebody gave me credit for starting a program in bioengineering here. And I started a lot of things here. But I never concentrated on any of them. My idea was to get a program going and get someone behind it and push them on. And fortunately we had outstanding young men who came in and did so." The Chemical Engineering Department remembers Johnny's deanship very favorably: "Dean McKetta was most active in developing new faculty, encouraging curriculum improvements, and soliciting outside funds for the engineering college."[8] He strengthened his engineering foundation, which provided industry money and advice to the college. A well-funded university can enable graduate students to do cutting-edge research; it can give the gift of time and focus to its undergraduates. UT was fast becoming this caliber of school.

He was good at asking thoughtful, hard questions and devising simple answers, and by doing this, Johnny instigated major changes in the curriculum. He was always sensitive to the seismic shifts underground. He paid attention. He listened. In the 1960s, undergraduate students were starting to feel cheated—they were no dummies: they could tell that the department's focus was on research dollars and graduate students—and they were starting to talk about it.[9] He saw that the teaching was beginning to sag in the department while the professors focused on their research. As dean, Johnny remedied this. He hired a teaching expert, Dr. James Stice from Arkansas, to come to UT to teach the professors how to teach. This was the start of his famous Teaching Effectiveness Program. The professors each took a weeklong teaching class from Dr. Stice, and then they were video-recorded in their classrooms. They would watch it and discuss it afterward with Dr. Stice, seeing where they were and were not effective. It worked. Within five years, over a hundred engineering colleges had adopted this method of teaching professors to teach.

Johnny's legacy rests on his wholehearted insistence on the closeness between students and faculty. This was always an ideal close to his heart. For this reason, he insisted that all his faculty members wear name tags—a practice he himself still follows and one that he has popularized in his retirement home: when I visit these days, many people wear them. When his professors balked at this rule, Johnny responded severely. "I said to my faculty, it's up to you to wear them. But if you didn't wear it, I'd consider it the next time I considered your salary increase." As dean, Johnny dismissed the notion that some students were simply unteachable. He told his faculty, "I know what you've all heard. 'Look at the person on your right. Look at the person on your left. Two of you won't be here at the end of the course.' I don't want anyone in my faculty to ever say that. If I hear that—and I can prove it—you're going to lose your position in the college. If you can't teach a person, I don't want you on my staff." Severe, yes. But he got the point across that without students, there is no university.

In recent years, the department has given out burnt-orange T-shirts with a McKetta quote on the back: "A student you befriend is your friend forever." He had been saying this since he started teaching in 1946, and this was his greatest legacy in the department. Yet this respect for the student was not something that was widely being practiced. "I was emphasizing things that were unusual—like be good to your students. Consider your student as a human being. Make special efforts so the teaching of your student is foremost in your mind." Johnny even encouraged the hiring of a number of UT alumni. One of these hires, Ervin Perry, made headlines in 1964 as the first African American to be hired as a professor at UT—or at any white southern university. Johnny saw the great work Perry was doing as a PhD student and teaching assistant in civil engineering, so he suggested that the engineering faculty vote for Perry to join their ranks.[10]

Johnny's tenure as dean left a huge impact on the University of Texas: he extended his wonderfully organized mind, his knack for devising small daily methods for bettering himself, his love and respect for all people, to the entire engineering department. It was a corralling of his best skills, put on a university-sized level. It was a rare and beautiful form of scaling up. During one of his speeches (October 1966, shortly before his fifty-first birthday) to the full engineering faculty at a UT Teaching Effectiveness Colloquium, a short excerpt from his speech "went viral," as we would say today: deans, chairmen, and presidents from universities all over the world asked for copies. It was not about research, funding, or industry advances; it was, at heart, about students:

> When one accepts a position as a university faculty member, he should expect to write proposals for research, equipment, and special projects; to

publish articles, reports, papers, and books; to keep up-to-date in his professional field; to serve on councils, boards, and committees; to maintain the best possible relations with alumni, legislators, and the business and industry of the region—in short, to be a responsible member of the community and to participate in many of its activities.

But we all know that these many activities must never overshadow our greatest concern—the student. If our responsibilities to, and concern for, the student ever become secondary, we will be violating the trust we accepted when we joined the faculty.

His students felt this investment, and they rose to the bars he set for them. They kept in close touch too, and Johnny and his colleagues were so proud when their graduates wrote home with news. And always, there was news: The students who had passed through the University of Texas were beginning to run the world of engineering. The world was advancing on their shoulders. "Every field had somebody from my class that was up among the top—in computers, bioengineering, process dynamics, optimization, you'd find several of my kids. The only trouble was they were all men."

Ding ding ding! This started another initiative in Johnny's tenure as dean. The intention was to introduce women to engineering. Johnny took the "if you get a bus, they will come" way of thinking: he rented a school bus, hired some drivers, called principals at local high schools, called local chemical companies, and got to work playing one of his favorite roles: The Connector. He arranged for the bus to pick up high school girls and drive them to the chemical plants for a half day of learning what work was being done there. And a new "McKetta Method" was born. Pre-college young women were given the chance to see close-up what an engineer actually *does*. The program was a tremendous success. The vice president of Exxon thought it was brilliant and said, "Johnny, I'm buying you a new bus and sending you fifteen hundred dollars a month for the expense of the new bus, and I'll provide a driver because your idea is beautiful—we need more girls in our field." Dow Chemical also offered to help fund the program. Everyone was behind it.

The program ran for three years and covered many Texas high schools. And like many of McKetta's methods, the system spread and lived on: a good system is always contagious because it is a means toward an end with actual steps that can be replicated. And this particular system spread all over the world. Many schools began similar programs, and in the years since the girls-on-a-bus plan began, the AIChE has started an annual "Introduce a Girl to Engineering Day," complete with a call for role models and a countdown on its website. By 2015 women made up about a quarter of UT Cockrell School of Engineering students.[11] In 2013, 11 percent of all chief executive officers in the chemical business were women[12]—still not enough, but definitely an improvement.

Johnny worked on a large scale to give his students opportunities, as he himself had been given. To this end, another of his early initiatives as dean was called the "Cooperative Engineering Program," which continues today. Johnny set it up, checked to make sure all the systems worked, and then handed it off to a colleague, Joe Bruns, to keep it going. The program gave students the chance to do two semesters of full-time work with the same employer and get school credit for it. In other words, it gave engineering students hands-on experiential learning, as well as a decent income, and it also set them up handsomely for potential jobs after graduation. His background in beginning such a program dates back to his own relationships with local businesses. Recall that in the late 1940s and 1950s a good deal of Johnny's time was spent solving problems for local companies by serving as an expert witness and offering his professional advice as a consultant or board member. While across the country many professors were sitting around waiting for federal funds, Johnny set a precedent at UT by hustling around Austin, earning bits of money here and there, forging relationships, putting his engineering expertise to use through helping local businesses, doing work for them in his laboratories, and at times publishing the results. This meant that he had wonderful relationships with these businesses, as well as a serious pipeline connecting his students to these companies: the students needed work; the companies needed workers.

But lest he tilt too far in the direction of student well-being, he also made sure that his professors were flourishing. Johnny developed a block system with two of his colleagues, offering the students a "guided selection of seven courses" that included technical electives and allowed students to navigate their options with greater choice. This new system benefited the professors too, offering them greater freedom to teach courses that interested them and complemented their research.[13] Johnny also started a "Resident Scholars Program" to draw luminaries from the engineering world into UT's School of Engineering for year-long positions. In this way he brought the outside world in, inspiring professors and students alike. As part of his recruitment plan for permanent faculty, Johnny worked to welcome professors in at the assistant professor level so they would remain at UT and develop loyalty to the department, as he himself had, providing a solid root structure for the future. Professors valued him as dean because he so obviously valued *them*. The department expressed the belief that "the University's goal is to produce scholars, and it should be obvious that the faculty itself must be scholarly. There is no real value in having a scholar on the faculty who cannot impart his knowledge and enthusiasm to the students."[14] Johnny worked hard to help support his professors in enacting this balance: a good teacher is also a good researcher, both imparting and producing knowledge.

Johnny listened to his colleagues and helped realize their wishes. For many years, UT liberal arts had had an honors program (Plan II), offering a select group of students smaller classes with more direct contact with the professor. The department history narrates, "When, in 1964, Dr. Rase asked Dean McKetta why Engineering couldn't do the same, he responded in his usual enthusiastic fashion by saying, 'Let's do it.'"[15] Thus, the Freshman Engineering Honors Program was born and fifteen years later extended to a four-year honors program, attracting students from all over the United States and the world. In an article published in *Engineering Education* in December 1969, once Johnny had moved from the position of dean to vice chancellor, he tallied up the results of the changes made: At the end of his deanship, nearly 90 percent of engineering undergraduates were in good academic standing, up from 57 percent seven years before. In that same time period, the percentage of engineering students on the honor roll jumped from 8 percent to 21 percent, even while "admission requirements remained the same." But this was not at the expense of professors' research; Johnny pointed out that during that time "the number of papers published per faculty member increased twofold. The number of books published increased fourfold, and the amount of total research dollars increased almost sixfold."[16]

Johnny also modeled for his faculty and students the need to be part of professional organizations. He often drove with a carload of other professors to the monthly meetings of the South Texas chapter of AIChE. His travel became both a habit and a constant source of stories. Known fact: if you do interesting things and describe them to people, you will remain an interesting person. As dean, he remained on the board of directors for Gulf Publishing, and one of these trips—at a Gulf Publishing Editorial Conference—remains an example of one way that his role modeling took surprising shape outside the classroom. The conference took place in Fort Clark in South Texas, very close to Mexico; the engineers and publishers entertained themselves one evening in Piedras Negras, a Rio Grande border town, one of seven border towns that has a "Boy's Town," or a *zona de tolerencia*, and you can probably imagine what behavior is tolerated. I love the way my grandfather describes it in his autobiography: "one can visit and not partake of the availability of prostitution." Like Odysseus while passing the island of the Sirens, Johnny all his life had liked to come close to trouble but keep himself tied to the mast so he couldn't join in.

It was 1964, a year into Johnny's deanship. A dozen engineers and advisers sat around a large table near a "horrible" dance floor show that involved a "lady dancer, a duck, and some grains of corn." Several naked "girls" were hanging around too, and one was sitting jointly on the laps of Johnny and one of his colleagues. Across the room Johnny spied three of his PhD students, and he waved them over and paid for their drinks. His students were gawking the whole time; from their perspective, imagine seeing your dean in a tawdry town at night with a dancer on his lap.

Back in Austin weeks later, at the annual engineering picnic now hosted by Johnny and Pinky at their house on the lake, one of these students came up to Johnny, grinning wickedly and offering a proposition: "Dr. McKetta, if you are easy with me on the oral exams, I won't tell Mrs. McKetta where I saw you last weekend." Johnny immediately responded with the kind of ironic hero's swiftness that left the student dumbfounded:

> I called Pinky over and said, "Honey, Bobby was one of the three boys in that dive in Boy's Town last week." Bobby froze—he turned brilliant red—and mumbled something and walked away. Later on he asked me,

"Why did you ever tell Mrs. McKetta about that?" I told him the following, "Bobby, if you have never learned anything working under my supervision, you must learn that every time you leave town or are away from home, come home and tell your wife every single thing that's out of the ordinary because there are always SOBs like you that will threaten to tell her."

The lesson held fast: Precisely because the world is an untrustworthy place, make yourself as transparent and trustworthy as possible. Then you can trust everybody. And being transparent at home was easy with a spouse as tolerant as Pinky. Knowing her sense of dry wit, she likely responded to the Boy's Town story by saying, "I hope you tipped her."

Humor, of course, always played a part in his tenure as dean. When he received the W. K. Lewis Award for Chemical Engineering Education in 1964 from AIChE and was expected to make a speech, he bought a small battery-operated "laughing machine" and began the speech with a joke: "When I received word that I was going to be the W. K. Lewis Award winner I immediately called my family together to tell them the news. I taped their reactions. I want you to hear them." Then he hit the play button for his laughing machine, and hoots and guffaws roared across the hall. The audience laughed and laughed. He dished humor out, and his colleagues responded in kind. That same year, Johnny spent a few days in the hospital for some surgery on his right elbow. The engineering faculty telegrammed him at the hospital: "Best wishes from your engineering faculty for a speedy recovery by a vote of 85-75."

Johnny was by now known in the worldwide engineering community as a marvel of American scientific progress: productive, happy, and willing to work hard. The Venn diagram of his life was the intersection of scientific hard discipline, love, and humor. He focused his energy on advancing his university. He did it all while steadily and stealthily working on his encyclopedia in the mornings so he could spend his day devoted to the university and its people.

He was busy—busier than most fathers. Still he made time to pursue activities with Pinky and his sons. With Pinky there was always cribbage. With his sons, there was coin collecting, a hobby he took up the year he returned from Houston—first rare coins, then coins with dates of family birthdays. His kids joined him at collection fairs and helped him sort and roll.

Johnny enjoyed being dean for a few years, but at the end of his first term he asked Harry Ransom, the president of UT, if he could go back to classroom teaching. Ransom persuaded him to stay on as dean for another term. Two terms was the limit. Then in the spring of 1969, Ransom called him again. He said, "Johnny, we want you to be dean a third term. The Board of Regents approved a third term."

Johnny responded, "Harry, no. I want to be back in the laboratory. I've got fourteen PhD students, and I want to be fair to them. I want to go back to the lab. I want to teach. That's what I love to do." But Ransom wasn't put off for long. He called right back. This time Ransom wasn't calling about the deanship anymore. He had a better idea: "Can I borrow you for a year to work for the whole UT system?"

Ransom proceeded to explain that, as chancellor of the UT System, he had four new universities to start in the upcoming year,[17] and he believed Johnny could help him do that with ease and efficiency. If Johnny would help him by serving as vice chancellor for that one year, his main duty being to oversee all of the presidents in the rest of the system, then he could go back to teaching afterward. Johnny said okay. But he requested a letter from Harry Ransom stating that the term would run for only that year. He would take the position but would leave by September 1, 1970. The letter was signed by, among other people, Frank Erwin, who was the chairman of the UT Board of Regents.

This was a familiar name. My grandfather had met Frank Erwin before—back in 1949. Back when Johnny and Pinky bought their new house on Perry Lane, Erwin was their lawyer's young associate who did odd jobs such as buying the McKettas fire insurance and helping Johnny gather samples for an expert witness job. Johnny's first thought when he saw the name was, "That's the same kid who used to work for me!"

But in the years since doing work for Johnny, Erwin had decided he was done working for—and cooperating with—people. Now he wanted to be the person who told other people what to do. This is of course an evolution that makes sense; it's also one that caused particular trouble at the University of Texas in 1969–70. A *Daily Texan* article titled "Conflict Marks Frank Erwin's Career" recounted a protest that involved students blocking the entrance to the administrative building using limbs from trees cut down in the first stadium expansion.[18] Johnny recalls, "When I got to the vice chancellor's office, I found that Frank Erwin and Harry Ransom weren't speaking. Frank and anyone who worked with him weren't speaking."

His office in the Chemical Engineering Department: one desk against the wall for work, a bigger one in the center of the room for meeting students, circa 1969

Two weeks into Johnny's new term as vice chancellor, Ransom came into Johnny's office and sat down looking beleaguered. He said, "Johnny, sit down. I want to talk to you. I've resigned. They now have a deputy chancellor, a friend of Frank Erwin's. You're still vice chancellor." Johnny took in this information and did the most sensible thing he could think to do. He went to the office of Norm Hackerman, the president of UT and also a former chemistry colleague. "I went to Norm, and I said I have bad news." Norm's response? He was not surprised. He said that Frank Erwin was just in his office yelling and cursing. Norm's next words came as a tremendous surprise: "I'm telling you, Johnny, I'm leaving. I'm getting the hell out of here." And Norm Hackerman resigned and became president of Rice University.

When Johnny saw that the heavy boat of UT administration was clearly starting to sink, he went back to Ransom with a heavy heart and said, "I think I should resign, too." But Ransom—brave, loyal Ransom, even though he had just resigned (which Johnny believes he was coerced to do) from his beloved university—admonished him: "Johnny, you can't. The university is bigger than you and me. If word gets out that there's trouble between Erwin and me, and that Hackerman is leaving, and then if word gets out that you've leaving, there'll be hell. You said you'd stay a year." It's true. He had a letter that contracted him to the vice chancellor's position for one full year, no more and no less. Johnny admired Ransom for his loyalty, and he abandoned all thoughts of leaving and got to work: "I hired Bill Livingston and made him my right-hand man. We got the things started, got the staffing done and all that stuff." But they were working against odds: the deputy chancellor Frank Erwin had hired had no real idea how to run a university, and the UT Board of Regents was a mess because Frank Erwin was in charge of it and loved power and was arbitrary in using it. He especially loved to fire people.

Johnny's face-off with Frank Erwin was bound to happen eventually. It happened one spring day when Peter Flawn, then professor of geological sciences and director of the Bureau of Economic Geology at UT, rushed over to the third floor of the Tower, the site of Johnny's office. He brought news that a drunk professor was lecturing to the students in the History Department. The story Johnny tells of the encounter runs like a comic act.

Johnny entered Erwin's office and stood there until Erwin looked up from his work. He then explained the problem.

"Go stop him," Erwin told Johnny flatly.

Johnny, following protocol, said, "I'll tell the university president to tell the head of the department."

Frank Erwin blinked, and then roared, "You do it!"

Johnny would not do it.

"Then you're fired!"

Johnny kept his calm. "You can't fire me."

"The hell I can't!" Erwin yelled. He was used to getting his way.

Johnny retrieved a letter and showed it to Frank Erwin. "Look. I have a letter saying I'm here until August 31. From Harry Ransom. And look! It's okayed by Frank Erwin."

"You son of a bitch," Erwin said.

"Remember this letter," Johnny told him.

So it was, in the end, through good record keeping and the ability to stand up to a bully—two skills learned from his childhood—that Johnny got around Frank Erwin. Johnny finished out his year as vice chancellor with a new group of lifelong friends (not including, obviously, Frank Erwin).

Johnny also, sadly, lost his father that year. His father, still in Pennsylvania, had remarried and was living a happy life, admiring his son's feats from afar, writing him letters in enthusiastic but broken English, saying things like, "We are as usually try to be happy; regardless of our age as it is the way of life which is so precious to all of us."[19] He was active too, still working as an electrician and doing maintenance around his own house and neighborhood. When he was in his late seventies, John Senior fell off a roof that he had been repairing—and he recovered splendidly. But he went too long without cleaning his chimney, and one night he asphyxiated in his sleep from the smoke. Of all the deaths to take a man of his survival ability. It was sad for the family but heartening that his death was an accident—for it seemed that the genes in the family were destined to keep going for a long time.

Knowingly or unknowingly, Johnny was continuing his father's legacy, churning one experience into another. In his father's case, coal mining led to electrician work, which led to a continual rise of helping modernize towns by installing electricity; with each success, he could rise to a bigger challenge, a bigger town. Johnny's work as a teacher and in the laboratories led organically to his work as an expert witness and with Gulf Publishing, which led to more intensive consulting work and the encyclopedias, which led in part to AIChE president, UT dean, vice chancellor, and onward through his life. Each opportunity expanded his skills, making him ready for the next opportunity. The use of one experience to create the next is something akin to a law of nature. It is like needing some yogurt to make more yogurt. Each experience in itself was a pleasure and a useful occasion. But what is impressive is how he fermented them together, turning each experience into a new stepping-stone for the next time he was asked and could say yes.

INTERLUDE=

At Westminster one morning after I battle rush-hour traffic for a short visit with my grandfather, I congratulate him on a bit of news: the UT Ex-Students Association (the "Texas Exes") polled their alumni in 2013, who responded that Dr. John J. McKetta was one of the "Texas 10," a group of their most inspiring and best professors.[1]

He smiles and kisses me. His hands shake after who knows how many cups of coffee, and his hand hovers near his portable phone.

"How many students' birthdays today?" I asked him.

He peered onto his desk, where several spreadsheets lay. "Six today, honey. One student from my class of 1947, and he is ninety-eight years old and still alert. I have one other student left from that first year of teaching, but he has zero knowledge now. He hasn't got anything left."

"How sad," I say.

"Honey, it happens to us. And I can feel it happening to me."

This is hard to imagine for a man who still remembers names, dates, and the rich, nuanced texture of memories. But I believe he is telling the truth.

We talk briefly about his friends in Wyano. They're gone too. So are all of his mentors, his double cousins, and his older sister, who lived well into her nineties. I know most of the men from Wyano, Pennsylvania, are all dead now—what about the women?

He tells me that one or two of the men are still alive, and that of the women, he says, "Those who were lucky to marry someone and leave, they left. I don't know what happened to those. I don't travel anymore, honey. My breathing is too hard."

Then he shows me another spreadsheet. This one is not of students—rather, it is a spreadsheet of all the people at Westminster whom he has had dinner with and all the ones who are currently on his schedule. It warms my heart and I understand what I inherited. I have files of spreadsheets labeled by the year. I know where everything is, always. My dad is the same way, tracking his weight, his favorite sumo wrestlers. Like father like son like granddaughter. Like great-granddaughter, too: I see the same collector's impulse, the natural archivist who likes to write things down as a way to be in control of her life, in my five-year-old daughter.

I share this with him. And I congratulate him again on being the most inspiring professor.

"Thank you, baby doll." He beams now. He taps the phone. "I am now patting myself on the back but happily."

TEN═AIR
Piloting + Policy

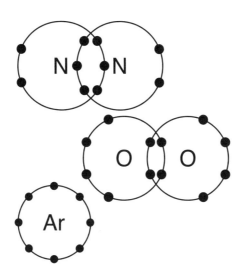

As Johnny approached his own midlife years, the question that kept him awake was the question of energy—both his own energy and energy on a larger scale. How to sustain it? What habits or practices will spend energy smartly when it is—both personally and industrially—a diminishing resource? Johnny knew that he did not have as much energy in his sixties as he had had in his twenties. He loved teaching and being with people. These things gave him energy. How to generate more? Likewise, America was consuming energy at an unprecedented rate, and the media were starting to run stories that soon all our energy-producing resources would run out.

He began to form a thesis, which grew in part from a rising concern that the government was laying down brickwork to regulate the chemical industry—but in Johnny's mind, the government was acting not as

Receiving the Engineer of the Year Award in 1969. Pinky sits in a wheelchair, owing to a broken leg from getting tripped by a dog.

a solution but as part of the problem. The book *Silent Spring* had come out in 1962 while Johnny was still dean, and it spoke to the American overuse of pesticides and the consequential killing (silencing) of birds. The author criticized the chemical industry for harming the earth and criticized the government for letting it happen. The book helped spur on the environmental movement, which resulted in the formation of the Environmental Protection Agency and the passing of the Federal Clean Air Act, both in 1970. This meant that the petrochemical industry was about to become a lot more regulated. Clean-air enthusiasts were claiming that the country could learn to be more efficient (Johnny agreed) by using only solar and other renewable energy sources (Johnny disagreed). But chemical engineers believed it would take more fossil fuels—petroleum and coal—to keep the modern world rumbling along; they also hoped to explore the promising alternative of nuclear energy. On the other side, the environmentalists, led by a young Ralph Nader, were cry-ing out against the further nuclear and petroleum explorations that the chemical engineers were seeing as the only realistic options. It was a dif-ference in agendas that seemed impossible to reconcile.

The first problem, according to Johnny, was that the environmental-ists were not chemical engineers and didn't fully understand the issue. The second problem was that the government listened to the environ-mentalists about slowing down development of nuclear energy and fur-ther attempts to harvest more petroleum and coal, while at the same time refusing to place any regulations on how the American people guzzled energy, so pretty soon chemical engineers were facing a gridlock. The people who were demanding "zero energy" were not the ones responsi-ble for generating the energy. Chemical and petroleum engineers were.

And now America was running into all sorts of roadblocks. Johnny said that in this volatile energy landscape, "I was concerned about the coming energy problem and was flooded with requests to speak." He be-gan to take his show on the road.

Public speaking was nothing new—he had been speaking publicly for a long time to groups in his profession, being by now a known quan-tity in front of any AIChE audience, any administrative audience, or any class of students. But Johnny began speaking to the general pub-lic, giving what his colleagues refer to as his "famous energy lectures." These lectures felt like a natural summation of his work thus far: his ex-pert witness work combined with his encyclopedic knowledge of what was going on in the fields of engineering, now mixed with the logisti-cal expertise from being a university dean and vice chancellor, allowed him a prime vantage point to see and understand the entire issue of how America was gaining and spending energy.

What he saw worried him. He saw that people were using too much energy for unnecessary things, such as air-conditioning to cool the in-side of their cars. He saw that this would only increase, and America needed to think more broadly about where its energy could come from. He saw a problem, however: The government was afraid to make any significant laws to rein in ordinary people's energy use, but Congress was adopting legislation that affected how fuel could be obtained. So the American people's use of energy was increasing rapidly, but the chemi-cal engineers' ability to create more energy was being halted by the legislation. Johnny began to lecture on this, to write articles that would be published in popular newspapers and journals throughout the world.

He began to receive offers to become president of universities and corporations. More than thirty universities asked him in the year that followed his vice chancellorship to be their president. He said no to all, and it especially tickled him to be able to say, "Thank you, but I have a policy of never accepting a presidency at any university that turned me down as a freshman." But the truth was that UT was his home, and he didn't want to uproot, to see the world he had built, his small community, vanish into thin air. He was also offered many industrial positions as president of various oil corporations, and he was asked to be on many more boards of directors. He said no to the presidencies. As for the boards, he said yes to Gulf Publishing, Chemical Consultants, *Journal of Heat Transfer*, and a few others—and of course he continued serving on the board he was most honored to join: Tri-State University, his alma mater, which would later name its chemical engineering department after Johnny.[1] He said no to all the rest, holding fast to his self-appointed rule of capping his board memberships at ten.

He also received requests from presidents of the United States. First, in 1972, President Richard Nixon called to ask him to serve as chairman of a newly set up National Energy Policy Commission composed of seven energy experts from across the United States. "Naturally," Johnny said, "I accepted this very nice honor and onerous chore." This position gave him a further platform to reach audiences with his arguments about energy and the environment. In a *Chicago Tribune* article in June 1972, Johnny was quoted as saying that the energy crisis isn't merely approaching—"it's here."[2] He reminded Americans that our nation's energy consumption had doubled since the 1950s and was likely to double again by 1985. He noted that energy was being used faster than the main sources—oil and gas—were being produced.

In this way, Johnny's public opinions educated the presidents and shaped American policy, even if they didn't shape it as much as he had hoped. During the next presidential term, President Gerald Ford asked Johnny for energy advice, which Johnny was more than happy to give. What Johnny as an individual could do was to continue sharing his vision of a solution: he wanted tighter regulations on how American citizens used energy, and he wanted looser regulations on how American chemical engineers could create it.

When Ronald Reagan, while governor of California, called, Johnny was outside mowing his lawn. Pinky came running up to him. "The governor of California is on the phone," she panted.

Reagan, who was an advocate for growth in the petrochemical industry, asked, "Is it true that grass puts out more carbon monoxide than a chemical plant?"

"Yes," Johnny responded.

"Can you substantiate that?"

"You betcha."

This point—that plants might produce more air pollution than cars—became a staple in Reagan's speeches as he approached and entered the White House. Reagan continued calling on Johnny as an expert on energy and how America should use and generate it. In this way, Johnny's advising of presidents used the same skill set he had honed as an expert witness, though the verdicts were shaping energy policy rather than merely affecting individual businesses.

Johnny became well known for his predictions, which the years ahead consistently proved right. Lecturing about energy became a way for him to teach to larger audiences—and in many cases, audiences whose opinions would shape world policy. He was invited in 1973 to speak to the British House of Lords about the energy situation and the Saudi Arabia embargo. For that speech, he was trained by the State Department on how to behave and to keep his speech under nine minutes. Good thing he was trained, because he was folded fast into British tradition: for his speech he wore a wig (seriously, not as a joke) and was transported there first in a limousine and for the last bit of the journey where people could see him, in a carriage drawn by six horses. Then he went inside and told the House of Lords exactly what he thought England should do.

==

In great part, his rising influence was a joint matter of his own energy matching the nation's. He was riding the wave of the times. The United States in the 1970s was feeling confused about energy. Energy came at a higher cost, both in terms of the price of oil and a new awareness of environmental pollution. The price of oil seemed to be, mostly, out of ordinary people's hands, leaving Americans feeling helpless. But the global powers that exported oil weren't getting along, and the Americans trying to fill their cars at the gas station were the ones affected. In 1973,

Saudi Arabia called it quits, proclaiming an embargo because it was furious at the United States for getting involved in the October War, or Yom Kippur War. During that war, Egypt and Syria attacked Israel, and the United States supported Israel, providing planes, tanks, cars, and artillery. To punish the United States for meddling in somebody else's affairs, Saudi Arabia cut the United States off from oil. This embargo meant that the cost of a barrel of oil in the United States immediately rose from three dollars to seventeen dollars. It didn't stop there: five years later, the shah of Iran was deposed, Iranian oil fields shut down, and Iraq and Iran went to war. Oil rose to twenty-one dollars a barrel. Importing energy wasn't working out.[3]

But making energy locally wasn't much easier. There was also a suspicion of big oil companies earning gluttonous profits, so Congress initiated a hefty tax to make sure this didn't happen. The result? The cost of raw materials rose, but oil companies couldn't raise prices accordingly because they were constrained by the taxes. They exported their products to avoid the taxes. Suddenly there were long lines at gas stations and a sense of scarcity in the air. America couldn't import oil from Saudi Arabia anymore, and American oil companies were sending all their oil out of the country, so where would our energy come from and how much would it cost? These were the questions keeping newspaper-reading Americans awake at night in the 1970s.

Into this landscape of energy confusion came John J. McKetta with his clarifying lectures. He began each one by telling the audience that he was a family man with a wife and kids, and he wanted to keep the environment in good shape for them. He explained that the energy shortage was a very real thing and why chemical engineers needed to be left alone to do their work. He also advocated for an expansion of offshore drilling in the Gulf of Mexico, something that Johnny had partly enabled, for his McKetta Method of determining conditions in a well made deep-sea drilling much easier and more cost effective. His equations could accurately predict what the drillers would find, both the amount of liquid and the cost of removing it. This type of drilling was much more expensive than traditional land drilling, but Johnny got interested in it early and advocated for more of it. It was a practical matter of percentages in his mind: drilling for oil was safer for the workers than obtaining energy in other ways, such as mining for coal. To determine this, he simply

His photo for the 1973 Crain Award

looked at the fatality percentages: he observed that after 1950, less than 0.01 percent of petroleum industry workers were killed on the job. Compared to other ways of obtaining fuel, he felt that this was a good one.

Responding to the pollution charges, he countered that America's air-quality standards were stricter than many worse-polluting overseas countries and that it all mixes together in the world atmosphere. He asked his audience to consider all the unused coal and fuel buried under American land and water—it went untouched, while we wasted energy in importing oil. His work was helping determine the US relationship with its own energy sources. Johnny McKetta's lectures were a mixture of moderate advice for small systems that could make a difference—a topic he knew well across the board—and relief: letting people know that much of what they worried about was simply not worth the worry. He explained for the nonscientific community what *was* a crisis and what wasn't, and what they should do about it.

He spoke out vehemently against the extreme environmentalists. Simply put, the American public suddenly felt very informed and very opinionated about energy. Oil and gas, it turned out, had some rotten side effects. But the American people *wanted* cars. They *wanted* air-conditioning. They *wanted* lights to read by and nice-sized heated houses. They also wanted the earth to last long enough for their children's children's children. And their wants seemed at cross-purposes with each other. The environment was starting to suffer visibly, and the extreme environmentalists argued that Americans could still have the life they wanted without polluting the earth. Chemical engineers argued back that coal and petroleum combine to provide over 80 percent of America's energy—yes they pollute, but the cleaner options, such as solar and natural gas (comprising only 15 to 20 percent), though rising in use, still weren't enough.

To provide Americans with less-polluting energy, chemical engineers urged the government to let them explore promising alternatives, such as nuclear energy, but environmental groups proved such an effective lobbying force that many alternative sources were shut down. It didn't help the engineers' case that later, in 1979, one of the largest US nuclear power plants, Three Mile Island, experienced a nuclear meltdown. There were reasons why Americans didn't trust what the chemical engineers were saying. Petroleum, even with its shortcomings, was a known quantity. We know what to expect with a familiar dragon. Johnny continued to promote solutions that the chemical engineering professionals believed were best—but these "unknown dragons" didn't get traction.

Yet each new president knew that energy was an American problem, and each one tried to address it in his own way. President Jimmy Carter believed that solar would be the energy of the future, and he proposed a plan that would scale back on petrochemical production. In a *Hydro-*

carbon Processing article in 1977, Johnny acknowledged, "Some details within the Carter plan are commendable: a single energy department, conservation, more use of coal." But Johnny vehemently argued that more governmental rules would make the problem worse, stating, "The Carter plan recommends more governmental rules to alleviate an energy problem worsened by earlier, senseless and inflexible governmental rules."[4] Johnny made an important distinction: America was not running *out* of oil and gas; we were running low on proven reserves because we hadn't been willing to drill for oil in the Gulf of Mexico shale and tar sands or use enhanced recovery methods to produce more oil. Basically he was saying "back off!" to the government, insisting that chemical engineers could regulate their industry better than the government could.

Whether he was getting his way or not, the energy world saw that he was trying mightily. He kept being appointed chairman of energy policy committees, from the National Air Quality Management Committee to the National Hazardous Waste Committee and the National Carbon Dioxide Greenhouse Committee. He helped found the National Council for Environmental Balance. In 1975 AIChE awarded him its National Service to Society Award "as tribute to his work toward informing the public on the topics of energy and sensible environmental balance." This news traveled back to Uniontown, Pennsylvania, and was published in an *Evening Standard* article, "Nation's Top Honor for Former Resident."[5]

The following year Johnny received the first Triple "E" award from the National Environmental Development Association for contributions to national issues concerning energy, environment, and economics. That year he was named the Outstanding Engineering Educator in the nation by the American Society for Engineering Education. Soon afterward, a permanent professorship was established at UT, the John J. McKetta Energy Professorship, followed six years later by a $1 million John J. McKetta Centennial Energy Chair.

The US presidents changed, but Johnny stayed in the same place, doing the same teaching, lobbying, and encyclopedia-making work. Soon enough he was advising President George H. W. Bush on energy policy, flying both to Washington, D.C., and to the Bushes' Houston home on the weekends. He often made a football analogy: "The situation we're in right now is equivalent to a Michigan State–Notre Dame football game and Michigan State is ahead 19 to nothing with 12 seconds to go and Notre Dame has the ball on its own 10-yard line. . . . Someone is trying to plot the strategy of what they do to win the game; whether they ought to have an end run or pull the old statue of liberty play. Well, it makes no difference what they do, [Notre Dame is] not going to win. It's similar in the energy picture. Nothing is going to remove the problem."[6] It appeared to all that cheap energy had run out and the crisis was deepening. Congressman Mike McCormack wrote, "The one certain thing about energy is the confusion that exists almost everywhere. But one concept has emerged that has almost universal acceptance— namely, that we must reduce waste in our use of energy."[7] And of course John J. McKetta weighed in:

> The entire country, with the exception of the U.S. Congress, finally became concerned about the energy crisis in September 1973 when the oil embargo was imposed by the OPEC countries. Do you know that your Congress has not put an extra drop of energy into our supply tanks since that date? I mean that none of the legislation they have passed helped to improve our domestic energy situation. In fact, many of the new regulations have *decreased* our supply of domestic energy.[8]

He was working to change how Americans thought about energy. In so doing, he was placing chemical engineers on the map as a real lobbying voice, a wise and logical voice that could advise countries. He was seeking a tricky balance: he had to show people that the situation was dire enough that change was needed, while also reminding them not to panic and shut off energy options out of fear. His 1970s lecture titles reflect these tensions, such as "Why the U.S. Will Not Achieve Energy Self-Sufficiency," "The U.S. Energy Problem: America's Achilles Heel," "The Bright Future of Man," and "Let's Not Cry Wolf: Earth's Population Is Not Doomed."[9] Johnny argued that people should take good care of the earth. He also believed in the earth as a means for supporting its people.

═

In anticipation of sharing his vision of sustainable energy and the travel it would require, Johnny had begun learning how to fly during his deanship. Although the trips that stand out in his memory often took place overseas, much of his travel was local. His oldest son, Charley, who by this point was serving in the Marine Corps, already knew how to fly. "Try it, Pop," he said, "you'll like it." In 1965 Johnny began taking flying lessons on a single-engine Cessna airplane. What astonished Johnny as he worked toward his flying certificate was the teaching method for flight: "Whenever I put my hand or finger on the wrong instrument control, [my instructor] would hit my hand with a pencil or whatever stick they may be carrying. I knew that I would not be allowed to do that in class." Johnny passed his instrument and commercial ratings for flight; his new instructor used the same slap-hand technique.

Armed with a pilot's license and a small chartered airplane, Johnny began flying himself to many of his US speaking engagements. But "some trucks are faster than airplanes," he observed in his autobiography. Depending on the weather, his single-engine plane was subject to flying a lot faster or somewhat slower than ground traffic. But fast or slow, having their own plane gave Johnny and Pinky access to a whole new relationship with travel. They could go anywhere, anytime, on a moment's notice.

Requests for his time and expertise kept coming. Would he serve on the Air Force Institute of Technology Executive Committee? Yes. Would he be the committee's chairman? Yes. If he believed in the mission, he said yes. Interspersed with his travels to the more exotic places were trips back to the land of his childhood: anytime Johnny traveled within a few hours of western Pennsylvania, he made a trip back to visit his high schools and teachers. They were all so proud of their boy, their city's son, because, in his words, "Who had ever heard of a coal miner becoming the dean of one of the largest and one of the best Chemical Engineering Departments in the USA?" He stayed in touch with his teachers for their entire lives, accepting their requests to give commencement speeches at his former schools.

Johnny was flying all over the world to lecture about energy. But strife in the Middle East often made travel hard. In 1966, while he was still dean, Johnny had been invited by the Ministry of Interior of Egypt to advise on some problems with the Aswan Dam on the Nile River. He hired four US hydrologists to come with him, and this time Pinky joined him. When Johnny and Pinky arrived in Frankfurt, where they had their layover, they were met with a telegram: "Your host is in jail.

Please cancel your trip." He wired to the hydrologists not to fly over. Then he learned that the prime minister was dead, and one of the other ministers had taken over the government and was sentencing its leaders to either death or jail. Stuck in Europe but unable to move forward to Cairo, Pinky and Johnny decided to spend the week in Frankfurt, but—as all hotels were full due to an international furniture conference—they resorted to taking a room at a house of prostitution. Pinky shoved a chair underneath their doorknob to avoid any "funny business" coming into their room.

The trips were for work, but Johnny always made sure they added to his life. While representing the United States at the World Energy Conference in Russia, he made a special trip to Korotchenko, the town of his ancestors on the Ukrainian-Polish border. He wanted to see what was left, who was alive, and what he could learn about the world his father left behind. Johnny hired a driver and gave instructions to the area where his father grew up. He saw five homes on the border and looked hard at them all, not knowing which one had been his dad's. He asked the neighbors if they knew anything about the Miketa family. Nobody did.

While Johnny traveled, taught, and lectured, his sons grew up. Johnny said, after so many years of traveling alone, that he loved having his boys at an age where Pinky could travel with him. Both were still healthy. Together Johnny and Pinky traveled to most of the countries in the world and all of the American states. The two adored Alaska and often stopped in Anchorage on a layover between Japan and Dallas. When they did, they liked to stay for a weekend and take small boat tours, sometimes fish for salmon, and always marvel at the coastal areas. "We would lie in the grass and watch wapiti deer by the zillions jump over the newly laid oil pipeline." Johnny became a member of Tesoro Petroleum's board of directors in 1980, which meant a decade of annual trips to Alaska. Tesoro drilled for oil in Alaska and maintained two refineries there.

Alaska was an arena where many of Johnny's more controversial efforts played out. He believed that offshore drilling was the right way to proceed, for there was estimated to be over a hundred years' worth of oil on Alaska's northern coast. But the government kept tightening drilling restrictions, because any coastline is valuable and an important natural resource; marine animals live there and drilling would obviously disturb them, not to mention human enjoyment of their coastlines. But Johnny was an energy realist. His logic was that if you can't truly change people's energy-consuming habits, then the only way to prevent a major shortage and crisis is to keep drilling for oil where oil exists, doing it as safely as possible and in the meantime exploring other options for energy. He trusted the methods and had helped create them. Drilling, in his mind, would buy chemical engineers time to persuade the government to let them work on alternative energy sources.

But there were setbacks, and the public opinion of the oil industry was sinking. In 1989 the *Exxon Valdez* oil tanker struck a reef and flooded oil all over Prince William Sound on the southern coast of Alaska; nightly news showed seabirds and otters covered in crude oil. Johnny was invited by the US government to comment on the event and explain how such a thing could happen. He was not sympathetic to the sentiment that it was a tragedy and the coast was ruined. In his mind, the crash was unfortunate but not the most terrible thing in the world. There is a certain callousness to his response, and I asked him about it. He spoke about the weighing of progress versus accident and came out squarely on the side of progress, even if accident is a risk:

We are always saddened by any disaster, such as floods, explosions, mass killings, wars, coal-mine deaths, oil field accidents, et cetera. We are proud, in most cases, of the high percent of safe days in all these efforts, but the bad days stick out like a sore thumb because of deaths to our people. We are saddened, but this does not affect our morale because we know of the high effort to produce safe products for the benefit of mankind. Some of these severe events result from faulty efforts by man and that we dislike and try to change immediately. Some are from faulty equipment, especially under high pressure and temperature conditions, and these should be discontinued throughout the industry.

In his words, progress matters most, but every failure must become a lesson for how to be more careful. Offshore drilling was and still is a hot button. But it was something Johnny was very much in favor of. He spoke in some of his European lectures about how drilling would help secure energy in the future. When he spoke to the British House of Lords in favor of drilling in the North Sea, he met with some opposition, for many European political parties opposed it. Afterward he said he was disappointed because none of the countries followed his suggestions—except England and Norway, who both took his advice and began securing drilling rights in the North Sea, and their wells began producing two and three million barrels per day. The other countries grew interested after that, but the field was already occupied by the countries who acted first.

There were of course other times he was wrong. For instance, he refused to believe in global warming, even though today the American Chemical Society says in its position statement, "Comprehensive scientific assessments of our current and potential future climates clearly indicate that climate change is real, largely attributable to emissions from human activities, and potentially a very serious problem."[10] Johnny, like many others in the chemical industry, could not listen to the *Silent Spring* lesson because it went against the entire premise of what he had been trained to do. Even so, he tried to be moderate. He listened and contributed. He remained open to growth and personal responsibility, and he continued his work in advocating for his field and its causes.

Johnny approached life as both a realist and an idealist. His habits served his idealist dream for a fairy-tale happily-ever-after long life. But when it came to energy policy, he identified as a realist. This was how he distinguished himself from the environmentalists. He and they both wanted an unpolluted earth, but Johnny knew that energy had to be made. During this time, he was invited to speak at a conference comprising Ralph Nader supporters who were focused on the idea of "zero pollution"—but before he could finish his talk, Johnny got booed off the stage.[11] As it turns out, Johnny's predictions all came true. He predicted the 1974–75 scarcity back in 1960.

Johnny's message to the environmentalists and to the presidents he advised was clear: Money is scarce; be grateful for what you have. Be judicious in what you use to make energy and use all available sources; but chasing perfection is a waste of time.

The coal miner had not left him.

INTERLUDE=

"Djiedo," I asked, over coffee one Saturday morning. "Explain to an English major what the zero pollution debate was. Nader and others said, use no energy. And you said, that's impossible."

"Yes," my grandfather said. "You've gotta have something. The important thing was, I'd start every one of my speeches with 'I am interested in ecology. My wife, my children, need clean air to breathe, and I want them to have it. But I don't expect to provide them with zero pollution.'"

"What did you advise all the presidents?"

He sipped his coffee, jiggled his leg, fidgeted with a Texas penny. "I told them to be careful in the use of energy. Be careful in how much you use, how much you waste. Honey, if you wanted your business to continue, you've gotta have energy. Conserve it but keep looking for more—try to use other types. Hydrothermal. Use semisolid energy. Honey, I stopped worrying about that stuff a long time ago, in 1975 when they stopped listening to me."

"Who?"

"The environmentalists. They didn't care about the future of energy, and that was all I cared about, the availability of energy for the future. We have more oil than any country in the world, but we are sitting on it and don't use it."

ELEVEN=PISS & VINEGAR
Reputation + Retirement

$$H_2N \overset{\displaystyle O}{\underset{\displaystyle}{\|}} NH_2$$

$$\overset{\displaystyle O}{\underset{\displaystyle}{\|}} OH$$

ere comes God," one of his students said as Johnny entered the building.[1] Behind him, the sun generously poured its light, making his body look as if he really were some golden form of pure energy. This was the first class of the spring semester, 1976. He spoke to his students who were waiting in the hall, and then when the clock struck 8:00, he locked the door to the classroom, as always: latecomers beware. Then he wrote the number 183 on the chalkboard.

183? He waited to watch his student make sense of the number. When he waits, his face makes a funny sort of look. His blue eyes stay in action, resting in turn on each person in the room; his forehead raises a little, and his thin lips smile mysteriously. When he can't wait any longer, he explains to the class, "I'm on a diet. This is how much I weighed this morning." Then he began class, singling people out for their specialness, quizzing people, and telling stories. Perhaps it was that day, perhaps another day, when he took up an impromptu collection plate for an undergraduate who was wearing a stained, ratty sweatshirt and said to the student, "Jim, we only have seven bucks so far. Is that enough for a nice shirt?"

While his public life as a national energy adviser was still seething and breathing like a beast in the shadows, Johnny continued to show up for his orderly life as a professor. The teaching felt like a relief, something controllable and fun, a place where he could make a difference without the cross-forces of politics polluting his ability to do his work. Soon after his stint as vice chancellor, he was crowned the Joe King Professor in his home department. People loved this, for if you say it in the right way it sounds like the "joking professor," which of course he also was. But what he was becoming increasingly was the Energy Realist. Johnny saw through the panicked American sentiment and combated it with the facts he saw. For his lecture on receiving the Joe King Professorship, he chose the topic "US Energy Self-Sufficiency Will Probably Not Happen in Our Lifetimes." Self-sufficiency for Johnny was a big deal. It meant America being able to stand on our own feet, having enough resources to be a country of givers, not takers. This was one way his expectation of himself fed into his expectation of his department, his profession, and his country.

Johnny always had great poise and carriage, in part a result of his daily exercises. He was also growing into a distinguished older-professor look. His hair was beginning to silver, and as part of his interest in coin collecting, he began carrying around a small leather bag full of coins, pirate-style. His coins were silver-plated half dollars, and he used them for all sorts of reasons: from tipping for meals (stacking them into piles of five or ten dollars) to pretending to pull them out of children's ears. Johnny called them "Texas pennies," playing off the joke that everything is bigger in Texas. The children of his colleagues all have memories of receiving Texas pennies. His students remember introducing him to their parents and grandparents; one student recalls a swimming party where Johnny said to her father, "You have the boniest damn knees of anyone I've ever met!" and to her grandmother, "Hello, I'm Dr. John McKetta, and I'm one of the most handsome men you will ever meet."[2] He never failed to be outrageous. He still drove around in a burnt-orange Mercedes convertible, waving at people, then striding off to meetings in a burnt-orange custom-tailored suit. It was hard to miss him.

It was in this era, while he was working a full outside life as a presidential adviser and policy maker and a full inside life as a professor, that the God jokes began. One day a student slipped under his office door a poem titled "The Last Psalm." It began:

> Dr. McKetta is my Professor, I shall not pass.
> He maketh me to exhibit my ignorance on every quiz,
> He telleth me more than I can write down,
> He lowereth my grades.

The poem ended with an unavoidable certainty of having to "dwell in the College of Chem Engineering forever. Amen." Some of these jokes had to do with exams, for the professor is the one who passes eternal judgment on the mere mortal students. Other jokes were about Johnny's role in the bigger picture of chemical engineering.

One of these jokes took place in 1979 when Johnny was awarded the General Dynamics Teaching Award for the School of Engineering. This was a big deal, a serious occasion. Two of Johnny's graders asked permission to say a few words, and they delivered a parody of the Bible that told the "genesis" of how chemical engineers were made in six days:

> In the beginning there was oil, and the spirit of McKetta hovered over the oil. And McKetta said, "Let there be distillation, to separate the light oils from the heavy oils, each to their own kind. And the light oils shall be called Distillate and the heavy oils bottoms." And there was distillation, and McKetta saw the separation and it was good. There was vapor and there was liquid—the first stage.

And then, after four more stages of vapor and liquid, the joke ended with McKetta creating chemical engineers "in his own image and they were *very* good." The punch line was that on the seventh day he gave them a test. "And it was *not* very good."

Johnny's days continued to include numerous speeches, award acceptances, and advising work all around the world. Once in Tulsa in 1983 he was introduced to an AIChE section by Professor Frank Manning in terms of the success narratives of his life. It is a beautiful introduction speech, one that gets me in the heart each time I read it, and the one that Johnny himself claims as his favorite. While asking the question "what is success?," it runs down each avenue of Johnny's life, from a good marriage, to his rags-to-riches rise, to his publications, to his worldwide relationships. The speech ends—and I just love this—on an idea that relates, I think, to all the God jokes:

> While the above measures of success have much merit, I believe that true success is developing a stage of mind, an inner courage, your own personal "religion" if you like. Thus armed, you can meet the technical, ethical, and personal challenges of life. And better than anyone else I know, Johnny McKetta has withstood the tragedies of life and has not been spoiled by the pinnacles of success. Ladies and Gentlemen, my favorite success story: Johnny McKetta of Texas.

His own personal "religion" was indeed the backbone of his life. He trusted it, and he trusted himself, and for this reason the majority of conflicts in his life have been external, not internal.

But some of the jokes that surrounded him were less sacred and more mundane. There was the McKetta's Boys debacle in 1977. For years Johnny has said, "I'm so proud of all my boys." It is as predictable as a refrain. Anytime he was quoted in an article or an interview, he anachronistically referred to his students as "my boys." In response, some of his male students wrote a letter to the editor of the *Daily Texan*: "Although Dr. McKetta may be an expert in the field of energy, he apparently lacks any visible knowledge in basic biology. . . . Having lived 'a man's life' and having done 'a man's work' has blinded him to a present day fact—there are women in engineering." The letter goes on to state that McKetta's fixed habit of referring to his students as boys "may have been true back in the days of wooden ships and iron men; however, in these days of color TVs, high speed computers and rocketships to the planets—yes, even women are in chemical engineering." The letter was signed "The Women of Chemical Engineering."[3]

He was bested, in part. He was old world. His science was modern, but his manner and societal expectations were in many ways very, very dated. (Case in point: try going to a restaurant with him when the server has tattoos or is male with a pierced ear.) Yet he embraced change, for the only alternative was to move forward. He responded the following day by starting class with a disclaimer that yes in fact he knows the difference between a boy and a girl. "My mother explained to me that a girl is the one that has a yellow ribbon and wears a dress." Then he snidely added that nobody in his class fits that description. What is true of poker is true of life: "Fold or raise, raise or fold. Never chase."[4] The students raised. So had Johnny.

And the students kept raising. The next day all the chemical engineering women came to class wearing yellow ribbons and dresses. One member of that class remembers the day well:

> On the selected day, we girls met in the Ladies Room. We all had on dresses and had bows in our hair. We then waited until Dr. McKetta closed the door to the classroom; we were certain that he noticed that none of "his girls" were in class. We waited a few moments, once the door was closed, and then proceeded to file into the classroom, where we very properly greeted our beloved professor with, "Good Morning, Dr. McKetta." I believe it is the only time I've ever seen him speechless! After he complimented us on how nice we looked, he told the boys how they "looked like hell," but "don't the girls look nice?"[5]

That day the men in the class admitted to writing the letter to the editor. And several days later, the women rose again, this time wearing to campus T-shirts printed with the words "McKetta's Boys." He accepted defeat. He was wrong, and he laughed along with them at his mistake. The joke was just in line with the jokes he played: it was a funny public callout of a mistake, a practical joke on the joker. And he responded in kind, accepting a critique, making a joke, then changing course to accommodate the new order, and always making time for the student.

To many students, Johnny and Pinky acted in loco parentis—in at least one case attending a student's wedding when his parents couldn't come, sitting where the parents should have been seated, and then afterward giving the new groom and bride one thousand dollars for a honeymoon. "Johnny and Pinky told us, 'Savor each other before you start working for the rest of your lives.' Then they sent us a piece of china each year on our anniversary."[6] No matter what happened in the department, students remember seeing their professor take the high road. One former student remarked, "I never heard him say a bad thing about another professor. To him it was always about the department, and to many of us today the department and John McKetta are synonymous."[7]

Johnny continued inspiring his colleagues in addition to his students.

In 1984 when Donald Paul, former chairman of the department, passed on his chairmanship to Tom Edgar, Paul's advice to the new chairman was, "You should always talk to John McKetta and do what he says."[8] Though his reputation worldwide came from his research and his encyclopedias, his joy came from his families, both his departmental one and the one at home. For this reason he offered to teach without salary after 1985. "We didn't need it. But I'd still lecture when anyone asked." He taught about every important subject, at times opting for classes he wasn't familiar with so that he could keep learning. He also gave many lectures on good directions for department growth. His solutions always involved keeping in motion: "The worst thing you can do in any program is to stick to the program. You want it to widen."

His lectures were always enjoyable, and he continued giving them both at UT and elsewhere. One big one was part of the centennial celebration at Clemson University in September 1988. The president of the honors program, Jack L. Stevenson, wrote: "You made a big hit! People have talked to me from all over campus about the warmth of your presence, the positive content of your presentations, the hopefulness you brought to us from the broad and deep science perspective (with a sense of wit and understandability)." He could banter with the best and turn any mistake into a good time. After a lecture in Sacramento, a young woman approached him in a whirl of gush and fluster and said, "Oh Dr. McKetta, that was the most superfluous speech I ever heard. I would love to have a copy of it." And he replied in a beat, "I plan to write one and have it available posthumously." To which she replied: "Oh, the sooner the better."

The underwear anecdote that I told in the introduction is also part of *My First 80 Years.* Johnny recalls,

Early in 1977 I was invited to give the campus-wide Centennial Lecture at Texas A&M [UT's archrival in all things football]. I was very careful to be dressed in maroon and white, A&M's colors. Dr. Frank Vandiver, the President of Texas A&M, mentioned in his introduction how nice it was of McKetta to be so thoughtful to wear A&M colors. The audience clapped and cheered a little bit. When I got up to speak I told them that there was a little correction to Frank's introduction in that I was not dressed *only* in maroon and white. I then reached under my belt and pulled out the top of my shorts which were burnt orange, the colors of the University of Texas. The entire audience went wild.

This is his type of humor: masquerading as deferential but with a little kick at the end. Or perhaps we could call it a double masquerade, for it is truly gracious. He even went out and bought a maroon suit for the occasion. Rarely in his academic life was he not grateful for the opportunities given. He wanted to let people know; he wanted to say thanks. And he wanted to do it in a way that would always leave them laughing.

His sense of humor lent itself well to old age. Another of his double masquerades became imitating old people, a nod back to his college role of actor. In his old-person imitation (which he loves doing around the elderly, and at his retirement home he has many opportunities), he squints his eyes and gives his mouth an overbite to imply false teeth, and he fakes an exaggerated tremor. He also pretended to forget names, greeting men as "old what's his name," women as "Stella," and his grandchildren all as "Steve!" People in his family always suspected that he did this performance so that one day, when he himself grew really old, people wouldn't know if he's the real thing or an imitation. But now he's a hundred, and we can still tell the difference.

In a similar joke he pretends not to be able to spell. Every one of his ex-students can produce a note from him in classic misspelled English. "Wir so prawd of ya, hunny." "Hot Kawphy Pot: do not touch." Michael Poehl, first a student of Johnny's and later hired as one of Johnny's professors, keeps on his desk a framed note from Johnny that reminds him: "Meeschko—doan ferget June 6 Mundy is lunch at wimen's clubb" (with a P.S.—"doan you kum to work in morning?? I do!!"). Partly this misspelling was a game to amuse himself and his friends. And perhaps for Johnny, pretend has another level: He was born into a world so different from the one where he put his skills and charm to use. Nobody from his hometown could imagine this land above the clouds. His entire adult and professional life was, to his younger self, a great feat of make-believe. In fairy tales, any good game of pretend ends with fantasy becoming real. This is true. We see it every day. Pretend something long enough and you will likely get into the habit. And what is a person's life but a long, dedicated series of habits?

There are other parts to the story that I don't know, that nobody knows. What we see is the man created from his habits, the way water shapes limestone or a sculptor shapes clay. What is left is only the work of art, the man.

===

Things began to change: his secretary Ruth Crawford, after thirty years of helping things run smoothly, retired. In his good-bye letter to her Johnny wrote, "You have been the most loyal, dependable, faithful and capable right arm who could have ever stayed with me through the pro-verbial thick and thin situations."[9] He began teaching less, and his name became synonymous not with the funny man in the classroom who wore a stick-on earring, threw chalk, and wrote his weight on the board, but with the institution itself: a study room named after him, two endowed professorships, and soon the department as well.

There were losses, too. He returned to and often organized the re-unions of his high school class of 1933, and he watched the yearly loss of the men. Nearly all of the graduates stayed in the coal mines, except for a few who became farmers, and even though from the 1940s onward the mines were better ventilated, it still was dangerous work. At the fiftieth anniversary of his high school graduating class, only four men attended, Johnny included. There were fourteen women.

He watched his mentors move through old age and die of natural causes, as well as some of his earliest students. He began to say good-bye to the world of academia, to assess his gains and losses, and to think about retirement. His story as a professor was about to come to a close. To mark this shifting era, one of his students gave my grandfather a necktie that he still keeps framed on his living room wall: the necktie is spotted with chemical bonds that look like misshapen dots from a dis-tance, but a chemical engineer could assess and instantly recognize the elements of piss and vinegar. Since he first started work as a chemical engineer, he had used honey to push his agendas forward—but just as often he resorted to using piss and vinegar. As a whole, it had worked.

Johnny delivered his last formal university lecture as a University of Texas classroom professor in May 1991, at age seventy-six. He wrote a letter to his ex-students assuring them that he would still be available to them and that retirement was a relative term: he was working on volume 39 of his encyclopedia series and had two dozen more to do; he continued to serve on boards and committees and to lecture across the country on issues of energy. If anything, he was reassuring himself as much as them: retirement from teaching, the one thing he has loved most, would not mean that he was no longer a teacher; it meant that he could allocate his most important resources—time, energy—to spread his knowledge to the widest audience possible, as well as to keep a pied-à-terre in his department for students to come visit. He ended his note: "I will be in the ChE building almost every day that I am in town. Whenever you are in Austin, please drop into my office for a short visit. Keep up the nice work. I'm very proud of you all."

INTERLUDE=

There is a story about how my grandfather traveled far to see me when I was two years old. He was in Washington, D.C., and had just finished meeting with President Carter to advise him on his energy plan—and he took a train and then a taxi to our house in Arlington, Virginia, during a two-hour break he had before hurrying back to speak with the Senate.

He left his taxi waiting for him at the curb, and he burst into the house with exactly ten minutes to visit. I was playing on the floor with a record player.

"Elisabeth!" he said. "I've come to see you."

My reply? "Not now, Dan-Dan. I'm too busy."

My grandfather rocks with laughter whenever he tells this story. He thought it was great. He had interrupted me and I was obviously quite annoyed. He had sacrificed time and energy to see me—yet he did not mind, for he recognized in me the inherited trait he passed on to all of his family and his students: that focused work, that lost-in-project-ness, is a wonderful use of a person's energy. Tall credit to the man who found this funny, who had a solid enough self-concept not to be derailed by investing enormous energy to make time for a visit, only to be unceremoniously ignored by a toddler.

And clearly I *was* too busy. I believe he actually didn't get an audience with me, though he did with both my parents. By the time I finished my project and was ready to say hello, he was already off in his taxi to meet with the Senate.

TWELVE═COFFEE

Generosity + Centenarianhood

When he was within a year of turning eighty, Johnny tried out a new role: chronicler of his life. He wrote a casual and funny autobiography in vignettes titled *My First 80 Years* and gave out copies to his eight grandchildren, the oldest of whom was seventeen at the time of printing. Our parents chuckled and made jokes: "What about his *next* eighty years?" It was true that at eighty his energy had not diminished. He still traveled as much, taught as much, worked on his encyclopedias, called his former students each day, and woke up early and did all his daily exercises. He and Pinky still played their daily cribbage game over morning coffee. Pinky still usually won.

It had been a decade since he had tried to retire: he still taught and met students and alumni in his office with all the photos, memorabilia, and practical jokes. Both the faculty and the man himself wanted more of him in the classroom, so he kept teaching when asked, in addition to just being in his office every morning he was in town, five days a week, to meet with anyone who came in, wanting his advice on problems, personal or academic. He found new jokes to evolve with the times: one was a floppy disk covered with plastic spilled "coffee." He liked to keep it on his desk, next to his coffee mug, so that it could excite his visitors. The actor from his Shakespearean youth reappeared in these decades as he began trying to fool his friends into thinking he had lost his mind. One of his favorite "old-man senility" pranks was to walk around the office holding a stiff leash connected to an empty dog collar, pretending to be an old man who didn't realize that he had lost his dog.

He still worked after and before work hours on his many beloved projects. The genesis of *My First Eighty Years* came from a conversation years before over morning cribbage with Pinky: Would their new family members be interested in where they came from, knowing their family tree? He had contacted his cousin Charles Gelet about all the information he had amassed in his family Bible, and in the evenings Johnny and Pinky formulated this information into a family tree, which formed the first eight pages of the book. In response to questions from Pinky about his childhood, he compiled more anecdotes, which Pinky and Ruth Crawford typed. He took the whole thing to the university printing shop and had it bound like a class course package, with orange covers and a photocopied picture of his smiling face.

And on he went to the next project—a project whose generosity and simplicity remain legendary: as he and Pinky were financially comfortable in their retirement, he pledged to give back to the department all of his earnings since they hired him in 1946. This amounted to almost a million dollars. Then he asked his students to match it. The students came out in droves. This was their favorite professor, the man who called them on all their birthdays and who knew the names of their children and spouses and who had maybe even visited them in their hometowns. Students turned out recounting stories about Johnny. Bill Stanley, class of 1961, remembered a reunion when a student approached Johnny and said, "You don't remember me, but I am Duane Keele"—and Johnny stared at the student for about thirty seconds and responded, "No. You are Milton Duane Keele." Of course they would donate. Of course. The donations began pouring in, and the department would use them to grow its research, improve its laboratories, and work to change the world in even greater ways. As a result, in 1996 a plaque at the entrance to the building announced a new name: The John J. McKetta Center for Excellence in Chemical Engineering Education.[1]

As the McKetta Challenge gained momentum, his autobiography gained momentum too. He showed a copy to a friend at the Chemical Engineering Department, which led to their asking permission to distribute copies to donors to the challenge. This caused a ripple of nostalgia and laughter among his former students: reading about their beloved professor dropping out of school in first grade or kicking the priest in the shins. These students continued to return to the university mostly to visit Johnny—and Johnny, loyal to the school where he spent his life, encouraged them to give to the department in any way they could to help the students.

Having retired from classroom teaching, he still was asked to give frequent lectures at UT and other institutions on topics such as what chemical engineers should concentrate on or how departments should grow—these lectures continued until about 2003. His schedule left ample time for travel. In his seventies and eighties he and Pinky had places they still wished to see or see again. For Pinky one of these places was Plitvice in Croatia, a green and lovely spot where sixteen different lakes are linked by waterfalls. For Johnny one was the Galápagos, where he once was bitten by a blue-footed booby and the women in their tour group made such a tremendous fuss over his injury (you can bet that Pinky was *not* one of the fussers) that the men on the tour ended up borrowing their wives' lipstick and drawing their own "booby bite marks" on the backs of their legs. Johnny sparkled in travel situations for his charm and his ability—Tom Sawyer–style—to turn something negative into something that everybody sort of envies. Travel had always been high on their list of great loves, and this time it involved a new generation. At age eleven, each grandchild was presented with the option of helping choose a country to visit. The eleven-year-old trip was Pinky's idea, the logic being that it was a perfect age when everybody was toilet trained but nobody had yet reached adolescence with its attendant complications. These trips ranged from the Galápagos to Nova Scotia to Germany to Disneyland. Johnny and Pinky urged every friend of theirs to travel with grandchildren, for even into their nineties they talked daily about memories from these trips, getting to know the newest generation at close quarters.

My trip—to Germany—was instructive about the nature of my grandparents as social animals. My cousin and I went together and spent the trip on a tour bus with over sixty other people. All were senior citizens or near that age, excepting us two eleven-year-olds. From living with my grandparents for two weeks I remember two infamous Mc-Ketta Rules. One: At restaurants, if you didn't finish your meal, you had to pay for it (though when my cousin and I tested this rule, Pinky secretly paid us back). Two: The only excuse for not looking out the bus window at the scenery was if we were in the middle of a card game. Seriously. Reading was fine in the hotel room but not on a bus. Aside from that, anything was permitted. These were his rules, of course. Pinky never trafficked in rules, though sometimes she helped erode them, standing up quietly for the children. As a couple, they spread magic, complementing each other. Whenever Johnny bristled in impatience at some imperfection, Pinky's calm nature quieted him. She'd grab him by the hand and say, "Johnny, relax." She softened him—and greatly because of her work as his tempering agent, fellow travelers wanted to be their friends.

Quickly John and Pinky became the social centers of the tour. Fellow travelers always wanted to sit at their table during meals and talk with them on the bus (while looking out the window, of course!). Because my grandparents were master card players and always traveled with several decks, it seemed that every meal finished with a game of Blackjack or Twenty-One. We bought cologne in Köln, heard Pied Piper stories in Hamelin, admired cuckoo clocks in Triberg, did the chicken dance in a Biergarten, and ate ice cream at every stop. We visited concentration camps, which frightened us in a way that neither my cousin nor I ever forgot. We were allowed to pick up pieces of the freshly fallen Berlin Wall. My cousin and I were awed when our grandmother could shuffle cards with a perfect bridge finish and take six big vitamins in one swallow without water. We were also awed when a waiter overcharged us and our grandfather looked down his nose at the man and called him a "horse's ass." Later we knew to be truly awed when both John and Pinky carried on many-years' correspondences with friends they met on our two-week trip.

While to his family he was a traveling granddad, to the engineering world he was still a major contributor. Until 1989 he remained on the board of the Acid Rain Task Force. Its conclusions led Reagan to request funds to address acid rain by reducing sulfur dioxide emissions. From 1982 until 1987, Johnny served as a member of the Interagency Task Force on Acid Precipitation, appointed by President Reagan. This board oversaw the National Acid Precipitation Assessment Program, created to find hard data on what was perceived as a growing environmental problem, one that was straining relations with Canada. Its findings informed the Clean Air Act Amendments of 1990, establishing a framework to reduce the nitrogen oxide and sulfur dioxide that contributed to the problem, a program that has successfully abated acid precipitation up to the present day.[2] He served two years in the early 1990s as president of the Retired Senior Volunteer Program, of which he was a member for two decades, and he also served a year as president (and later six years as treasurer) of the Retired Faculty and Staff Association, which he joined at the time of his "retirement."

More awards came in. In 1989 the American Society for Mechanical Engineers gave him the prestigious Herbert Hoover Medal for "his accomplishments in energy conservation and environmental protection, resulting in the betterment of mankind,"[3] a humanitarian honor he shares with Herbert Hoover, Dwight Eisenhower, Jimmy Carter, Charles F. Kettering, Dean Kamen, and M. Hasan Nouri. Two years later, Johnny was named Tau Beta Pi Best Engineering Professor. He traveled to receive these accolades, always giving gracious speeches. Tri-State, since renamed Trine University, named its chemical engineering department after him in 1997. After serving on the Tri-State University Board of Trustees since 1957, in 2001 he was invited to accept an award for being a Tri-State "Pillar of Success." He accepted the award "with grace and humility." He said, "Five days a week, I park my car in the University of Texas parking lot and walk the 150 feet toward the building that bears my name. Each morning, as I walk toward that building, I am thinking of the morning that I walked toward Tri-State's Administration Building, hoping that the registrar, Raymond Roush, would let me register for classes. And each morning I am so grateful that he did."[4]

During his travels, he ran into former students. On a McKetta family vacation in 2000, a trip centered around Seattle, Vancouver, and whale sighting in the San Juan Islands, at a restaurant called Salty's, Johnny was met with an enthusiastic throng. It turned out to be the annual meeting of the board of directors of Tesoro Petroleum Company (a group that had previously included Johnny). The board members mobbed Johnny. They had seen his name on the restaurant host's wait list and waited in the entryway to ambush him and say hello.

In these retirement years, he began shedding objects—a normal response with age to the feeling that the objects that you once needed have served their purposes and can be let go. One such object was his coal-mining hat, which lived for so many years on the corner of his desk: his memento mori, a reminder that he was mortal and had better use his life well. Around 2000, Jim Fair, a professor at the department, was visiting Johnny—as professors did, to hear his insights and get advice on problems—and he noticed for the first time the dirty cap on the desk. Johnny explained its history and importance, and Dr. Fair asked if he could borrow it to show his students. Jim Fair died a few months later, and Johnny didn't want to bother his widow by asking for the cap back.

So that was the end of the coal-mining hat. It surely got thrown away, a piece of dirty borrowed junk. But its lesson had left the cap long before and gone to live inside Johnny. He no longer needed the cap to remind him to keep working, to work his way farther and farther away from the mines, to face life under the sun and keep investing in his life, loving its people, and above all keep working.

Age brought tribulations, but on they lived. Pinky was diagnosed with breast cancer in 1999 and had surgery but opted not to have chemo. The Texas McKettas came to visit her in the hospital, which annoyed Johnny to no end, for her convalescing coincided with a Longhorns football game and all of the chatter in her hospital room made it difficult for him to hear the commentary on the television replays. He hushed people, still formidable when he wanted his way—but in this case, his daughters-in-law hushed him right back. "Don't be a pill," someone said. "Sometimes life trumps UT football," someone else said. He agreed to mute the television. But still he kept his eyes on the game.

John and Pinky prepared carefully for old age. In the early 1980s, they had summoned their sons, fairy-tale style, to each choose one of the three most valuable investments that they had accrued over the years: the Tortuga House and land; eight unused acres on Lake Austin;

and a separate three acres on Lake Austin near Mansfield Dam. They didn't want their possessions causing trouble for their sons after their deaths. They remained in the Tortuga house, paying rent to cover ad valorem taxes; each time the taxes were raised, Johnny would complain facetiously about his mean landlord (middle son Mike) raising the rent again.

In the 1990s, Johnny and Pinky signed up for the waitlist for Westminster Manor, a retirement home in Central Austin where many of their close friends lived comfortably. Often they dined there with friends from the university, so the place felt familiar. Each time they reached the top of the list, they deferred—they loved their life on Tortuga Trail, and it still carried remnants of the life they cherished for so long: turtles bobbing their heads up in the channel, annual student picnics, enough guest space for visitors, animals wandering down from the thickety hills, the sound of the lake lapping the shore at night, and loyal neighbors on both sides. They deferred their spot for over a decade. But at last, as he reached ninety and she eighty-five, they decided it was time to move.

I went over to the Tortuga house often. In between luncheons and visiting students, Pinky spent hours cleaning out the house, while John engineered a to-scale graph-paper drawing of their new apartment, as well as paper pieces of the furniture they would bring. They kept the model on the orange-felt pool table, and both worked at the problem of moving the paper objects around and wondering where they would fit in the new apartment. When discussing their move, Johnny jiggled his feet, impatient to move to the next place. It was clear that the more introverted Pinky was sad about the loss of space, privacy, and their life as they knew it. Fifty years of their life together had taken place in this house: and now that life was ending and they were joining Westminster, where many other glorious Austin lives were coming together to end.

One day I caught my grandmother in the process of emptying out her files. I sat on her bed and offered to help. She had kept for the good part of a century two scrapbooks of clippings on Nelson Eddy, a heartthrob singer of her childhood; recipes and ideas for the garden; essays she wrote in college; receipts; letters. I stuffed things in the trash while she sorted. "Throw it all away," she said at last, without emotion—in this way and so many other ways proving that she was the stark opposite of Johnny, whose archivist's heart would have felt the need to put each item into the appropriate file and arrange them all into a binder set for the McKetta Study Hall. I asked my grandmother if I could keep her college papers to read.

"Okay," she said. "If you throw them away when you're done."*

Johnny and Pinky left the house on Tortuga Trail in early June 2006. It was a hot spring day. The Tortuga house was an empty shell. The movers had come, but late, and Johnny was impatient. The heat oppressed everyone. Pinky waited in the airy, lifeless house, listening to the familiar rhythm of the lake waves. I'm sure they knew then what was going to happen, though they did not talk about it. Soon the house on the lake would be gone. What was in the 1950s an architectural marvel, so carefully crafted down to the flying geese sculptures above the fireplace, would be demolished. Soon the three acres of mown grass would give way to a villa-sized megahouse for a couple of Austin transplants. Neither of my grandparents would ever drive back to look at Tortuga Trail again. They knew this. But their way was to look forward. It was not their house anymore. Not their concern.

What was still Johnny's concern, however, was that the young moving truck drivers did not understand the geometry of their job. They had driven the truck through the narrow orange gates and into the driveway, packed it up with furniture, and then could not drive it out without backing into the limestone cliffs across the street.

Picture my grandfather. The early summer sun shining down on his white collared shirt, his polyester slacks, his thin white hair. He knew he could have done it if he were behind the wheel. He directed them and grimaced and chided them for getting it wrong. He knew angles better than anyone, but he did not have the permit to drive the truck himself, and the movers (themselves not engineers) could not understand the physics of his instructions. Naturally the movers ignored him—they were professionals and he was a frustrated old man.

So back and forth, back and forth the moving truck shuffled. So ungainly and ineffective, and so deeply frustrating to my grandfather, who was not above cursing at these people who, if he had his way, he would

---

*Note to self when I am in my eighties: never, never, never believe a grandchild who promises to throw out something of yours. She won't. She simply cannot.

have pulled out from the truck so he could do it right. My mother was with me—she urged Pinky into the car so they could leave for Westminster and get out of the sun. She tried to coax Johnny too, but he was too busy hassling the movers and making sure they did their job. His frustration was visibly rising.

That was my last memory of the house at Tortuga. The sun, the water, the flat empty house, the expansive lawn, the end of an era, my grandmother at peace with the lake to her back, and my grandfather so angry he could spit at the truck drivers as they nearly missed (again!) butting into the tall white cliffs.

=

Living at Westminster proved the right choice for a man who had always loved universities. It was a tiny campus itself, a five-story building with apartments like high-end dormitories, a dining hall with people who ate together at small tables. It had plays to act in, singing groups, daily lectures and workshops, exercise classes, a hair salon, a gym. It was a place, Johnny remarked with satisfaction, "where you can be busy one hundred percent of the time." It was a microcosm of the world, and like a college, it was a place where a class of people all go through the same life stage together. Many of the residents were former university professors and spouses, so there was an air of reunion about the place.

Johnny was not the oldest, but he was far from the youngest. He was certainly one of the most energetic. He and Pinky participated. They ate their meals in the dining hall and made new friends. They penciled events into their daybooks, going to Tuesday-morning donut hour and joining the welcoming committee for new members. They visited their daughter on Saturdays and went to their favorite diner, Frisco, afterward, where so many of their friends worked and expected them each week. They drove around town in a white sedan with orange Longhorn stickers all over the back window and occasionally with a pair of white horns stuck to the car's frame to mimic a giant white Texas Longhorn (usually, though, one of the horns had fallen off). Johnny also wore a name tag every day, just as he expected his professors to do in the 1960s when he was the dean. This meant that nobody would hesitate in approaching him, asking him anything. His white hair thinned on top, but his body remained strong: he still did his morning exercises, though fewer and less rigorously. Though Johnny began going to the university less often, his time remained in high demand. He kept his tiny daybook filled from hour to hour with visits from old friends, students, family members distant and close. He drank endless cups of coffee with them in his apartment.

Pinky stood by his side but seemed a little exhausted by the rush of daily events. Her nature was more introverted, more intellectual and less social—her great loves were books and birds. When they moved, I gave my grandmother a book of poetry about birds, and her wry thank-you while we waited in line for Westminster dinner buffet revealed a lot about her feelings toward the life of constant interruption: "I put down your book to answer the door, then to answer the phone, then to answer another knock on the door. Finally I gave up on reading altogether, but then nobody came." While Pinky made peace with the interruptions, Johnny found them stimulating. He wanted to be at the center of things, wherever the center was. He had learned to use a computer, even though many friends his age had not. Pinky's interest was zilch. Her life had been fine without one for over eighty years. Why complicate things? Johnny, as one might expect, found personal computers revelatory. Excel spreadsheets! Databases galore! He continued to track the things that mattered to him: his daily weight, his dinner dates, his over six thousand ex-students' birthdays. He kept an office in their apartment and spent time there every day, calling students and corresponding. His home office, like his office in the university department, has file cabinets and three-ring binders full of his papers everywhere. Truly it is a mine of files. Veins of precious metals in the form of big blue binders, held together with aging coppery brads. Binders reaching the ceiling, stretching on long shelves from wall to wall. The first thing you'd see when entering his office is, on his computer, a screen-saver banner that reads, "I LOVE YOU PINKY!!!!!"

His incredible desire to be in control of his information, to make spreadsheets and track things, even things as small as whom at Westminster he has had dinner with and whom he still wants to meet, seems worth a pause. Even at ninety he remained a man of method. It seems to be about being in control of information, being compulsively organized, having a plan, knowing what the future holds if we just comply with whatever is on the list. We may live forever if we follow the spreadsheet, if we use it like a bright headlamp lighting up the darkness. There is salvation there, in having a plan, for his plans pin him to his future instead of to the dirt below his feet. There are no spreadsheets in the black gape of the coal mine. It has been over seventy years since he left the Pennsylvania underground, but I would bet a Texas penny that his lists, plans, and spreadsheets all have to do psychologically with increasing the distance between past and future. Spreadsheets are for people who don't trust their present but who trust their discipline to change their tomorrow. Spreadsheets might keep him alive for a long, long time.

It was clear that Johnny had mastered old age. When his students visited, sharing their stories and seeking his advice, they now regularly asked advice about a new topic: "To what do you and Pinky owe the length of your extraordinarily long lives?" Johnny came from long-lived stock, but in Pinky's family people died before age sixty-five. I have heard this story from so many students, but still it surprises me. Whenever they were asked how they lived so long, their answer was "CoQ10."

"CoQ10?" I asked him during a visit to Westminster.

"Honey," my grandfather said, "the body is a big chemical plant." He explained that CoQ10 is used by the mitochondria in our cells to produce energy. "As we age, that ability diminishes. Baba takes about two hundred milligrams. I take a little bit more."

It was not the answer I expected—nor, I suspect, that his students expected. He was not a health food nut or a vitamin nut. He never wore sunscreen, and he was openly scornful of organic food, his logic being that anything with carbon in it was organic, so anything labeled as such was a hoax. Also, there are so many big, lifelong things he and Pinky did right: they kept learning; they kept in touch, kept loving, kept happy. These things kept their lives epic and kept them alive. It felt like a joke, this CoQ10. But then, all of Johnny's solutions seem to be simple things, done day after day.

There was more: It turned out that one of Johnny's friends in the UT Pharmacy Department had discovered the chemical CoQ10 in the hearts of animals. There was a correlation between it and the strength of the heartbeat. Later this pharmacy professor became a leader at Merck. "He was keeping people alive longer, honey," my grandfather explained.*

In 2008, my husband and I began a two-year tradition of having Fri-

*I asked a doctor in town if he thought I should take CoQ10. He blinked. "Uh, no," he said, "not unless you've had a liver transplant." I bought some anyway. Just in case.

With Pinky at the author's wedding in 2008

day-night dinner at Westminster. It was a way for my husband to get to know my grandparents, and it was fun to see their lives in action. Also we learned that grandchildren are the most valuable dinner visitors. When we were there, Johnny and Pinky had currency—everyone stopped to see what young people they had brought in. After talking to us, the Westminster resident would usually ask Johnny, "Well, how are you and Pinky doing?" His reply stayed the same every time: he'd look them baldly in the face and say with utmost gravity, "We are speaking again."

But the natural fact of being in an environment like Westminster is that all around every day, people begin to die. Death is always in the conversation, occupying a seat at every dinner table. One Friday night we met at dinner a lively woman named April, who paused at our table, laughing and joking, and she patted my grandfather on the back. After dinner, I heard someone say that April had fallen and broken her hand. "She had to go to Health Services," people whispered in the elevator, and this was important because going to Health Services was feared by many residents as being a one-way street. You see the turn of lives quickly, and each one matters.

Around this time, when she was nearing ninety and he ninety-five, Pinky began to talk often about dying, a concept that felt foreign to Johnny. Nobody in her family had lived past sixty-five, so she felt astonished and—because her body was in near-constant pain from stomach-aches and sore muscles and feet—she also began to feel impatient. She got a little scooter and zoomed down to dinner. Johnny hurried her to zoom faster, because he was still quick on his feet, nimble and muscle-toned. The way he kept pushing on to live longer was not her way. When Pinky turned eighty-eight and my mother said, "At this rate you'll live to one hundred," Pinky replied: "I'd better take up smoking."

Johnny, on the other hand, seemed to live on an ageless planet. When he got a pacemaker at ninety-five, he asked the cardiologist how to change its battery. The cardiologist responded, "This battery lasts ten years! You don't need to worry about that." To which Johnny repeated his question: "And after ten years, how do we change its battery?" His family lived long. Recall that his father, healthy all his life, died at age

Greeting his former neighbor, John Trimble, at his ninety-fifth birthday celebration at the Four Seasons Austin

Blowing out candles on his ninety-fifth birthday cake, surrounded by grand-children and sitting next to Pinky

eighty *not* by falling off the roof but by having a dirty fireplace flue. His sister, Anna Mae, had lived until age ninety-four and was perfectly fine and strong until a year before she died. He visited her about every two months. His family lived long, and the exceptions were the horror stories.

To honor him at age ninety-five, and to honor his many contributions to the University of Texas Chemical Engineering Department, the university initiated a fund-raiser to rename the whole department after Johnny McKetta. The university lit up the UT Tower in orange to mark the occasion.

All eight of the grandchildren flew to Austin from their adult homes: we flew from Seattle and Boise; Boston and LA; Richmond, Virginia; and Loveland, Colorado. It was October 2010, Johnny's birthday month. Austin was still warm but comfortable. The lake was smooth, ringed with afternoon runners. The bats at Town Lake were starting to migrate south to Mexico. The days, though still beautiful, were getting shorter.

Over a thousand people, all people he would call his close friends, wanted to come, but the biggest dining room at the Austin Four Sea-

With Pinky at his ninety-fifth birthday party

sons held only 650. Many people whom he wanted there simply couldn't fit, because there was no other venue in Austin where a party could be held that could fit all of his friends. (It brings a new perspective to their home on the lake: it would take three acres to fit everyone!) Lines and lines of his former students, friends, and neighbors came. Energy CEOs flew in from all over the world. I waited in line with my husband and a clumping of cousins.

Pinky was on oxygen by that point but refused to bring her oxygen tanks to the party, despite the efforts of everybody.

"It's for your health!" her daughters-in-law told her.

"I don't care," she said.

It was Johnny's party and Pinky wanted to look nice, as youthful as she could at nearly ninety. She beckoned me over before the party and gave me a pair of Greek key pierced earrings she had bought but believed she would never turn into clip-on earrings. She had never pierced her ears, though she wore tasteful clip-on earrings every day and frequently bought earrings and had the posts removed. It seemed in an unspoken way that this party was to be her swan song. After it she could rest. To the party, Pinky wore a bright suit, aqua-green. Johnny wore orange pleated pants and an orange blazer over a crisp white shirt and an orange tie. He also wore orange shoes.

It was a wonderful party. Friends from all eras of Johnny and Pinky's life came to celebrate them. All of the photos from the event show the same thing: Johnny laughing, his arms tightly around his friends. Pinky sitting nearby, in quiet conversations with people. Old friends, new friends, the children and grandchildren of friends. One former student showed Johnny his orange socks. Johnny pointed down to his own orange shoes. Another man came over to show off a University of Texas tie. Johnny pulled down the top of his orange pleated pants to show his Longhorn-dotted underwear.

Dinner was accompanied by a slideshow of photos, a twenty-minute video of interviews and toasts from family and former students. The master of ceremonies spoke of Johnny's life of love and accomplishments and then said, "Pinky, raise your hand!" She hesitated, and Johnny held her arm and everyone laughed as he raised it for her. They served Mississippi mud pie for dessert, which everyone remembered from the picnics. There was a cake with candles. The grown-up grandchildren clustered around their grandparents.

A portrait of the great man was revealed. The university manufactured fifteen hundred brass Texas pennies with his face etched onto them and gave one to every person who attended and the rest to interested others. The face side reads: "Texas Penny, John J. McKetta, Jr., UT Dept of Chemical Engineering." On the reverse is engraved a huge "95" with the words "Challenge for McKetta honoring a legacy of Excellence." Johnny still carries his in his pocket every day. I still have mine on my desk.

It was a party everyone would remember. Everyone seemed at their best, their funniest, and most loving, and the whole event reflected the qualities Johnny and Pinky brought to their community and the university. As it turned out, this late October day in the hotel ballroom by the lake would be the last time the entire McKetta family would all be together.

After the party Johnny jogged forth into Christmas and the New Year, exuberant and hearty, full of plans and projects. Pinky was struggling. Her family encouraged her to go on more medications, get surgery for her foot and stomach pain, but she was stubborn. She would go into hospice care January 3 and die a month later.

Her last month they spent quietly, resting, playing cribbage. On February 3 Austin experienced an unexpected ice storm, and Pinky's hospice caregiver, Violet, slept on a cot in Johnny's office because it wasn't safe for her to drive home. In the morning, Pinky asked Johnny if he had called a certain student on his birthday yet. He hadn't—he made the call. Afterward Pinky and Johnny did the *New York Times* crossword together—he filled in the ones he knew first, and then she, the word lover and great reader, supplied the rest—and they had their morning coffee and then Pinky said, "I wonder how we can make Violet more comfortable here. I think we can get her a bed." Then she kissed Johnny and closed her eyes and never woke.

All the grandchildren flew in again. The Austin State Supported Living Center, where Mary Anne lived and where Pinky had donated so many volunteer hours, held her memorial service in their chapel. Johnny's grief took shape in frantic-paced action. Everything he wanted to do very fast and efficiently, from passing on her jewelry to family members, to getting to the ceremony. It was his way of trying to gain some control in the face of the most gigantic uncontrollable situation: the loss of this person who gave structure and love to his days. When disaster hits, trust your procedure.

Pinky's ceremony took place in a sunlit chapel in the middle of the school campus. About three hundred people attended. Most people remember it as a poignant and peaceful day: nearly a dozen eulogies from the McKetta sons and grandchildren and several friends. People spoke of her generosity, her love of words, her loyalty. People noted how it was fitting that her last day she completed the hardest *New York Times* crossword puzzle of the week. It was fitting, too, that her last words about making her nurse comfortable were generous, other-focused ones. The eulogy that made the most people laugh and cry was given by John McKetta IV, the youngest of the grandchildren.

He stood up, tall and smiling, with a dark mop of curls inherited from Pinky. He had notes, but he hardly looked at them. He looked at Johnny the entire time he spoke. He began:

I read a lot. I'm not bragging. I'm unemployed, so it's sort of what you do. Most of what I read are fairy tales and folklore. And I want to talk about fairy tales today. I want to talk about how they end. So if you'll bear with me:

You've rescued the princess; the dragon is slain; the ice is melting; the witch has been banished; for reasons you don't entirely understand, the dwarves have decided to return to the mines, because they kind of liked it there. And you're standing there. Looking at the Love of your Life. And you realize that the sun is starting to set behind you. Now at this point you have two options: you can hold hands and walk into that sunset, or you can kiss. It doesn't matter which ones you choose; either way we say the same thing, which is that from that moment on you will live happily ever after. And I want to talk about that. I want to talk about Happily Ever After 'cause I think I know what it means.

John IV went on to talk about the life of Johnny and Pinky, and what an incredible fairy tale and love story it was. As he spoke, he kept his eyes on his grandfather, who was the unspoken "you" in the fairy tale. He named familiar details that made people smile and wipe their eyes: "There's coffee and card games and Greek key and turtles and bowls of peanuts and Mississippi mud pie and oatmeal that has to be made this one specific way, and all of these things that let you know that this life is yours, and nobody else's." He ended:

And one day, after sixty-seven years of love story, one day, when you're ready, when it's time, you're sitting in your room, talking to the Love of your Life, and you look down and you see that hand that you've held every day for sixty-seven years, and it's still so pretty. And you look up and you see those eyes. And you close your eyes and you smile. And you go to sleep. And there's no pain, and it's not scary. And you know that the joy, the happiness you have created in this world, the love that your love story has inspired, it's here to stay. You have made smiles, you have made wonder, you have made magic. You have lived Happily Ever After.

This eulogy resonated because the fairy-tale part, while make-believe, is actually true: it was for his grandfather that John IV wrote this talk, and Johnny's fairy tale has worked out better than he ever could have imagined. The dragons in his life were poverty and the coal mines. He bested both. And he would spend the rest of his very good life still in love with the princess. This eulogy made one thing perfectly clear: Johnny was safe, now, from an unhappy ending.

=

Pinky, though gone, was still very much a presence in his daily life: The funeral home gave him a quilt with Pinky's face printed on it, which he keeps on his bed. His computer still has its same screensaver, the banner still saying, "I LOVE YOU PINKY!!!!!" He says he dreams of her every night, and these dreams eventually grew to include Mary Anne, who died a few months after her mother.

At first after losing his wife, he lost weight. He slept later and later. Basically he folded. He still went to the office and called students, but he had less energy. So many of his daily habits had grown up around her that he didn't see the point of continuing. She was his cribbage mate, his meal companion, co-traveler, his best friend, his "security blanket," as he often said. His family watched. We held our breaths. This was it, this was the story of the great love, how one goes and then the other gives up.

But then, six months later, he met someone. One night when he had gone down to dinner alone and sat at the table of a half-dozen strangers, one woman, a robust, bright-lipstick-wearing, lively woman named Susan Clevenger, said, "Only a man can go sit at any table he wants. A woman couldn't do that." And Johnny, ever debonair and ever a ladies' man, said, "From now on, we will have dinner together with new people each night." Susan was vivacious and she laughed often. Her memory was fading, but she made up for it with tremendous charm, greeting the people she met with the words, "Oh, so good to see you! Now, tell me about everything." And then she'd ask questions based on the information you had just supplied. Her default response: "Isn't that nice!" If it was something you told her with enthusiasm, she'd say "Isn't that nice!" with heart and verve. If it was something unfortunate, like a funeral, she'd twist the phrase slightly, adapting it for silver-lining purposes: "But isn't that nice that so many people came to the funeral." She brought charm, laughter, companionship, nightly card games, and a captive audience to my grandfather, and by summer's end he had regained his weight and refilled his appointment book. We, his family, breathed relief.

But still, through the loss of his wife and through his nearing of age one hundred, his life tunneled in. He saw fewer people. His hearing diminished, making conversations hard, though he tried not to get frustrated. Still, awards arrived. In 2012 there was the Donald L. Katz Award from the Gas Processors Association—an award named for Johnny's Michigan mentor and dear friend and given to Johnny for his lifelong work in gas-processing research and education. The department planned a party for both his one hundredth and theirs, in October 2015. When members of the Chemical Engineering Department asked—bravely, for it's never easy to talk about death—how they could best contribute to a memorial of him, he responded, "Honey, talk to Mike. I won't be there."

I called him every Friday. And I continued asking him questions, trying to get a clear picture of his life as a whole. Its lessons. Its myths. How it all stacked together, every life choice: He could not have come to UT if it weren't for Michigan and his industry work. The encyclopedia wouldn't have happened if he hadn't spent those two years at Gulf Publishing. He couldn't have been the public figure he became without marrying Pinky; the house on the lake and the parties and the community volunteering were her offering. He would not have become a man of the world if it weren't for his sons, for whom he wanted to model travel and worldliness. He might not have kept his humility and vulnerability if it weren't for losing his brother, his mother, his uncle that awful month, and if it weren't for his daughter, Mary Anne, being born the way she was, with an unfinished brain. He wouldn't have remained healthy until a hundred if it weren't for becoming a boxer under Red Richardson, resulting in the daily exercise regime. He wouldn't have lasted so long in all of his roles, loved all of his work, poured love into all of his living people, if he hadn't first been in the coal mines. Life under the sun never got stale. So it all became a factor of something else: his choices, together all making a life.

On October 17, 2015, Johnny McKetta turned one hundred. The University of Texas marching band spelled out "McKetta" on the field during a Texas football game. The UT president threw him a small dinner party. The McKetta Department of Chemical Engineering hosted a tailgate party honoring Johnny and the department's joint centennial

Greeting fans at age ninety-nine during the ceremony for the renaming of the UT Chemical Engineering Department in his honor

Laughing with students at the department renaming ceremony

Wearing full orange at the tailgate party celebrating his one hundredth birthday and the McKetta Department of Chemical Engineering's one hundredth anniversary

"McKetta" spelled out on football field during centennial celebration

birthday, and alums of all ages traveled as if drawn by the magnetic force of wishing to see their teacher again. Many photos exist of this party of Johnny with the newest generation of engineering students in their teens and twenties, smiling next to the old man, dressed in orange, sitting in a wheelchair, who gave his name to their department.

His family traveled for a family celebratory dinner. In the sunroom on the fifth floor of Westminster Manor, thirty McKettas and a dozen members of his companion Susan Clevenger's family came together for cake and champagne. At the party were his five great-grandchildren, playing games on the floor and chasing each other around the elevators. When it was time for the toasts, a series of beautiful remarks were made, familiar stories retold to honor him and to remember Pinky. Johnny, dressed in full orange regalia, sat next to Susan. At the end of each toast, he smiled deeply and lifted his champagne glass. When there was a break in the toasts, he said, "Thank you all for the very nice toasts. It's too bad I couldn't hear a single one."

His admission led to a great roll of laughter. But it was true. He could hear that we were saying great things about him, but he was no longer able to hear what they might be. But even with the slings and arrows of old age and failing health, he remained charming. At a Mexican restaurant celebrating his birthday the following day, Johnny was brought a slice of tres leches cake with a candle and we all sang the birthday song.

With his granddaughter Elisabeth (the author) and two of his great-grandchildren in his living room at Westminster Manor in Austin, 2015

The entire McKetta family and Clevenger family at Johnny's one hundredth birthday party, held at Westminster Manor, October 17, 2015

Clutching his heart in his "pretending to be an old man" charade after blowing out the candles on his one hundredth birthday cake.

He did his old man act, huffing and puffing and pretending to blow—and then he snuffed the flame out with his fingers.

It was dashing. It was unexpected. It was totally charming. He cut a big slice and gave the first one to Susan, who was sitting next to him. It was a triumphant act in a happy, happy day.

And I thought back to the fairy tale that the youngest John McKetta, my brother, had told at Pinky's memorial service. John was right: No matter what happened next or how much longer my grandfather lived, the fairy tale had taken shape and its happy ending had already happened. His worst fears have been met and survived. His wishes, such as they were, have already all come true—and the composite life has turned out better than he ever could have imagined.

=

Pick a day, any day, and you'll find him awake in the morning calling his students on their birthdays. More and more often he finds that they have died since their last birthday call. He talks to their widows or children, then crosses them off his call list. He wishes his wife were alive so he could wake her and tell her, *How sad, honey, that our boy William has died*, but she has gone along with them, and he is alone in his office when the sun comes up. This is his morning every morning, except the people are changing like a great parade, coming in and falling off. Does he stop and think, on an ordinary day, how much his department has grown around him, how both sprouted up from insignificant youths into international glory? Now University of Texas is referred to as "energy university" for all the innovations it creates. Perhaps he notices, as he finish his calls, that there is a space on the edge of his desk where the coal-mining cap used to sit. His inspiration, his memento mori. He doesn't need it anymore.

INTERLUDE=

Last time I visited him in Westminster was spring of 2016. "How are you?" I asked.

"I have less energy, honey. I never felt it until November. My memory is going too. I used to pride myself on having such a good memory." He laughed.

My dad was there too. They discussed a wedding of someone they knew.

"How many times were you a best man?" my dad asked.

Djiedo laughed. "Fourteen."

"Poor man tried thirteen times to get it right, and finally got it."

My grandfather laughed at this. His son's humor was his humor, too. "And only one divorce," he added.

My dad does quick math in his head. "Ninety-four percent is a good batting average."

"How many godchildren?" I piped in. I had just chosen godparents for my son.

"Oh, honey. I have no idea. So many of my students told me that they chose me for their children's godfather."

He told me again how every night he dreams about Pinky. About their life in Michigan all those wonderful years ago, strolling down the streets holding hands. "It is just like it's real." He recalls a few memories from my trip with him to Germany and of the other grandchildren's eleven-year-old trips. "At times you were a horse's patoot," he said.

"So were you," I told him.

He laughs and agrees. "And wasn't it wonderful?"

Then he says something that I hadn't, until that point, fully known or understood. "One of the things I loved best was to see each of you children when you turned fourteen. I always made sure to have lunch with each of you then. That was how old my dad was when he came over to the United States. I wanted to see who my dad was at that age, in those circumstances. I wanted to see how mature you all were."

"I certainly wasn't very mature at fourteen."

"Oh, you were. To me you were."

Then he said he had visitors in the afternoon and needed to rest. We said good-bye and kissed. I thanked him for the time spent and for sharing with me his life's stories.

"It's been a pretty interesting life, hasn't it?"

I said it had. He smiled.

That night after I leave, I look beyond Westminster toward Camp Mabry in the direction of the neighborhoods where he lived when he was my age, a young parent with a young family and an entire long life spread out ahead. And shining behind the military barracks I see the most beautiful pink sunset I have ever seen.

AFTERWORD

The real American Dream story, it turns out, is how to muster the energy to keep it going once you have arrived. Hence my book's title. Energy seemed the thing his life was about, as well as the resource he offered in greatest abundance. I went into this book thinking it would be a scientific biography, but it ended up being a story about love.

I write these final words in 2016, when Johnny is one hundred years old and counting. As I finish up this biography of my grandfather though his eras, in this era a very popular movie for kids involves a princess who possesses a form of magic that turns things to ice. Ice magic is definitely a good trick. My daughter, age five at the time of the writing, asked me recently, "What other kinds of magic do people have, Mom?"

John J. McKetta Jr. has one form of magic above all others: the magic of friendship. From childhood to centenarianhood, he would always be a good friend, drawing communities around him, investing in them, elevating them with his love. People would always remember the way he singled them out, making them feel uniquely deserving of love. He built an entire life, friend by friend, out of this investment. This, above all else, would be his legacy.

His love would have left a legacy for his university, but his work left a legacy for the world. When I spoke with engineers about this book, they referred to Johnny McKetta as "the premier chemical engineering educator" and "the most famous Ch.E. in the world today" and "The Godfather of Modern Chemical Engineering." They said, "He changed how we consume energy." In 2015, within a month of his one hundredth birthday, the American Institute of Chemical Engineers renamed their highest Donor Society "John J McKetta, Jr. AIChE Lifetime Giving Society."[1]

He worked hard. He also worked humanly. If I were to diagram my grandfather's life, it would be a triangle of work-love-play (with his early mornings and his exercises in the center, organizing him and sustaining his energy). He cultivated empathy, self-trust, and discipline: the three things I work each day to grow and the things I tell my students and children are the most important things. Because living a good life requires all three.

And his life is full of lessons on energy, how to mine it in ourselves, how to preserve and spend it wisely on the things that matter most: in his case, work, family, health. In our human quest to outsmart old age, there is a bevy of research being done on centenarians. What scientists find is remarkably consistent: Aside from some specifics about nutrition, the emphasis is on family first, finding a "tribe" of like-minded people with good habits, having a sense of purpose, moving the body regularly, and mitigating stress[2]—all elements of Johnny's hundred years. Johnny's life offers lessons to more than just the scientist. Like any fairy tale, there are morals at the end, however subjective. For me, those morals are many: Invest in people wherever you go, whether family members, colleagues, fellow travelers, or those who look up to you; follow the advice of those you admire; keep telling stories, keep a card game going, keep in touch with people, and by all means keep doing your exercises; cultivate a healthy pride in the life you've made; treasure your work and do it every day. Above all, energize yourself and pour love into your people.

Johnny carried a little piece of the world forward on his shoulders. He did it with discipline, routines, opportunities, good luck, and good love. Then he handed his piece off (like a rock of coal) and stood by while the world kept working, kept moving forward; his field of chemical engineering kept climbing, passing the baton from one person to another to another. He beamed at the passing of the torch.

We carry what we can. We take what is offered from the people ahead of us. We do our best to take care of it for the people who come after.

This was his three-act story. His life. It is all of ours.

The fairy tale has been scratching at the door this entire book, waiting outside like a good beast. Forgive me—I must let it in.

=

Once upon a time there was a boy who lived in a poor, rustic coal-mining village. The dusty earth grew nothing, but underneath the earth you could find treasure. Clothes hung on the lines. Coal warmed up the home. Whole families slept in a single bed. Mothers birthed babies in the spells between hanging laundry, as happened when this boy was born.

This boy grew up. He said aloud, *I want to live a bigger life than this.*

He made the barter for which he grew famous, trading everything he had for a handful of magic beans, as flimsy and foreign as a paper diploma. But the beans weren't magic until the boy took them in his hand. A beanstalk grew, brilliant green against the gray smoke.

Looking up, the boy thought, *I could fall. A giant might eat me. Any ally could turn enemy.* But he had been underground, survived the coal mines once, and he knew what was there. He knew too that the next and final coal mine would be death. Surviving the first meant that he would not be afraid of the second.

We all have our beanstalks. We remember our lives in terms of the great event that happened, the thing that changed us. And so Jack, or John, or any name you give him, would one day look back and see two disconnected eras. Before beanstalk. After beanstalk.

Did they share a single element in common?

They shared everything.

He climbed.

NOTES

INTRODUCTION

1. Jim Harris, telephone interview by Elisabeth McKetta, August 2014.

2. Cora Oltersdorf, "Never Ever Forget the Students," *The Alcalde*, January/February 2003, http://tinyurl.com/pt3b8tg.

3. "Challenge for McKetta," The University of Texas at Austin McKetta Department of Chemical Engineering, accessed August 2015, http://www.che.utexas.edu /challenge-for-mcketta/.

4. "Chemical Rankings," *U.S. News & World Report*, accessed June 2015, http://colleges.usnews.rankingsandreviews.com/best-colleges/rankings/engineering-doctorate-chemical.

5. Michael Poehl, interview by Elisabeth McKetta, Austin, Texas, August 2014.

CHAPTER ONE═COAL (*Childhood*)

1. The source for all ancestral history is John J. McKetta Jr., *My First Eighty Years*, December 1994 (unpublished). All uncited stories and quotations are from either *My First Eighty Years* or personal interviews during 2012–15.

2. *New York Tribune*, October 17, 1915, Binder 1: 1915–1951, John McKetta Archives, McKetta Study Hall, McKetta Department of Chemical Engineering.

3. A. H. V. Smith, "Provenance of Coals from Roman Sites in England and Wales," *Britannia* 28 (1997): 297–324.

INTERLUDE

1. Shaila Dewan, "Miners' Lives: Security, but Never Peace of Mind," *New York Times*, April 8, 2010.

2. Michael Cooper and Ian Urbina, "After Warning, Mine Escaped Extra Oversight," *New York Times*, April 9, 2010.

CHAPTER TWO═GRAPHITE (*Coal Mining*)

1. The death toll depended on the region, though the odds of a coal miner reaching his nineties were not good. A Uniontown paper in September 1930 reported eight

deaths. From 1870 to 1914, the Pennsylvania region averaged twenty-one fatalities a month (Albert H. Fay, comp., *Coal-Mine Fatalities in the United States, 1870–1914* [Washington, DC: Government Printing Office, 1916], http://tinyurl.com/ntbxwk6). In its 1936 annual report, the Bituminous Coal Division for Pennsylvania reported 190 fatal accidents (which average 15 a month for the whole region, or one every other day) and 2,049 nonfatal accidents causing disability of at least sixty days. There were accidents every workday, and these statistics do not count black lung, which killed many coal miners in the years after they retired. It would be a lucky thing for a man in the coal mines to live twenty years (http://www.coalmininghistorypa.org/annualreport /1936/1936_bit/1936_bituminous.pdf).

2. Raymond A. Washlaski and Ryan P. Washlaski, "Palmer Mine and Coal Docks," The 20th Century Society of Western Pennsylvania, June 15, 2009, http:// patheoldminer.rootsweb.ancestry.com/faypalmer.html.

3. *Klass Klassics*, Binder 1: 1915–1951, John McKetta Archives.

4. *Popular Mechanics*, August 1950, http://tinyurl.com/nzstzbq.

CHAPTER THREE=BLOOD (*College*)

1. "Dr. John McKetta, Jr. Honored at Spring Meeting," American Institute of Chemical Engineers Keynote by John J. McKetta Jr., May 28, 2013, http://www.aiche .org/news/institute/05-01-2013/dr-john-mcketta-jr-honored-spring-meeting.

2. "Crushed to Death beneath Shovel," *Morning Herald* (Uniontown, Pennsylvania), February 25, 1936, 1, https://www.newspapers.com/newspage/63637475/.

3. Mike McKetta, letter to John J. McKetta Jr., 1969, McKetta Family Archives.

CHAPTER FOUR=MERCURY (*Industry + Graduate School*)

1. W. W. Knight Jr., letter to John J. McKetta Jr., August 18, 1937, Binder 1: 1915–1951, McKetta Archives.

2. When I was interviewing my grandfather in March 2015, he said of Professor Moore, "His son lives in Pittsburgh and his granddaughter lives in Arlington, Texas. His granddaughter and her husband are visiting tomorrow."

3. Jane Nelson, *Positive Discipline* (New York: Ballantine Books, 2006).

4. Binder 1: 1915–1951, McKetta Archives.

5. George G. Brown, letter to John J. McKetta Jr., June 12, 1943, Binder 1: 1915– 1951, McKetta Archives.

CHAPTER FIVE=HONEY (*Love + Marriage*)

1. All quotes from Helen Elisabeth Smith are from unpublished files, McKetta Family Archives.

CHAPTER SIX═CHALK (*A Young Professor in Texas*)

1. John J. McKetta Jr., postcard to Helen McKetta, 1955, McKetta Family Archives.
2. Howard F. Rase and William A. Cunningham, *Chemical Engineering at the University of Texas, 1910–1990* (Austin: Department of Chemical Engineering, College of Engineering, University of Texas at Austin, 1990).
3. Ibid., 2.
4. Ibid., 18.
5. Ibid., 8.
6. Ibid.
7. Ibid., 67.
8. Ibid., 33.
9. Ibid., 38.
10. Natural gas is a waste product of oil production, and one of Schoch's research crusades was to figure out how to make it valuable.
11. Rase and Cunningham, *Chemical Engineering*, 35–36.
12. Ibid., 68.
13. Ibid., 84.
14. Pam Mitchell (spouse of Bill Galloway), e-mail to Elisabeth McKetta, May 24, 2016.
15. Michael Poehl, interview by Elisabeth McKetta, Austin, Texas, August 2014.

CHAPTER SEVEN═PETROLEUM (*Research + The Laboratory*)

1. Rase and Cunningham, *Chemical Engineering*, 84.
2. Ibid.
3. Helen Elisabeth Smith McKetta, letter to John J. McKetta Jr., 1947, Binder 1: 1915–1951, File: "Letters from de Pink," McKetta Archives.
4. Rase and Cunningham, *Chemical Engineering*, 117–18.

CHAPTER EIGHT═PAPER (*What Started the Encyclopedia*)

1. *Hydrocarbon Processing* Archives, Carnegie-Mellon Library.
2. A quick definition of polymers for non-engineers: Rooted in the Greek words *poly*, "many," and *meros*, "part," polymers are "molecular substances of high molecular mass formed by the *polymerization* (joining together) of monomers, molecules with low molecular mass." There are polymers both natural (such as wool) and human-made (such as milk-jug plastic). The study and synthesis of polymers exploded in the postwar period. Theodore L. Brown, H. Eugene LeMay Jr., and Bruce E. Bunsten, *Chemistry: The Central Science*, 8th ed. (Upper Saddle River, NJ: Prentice Hall, 2000), 440.
3. Dan Gilbert, "The Surprising Science of Happiness," TED Talk, January 2004, https://www.ted.com/talks/dan_gilbert_asks_why_are_we_happy?language=en.
4. Description of John J. McKetta, *Encyclopedia of Chemical Processing and De-*

sign, vol. 1, *Abrasives to Acrylonitrile* (Boca Raton, FL: CRC Press, 1976), http://www .amazon.com/Encyclopedia-Chemical-Processing-Design-Acrylonitrile/dp/08247245 18?ie=UTF8&keywords=encyclopedia%20of%20chemical%20processing%20 and%20design%20mcketta&qid=1465321890&ref_=sr_1_1&sr=8-1.

5. Now the Austin State Supported Living Center.

6. Tom Edgar, interview by Elisabeth McKetta, Austin, Texas, August 2014.

7. Michael Poehl, interview by Elisabeth McKetta, Austin, Texas, August 2014.

CHAPTER NINE═LIMESTONE (*Administration + The House on the Lake*)

1. Tom Edgar, interview by Elisabeth McKetta, Austin, Texas, August 2014.

2. Jim Harris, phone interview by Elisabeth McKetta, August 2014.

3. "Job Market Remains Bleak for Graduates," *Chemical Engineering News* 49, no. 45 (November 1, 1971): 26, pubs.acs.org/doi/abs/10.1021/cen-v049n045.p026.

4. Rase and Cunningham, *Chemical Engineering*, 104.

5. Ruth Crawford, phone interview by Elisabeth McKetta, July 2015.

6. "Department Head Close Competitor of Miss Engineer," *Daily Texan*, May 1, 1957, 5.

7. John J. McKetta Jr., letter to the Texas State Board of Registration for Professional Engineers, November 6, 1961, McKetta Family Archives.

8. Rase and Cunningham, *Chemical Engineering*, 129.

9. Ibid., 132.

10. Dwonna Goldstone, *Integrating the 40 Acres* (Athens: University of Georgia Press, 2012).

11. "Statistics on Women in Engineering," Cockrell School of Engineering, accessed April 14, 2016, http://www.engr.utexas.edu/wep/about/stats.

12. Alexander H. Tullo, "Women in Industry," *Chemical & Engineering News* 91, no. 34 (August 26, 2013), http://cen.acs.org/articles/91/i34/Women-Industry.html.

13. Rase and Cunningham, *Chemical Engineering*, 134–35.

14. Ibid., 137, 133.

15. Ibid., 149.

16. John J. McKetta Jr., "Teaching Effectiveness Program," *Engineering Education* 60, no. 4 (December 1969): 325.

17. Permian Basin University at Odessa, University of Texas at Dallas, University of San Antonio, and University of Texas at El Paso.

18. "Conflict Marks Frank Erwin's Career," *Daily Texan*, August 14, 1970, 2.

19. John McKetta Sr., letter to John J. McKetta Jr., February 27, 1965, McKetta Family Archives.

INTERLUDE

1. "Texas 10," Texas Exes, accessed July 2014, www.texasexes.org/awards/teaching -and-administrative-awards/texas-10.

CHAPTER TEN═AIR (*Piloting + Policy*)

1. "Energy Advisor to Four Presidents Put Students First," University of Michigan College of Engineering Alumni, 2013, http://www.engin.umich.edu/che/alumni/info/profiles/john-mcketta.

2. Kenneth Ross, "Energy Crisis Is Here: McKetta," *Chicago Tribune*, June 18, 1972, http://archives.chicagotribune.com/1972/06/18/page/119/article/no-magic-solution.

3. Rase and Cunningham, *Chemical Engineering*, 161.

4. John J. McKetta Jr., "Energy: Looking Ahead but Moving Backward," *Hydrocarbon Processing*, November 1977.

5. "Nation's Top Honor for Former Resident," *Evening Standard* (Uniontown, PA), July 6, 1976, 11.

6. John J. McKetta Jr., *The US Energy Problem: America's Achilles' Heel* (University Park: Pennsylvania State University Press, 1978).

7. Mike McCormack, "Putting Down the Scare Stories and Facing Reality," National Geothermal Data System, September 1, 1975, http://search.geothermaldata.org/dataset/putting-down-the-scare-stories-and-facing-reality.

8. "EEE Review," Binder: October 1975–January 1976, McKetta Archives.

9. John J. McKetta Jr., "Let's Not Cry Wolf: Earth's Population Is Not Doomed," *Mattoon (Il) Journal Gazette*, August 9, 1975, McKetta Archives.

10. "Global Climate Change," ACS Position Statement, accessed June 2016, https://www.acs.org/content/acs/en/policy/publicpolicies/promote/globalclimatechange.html.

11. "Nominated by Herbert H. Woodson, Dean," nomination of John J. McKetta for the 1992 National Medal of Technology, October 30, 1991, McKetta Archives.

CHAPTER ELEVEN═PISS & VINEGAR (*Reputation + Retirement*)

1. Jim Harris, phone interview by Elisabeth McKetta, August 2014.

2. Mary Blackburn, e-mail to Elisabeth McKetta, May 1, 2016.

3. "Letter to the Editor," *Daily Texan*, March 11, 1977.

4. James McManus, *Positively Fifth Street* (New York: Picador, 2004), 104.

5. Mary Blackburn, e-mail to Elisabeth McKetta, May 1, 2016.

6. Linda Harris, phone interview by Elisabeth McKetta, August 2014.

7. Jim Harris, phone interview by Elisabeth McKetta, August 2014.

8. Tom Edgar, interview by Elisabeth McKetta, Austin, Texas, August 2014.

9. John J. McKetta Jr., letter to Ruth Crawford, January 11, 1991.

CHAPTER TWELVE═COFFEE (*Generosity + Centenarianhood*)

1. Laurel Graeber, "A Professor Earns, and Returns, His Pay," *New York Times*, January 7, 1996, http://www.nytimes.com/1996/01/07/education/blackboard-a-professor-earns-and-returns-his-pay.html.

2. Public Papers of the Presidents of the United States: Ronald Reagan, 1987, http://tinyurl.com/jh4n2ee; and Paulette Mandelbaum, ed., *Acid Rain: Economic Assessment* (New York: Plenum Press, 1985), 232, http://tinyurl.com/gobsssm.

3. "Past Hoover Medal Recipients," American Society of Mechanical Engineers, accessed April 2014, https://www.asme.org/about-asme/honors-awards/unit-awards/hoover-awards/past.

4. *Tri-State Connections Magazine*, 2001, 1.

AFTERWORD

1. "Lifetime Giving Society Renamed to Honor John McKetta," AIChE Giving, accessed June 2016, http://www.aiche.org/giving/impact/stories/lifetime-giving-society-renamed-honor-john-mcketta.

2. Dan Buettner, "Power 9," Blue Zones, April 9, 2014, https://www.bluezones.com/2014/04/power-9/.

THANKS=COPPER

I wish I had Texas pennies to give to all the people who made this book possible. To my grandfather for sharing his memories over many years of meals, phone calls, and e-mails. To the entire McKetta family for their vast and open-minded support, especially Randy and Jeannie for talking chemistry, Terry for finding photographs, Sallie for proof-reading, Charley for responding to all my e-mails seeking stories, and Mike for helping with a hundred details great and small. To my parents, champions both: thank you for the world so high. To the donors who helped fund this book: Rex and Kathleen Bennett and Bill and Alvern Stanley. To Evan Mull, whose research connected all the dots. To Merle Thomas, Ruth Crawford, Michael Poehl, Tom Edgar, Don Paul, and Jim and Linda Harris for their recollections and advice. To Marisa Meier and Tom Truskett for their tremendous loyalty to both John McKetta and the department that bears his name. To Lynn Miller, who always gives exactly the right feedback at exactly the right time. To Kristi Gregory, Sarah Tregay, Kim Meyers Warren, first readers. To Maeve Cooney for her careful proofreader's eye. To all the Vixens for their inspiration, wonder, and wisdom. To James always and for more reasons than I can count. To the next generation of McKettas: keep climbing.

INDEX

Italic page numbers indicate photographs. JJM = John J. McKetta Jr.

acid rain, 58, 179

Advances in Petroleum Chemistry and Refining (ed. McKetta), 110–11

AIChE (American Institute of Chemical Engineers), *94*, 131–34 (*132*), 138, 140–41, 157

Air Force Institute of Technology, 159

air pollution, 19, 57–58, 153, 155–56, 162–63

Alaska, 160–61

"Alcoholic Breath Detector" exhibit, 97

alkylation, 83

alumni hiring, 136

anthracite coal, 8–9

antitrust laws waivers, 92

Army Specialized Training Program, 60

Aswan Dam, 159

atom bomb project, 60–61

Austin, Texas, 79, 96; airport, 133; Austin State School/Supported Living Center, 116, 191; birthday party at Four Seasons, 188–89; General Foods trips to, 127; JJM business relationships in, 138; JJM Lake Austin property, 121–25, 180–81; return to, 108; Scholz Garten incident, 87. *See also* University of Texas (Austin); Westminster Manor

autobiography. See *My First 80 Years* (McKetta autobiography)

awards. *See* honors and awards (JJM)

"Baba," Pinky as, 27, 67

Bair, Mary, 22

Baker, Ed, 61

Baytown, Texas, 91

benzene, 52, 54

best man, JJM as, 61

"Big Lab," 83

birthday calls to students, 4, 87–88, 117, 146, 176, 184, 191, 199–200

birthday skip rule for students, 87, 117

bituminous coal, 8–9

Blaney, Walter "Zany," 86

bleach, 56

block system for students, 138–39

boxing, JJM's love of, 3, 23, 44, 76, 88, 101

Boyce, Doc, 40

"Boy's Town" outing, 140–41

"Bright Future of Man, The" lecture, 158

brine, electrolysis of, 52

British House of Lords, JJM speech before, 153, 161–62

Brown, George Granger "Great God," 57, 58–59, 60

Brown, Jay, 95

Bruns, Joe, 138

Bureau of Industrial Chemistry, 83

burnt-orange color, JJM and: cars, 4, 166, 183; cover on autobiography, 176; McKetta T-shirts, 136; suits and shoes, 73, 123, *124*, 166, 190, *196*, 197; Tortuga house decor, 123, *124*, 181–82; underpants, 1–2, 4, 170–71, 190; UT Tower light honoring JJM, 188. *See also* football, JJM's love of

Bush, George H. W., 4, 157

camping vacations, 99, 107
Camp Mabry, 98
Carter, Jimmy, 156–57, 174
Cashmore, Bill and Ethel, 55–56, 70
Cashmore, Bill Jr., 56
catalytic cracking, 83
caustic soda (lye), 52, 56
cement, 81
Center for Excellence in Chemical Engi-
neering Education, 177
ceramic scrubbers, 57–58
chalk-throwing at students, 88, 100, 109,
117, 125
"Challenge for McKetta" campaign, vii,
4, 177, 190
Chemical Consultants board, 152
"Chemical Cow" exhibit, 97
Chemical Engineering Department
(Michigan Alkali), 51–52, 54, 59
Chemical Engineering Department (Tri-
State), 36, 40, 152, 179
Chemical Engineering Department (UT
Austin), 92, *143*; early history, 79–82;
founded in JJM's birth year, 79, 194–
95; under JJM as dean, 133–39, 142;
as one of top-five nationwide, 4; party
for JJM's hundredth birthday, 194–
95 (*196*); "Power Show," 97; renamed
for JJM, 4, 188, 194, *195*; reputation
for humor, practical jokes, 81, 96–97,
125, 128–29; statement on JJM, 92.
See also University of Texas (Austin)
chemical engineering field: early days
of, 79–83, 89, 107; *Encyclopedia for
Chemical Processing and Design* (ed.
McKetta), 4, 108, 110–15, 141, 172; as
trash-to-treasure, 81; women in, 168–
69; and World War II, 83–84
Chemical Engineering Foundation,
127–28
Chemical Engineering News, 126
Chemical Engineering Newsletter, 82
chloralkali process, 52, 56

Claude B. Schneible Company, 57–58
Clean Air Act, 58, 150, 179
Clevenger, Susan, 193–94, 197–99 (*198*)
Coal Carbonization (Porter), 35–36
coal mining, 1; children's fears of, 14;
coal-mining hours, 47, 60, 90; dangers of, 9, 11, 13–14, 57, 154, 172, 207–
8n1 (ch2); electrification of mines,
16–18; by European immigrants, 11;
Great Depression mine closings, 22;
JJM learning from brother, 31–32, 34–
35; JJM's description of, 37–38; JJM
studying chemistry of, 44; McKetta
Bros. & Sons Coal Company, 30–31,
44; Michigan Alkali recovering benzene from, 52; petroleum, natural gas
overtaking, 52–53, 154–55; during
Roman Empire, 11; "room-and-pillar
mines," 9; Upper Big Branch mine
explosion, 27; U.S. pollution laws
and, 155–57; in western Pennsylvania,
8–9, 65; wives of miners, 7, 9
coal-mining cap, JJM's, 48, 57, 114, 180,
200
Cockrell, Ernest (Cockrell Oil Company), 127–28
coins: JJM collecting, 119–20, 141, 166;
"Texas pennies," 5, 119, 166, 190
Coleman, Bill, 123
"Conflict Marks Frank Erwin's Career"
(*Daily Texan*), 142
conservation, energy, 18, 96, 151–52,
156–57
consumer economy, 92
Cook, Tex, 127
"Cooperative Engineering Program," 138
copyright fraud lawsuit, JJM assisting
in, 95
CoQ10, 185–86
cornet/trumpet, JJM playing, 24–25, 41,
45
cottonseed oil, 81
Cowsert, Mr., 122

Crain Award, *155*
Crawford, Ruth, 128, 172, 176
cribbage, 76, 78, 141, 175, 191
Cunningham, Bill, 82, 129
cyclization, 83

Daily Texan articles, 129, 142, 168
degrees and academic positions (JJM):
    bachelor's degree, 48; master's de-
    gree, 57–58; PhD, 58–59; accepting
    job at University of Texas, 79, 84–85
    (*84*); promotion to associate profes-
    sor, 89; as Chemical Engineering de-
    partment chair, 100, 129, 131, *143*; as
    dean of Engineering, 133–39, 142; as
    vice chancellor, 139, 142–44. *See also*
    Chemical Engineering Department
    (UT Austin)
dental procedure, JJM allowing room-
    mate to practice, 59
Depression, 17, 22, 30–31, 34, 66, 82–83
Dewan, Shaila, 27
Disneyland, 177
"Djiedo," JJM as, 27
Donald L. Katz Award (Gas Processors
    Association), 194. *See also* Katz, Don-
    ald Laverne
double cousins, 12–14 (*14*), 22, 45
double masquerade humor, 171
Dow Chemical, 82, 99, 137
Dudley, Ray and Frederica, 108

Eddy, Nelson, 67
Edgar, Tom, 127, 170
efficiency expert, JJM as, 54–55, 106
Egypt, 154, 159
Einstein, Albert, 61
electrification of mines, 16–17
electrolysis of brine, 52
eleven-year-old trips, 177–78
*Encyclopedia for Chemical Processing and
    Design* (ed. McKetta), 4, 108, 110–15,
    141, 172

energy: and air pollution, 19, 57–58, 153,
    155–56, 162–63; efficiency, 150; JJM
    as advisor to presidents on, 4, 152–53,
    156–57, 174, 179; JJM high-pressure re-
    search, 93; JJM lectures/articles on,
    94, 113, 151–59, 161, 163, 166, 173; nu-
    clear, 150, 156; oil embargo (1973),
    158; petroleum and natural gas as fu-
    ture of, 52–53; sustainability, 149;
    Three Mile Island meltdown, 156. *See
    also* petroleum
Energy Realist, JJM as, 166
Engineer of the Year Award (1969), *150*
England and North Sea oil, 162
environmentalism: acid rain issue, 179;
    after *Exxon Valdez* accident, 161; ver-
    sus consumerism, 156; Environmental
    Protection Agency, 58, 150; Federal
    Clean Air Act (1970), 58, 150, 179;
    JJM on, 150–58, 162, 163
Erwin, Frank, 95, 142–44
Ewing, Anne. *See* Anne Smith
Ewing, Ertinsa (née Shaver), 66
Ewing, William, 66
expert witness, JJM as, 95–96
Exxon/Humble Oil, 82, 137, 161

faculty, JJM's support for, 138–40
Fair, Jim, 180
family values, 19
Federal Clean Air Act (1970), 58, 150, 179
Ficks, David, 23
fifty-second classroom quizzes, 87, 126
Flawn, Peter, 144
football, JJM's love of, 23–25, 101, 129,
    170–71, 180, 194, *197*. *See also* burnt-
    orange color, JJM and
football analogy regarding energy,
    157–58
Ford, Gerald, 4, 152
foundations for research, 100, 127–28,
    135
Four Seasons Hotel, 188–89

fourteen, significance of age, 11–12, 202
Freshman Engineering Honors Program, 139
friction loss of fluid, 93
Frisco diner, 116–17, 183

Galápagos trip, 177
gas scrubbing, 57–58
Gatlin, Carl, 129
Gelet, Charles (cousin of JJM), 176
Gelet, John and Anna (uncle and aunt of JJM), 12–13
Gelet, Julia (aunt of JJM), 12, 45
Gelet, Mary. *See* McKetta, Mary (née Gelet, mother of JJM)
General Dynamics Teaching Award, 167
General Foods, 99, 127
General Motors, 100
Germany, 61, 79–80, 177–78
GI Bill, 84–85
Gilbert, Daniel, 114
girls-on-a-bus plan, 137–38
global warming, 162
"Godfather of Modern Chemical Engineering," JJM as, 203
God jokes, 167–68
Great Depression, 17, 22, 30–31, 34, 66, 82–83
Groppe, Henry, 88–89
Gulf Coast petroleum refining, 83, 92
Gulf of Mexico offshore drilling, 93
Gulf Publishing Company, 105–10, 113, 131, 140, 145, 152, 194

habits, JJM's lifelong, 47–48, 113–14, 117, 131, 171–72
Hackerman, Norm, 143
Hall, Tracy, 112
Handy, Burton, 36, 39–40
Harmon, Fred, 88
Harris, Jim, 125
Haun, James, 88
Haynes, Kevin, 2
helium, 80

Herbert Hoover Medal (American Society for Mechanical Engineers), 179
"his boys," 23, 168–69
Holst, Henry, 59–60
homemade cards, 49
honors and awards (JJM): AIChE Founder's Award, 133; AIChE Lifetime Giving Society, 203; AIChE Most Distinguished Service Award, 133; AIChE National Service to Society Award, 157; AIChE W. K. Lewis Award, 141; Allied Chemical Award, 78–79; board memberships, 152; Center for Excellence in Chemical Engineering Education, 177; Crain Award (1973), *155*; Donald L. Katz Award (Gas Processors Association), 194; Engineer of the Year Award (1969), *150*; General Dynamics Teaching Award, 167; Herbert Hoover Medal (American Society for Mechanical Engineers), 179; International Chemical Engineering Award, 4; Joe King Professorship, 166; John J. McKetta Centennial Energy Chair, 157; John J. McKetta Energy Professorship, 157; McKetta Chemical Engineering Department, 172, 188, 194, *195*; Outstanding Engineering Educator (American Society for Engineering Education), 157; "Pillar of Success" Award (Tri-State), 179; "Texas 10" poll, 146; Triple "E" Award (National Environmental Development Association), 157; W. K. Lewis Award, 141
honors program, freshman engineering, 139, 170
horned toads as pets, 130
Humble Oil/Exxon, 82, 91, 95, 99
humor (JJM), *41*, *42*, *53*, *85*, *132*, *199*; "Alcoholic Breath Detector" exhibit, 97; "Boys' Town" outing, 140–41; "Chemical Cow" exhibit, 97; God jokes, 167–68; hiding under desks,

100; homemade cards, 49; joke recommendation letter, 129; misspelled English, 171; mowing incident, 122; "old-man senility" pranks, 171, 176, 199 (199); piss-and-vinegar necktie, 172; prefeminist pranks, 96; runner up for "Miss Engineer 1957," 129; Shakespearean acting, 48, 101, 176; shoeless student, 128; "Stella" and "Steve," 171; "sympathy" cards, 49; UT-themed underwear, 1–2, 170–71, 190

Hydrocarbon Processing Industry (*Petroleum Refiner Magazine*), 92, 105–8, 156–57. *See also* Gulf Publishing Company

hydrocarbon research and applications, 4, 59, 92–95

hydrogenation, 83

hydrogen sulfide, 57–58

hydrothermal energy, 163

"Inspection Trip" class, 83

Interagency Task Force on Acid Precipitation, 179

International Chemical Engineering Award, 4

"Introduce a Girl to Engineering Day," 138

Iran, 154

Iraq, 132, 154

isomerization, 60–61

isotopes, separating uranium, 60–61

Israel, 154

Joe King Professorship, 166

Johnny Jay and the Kampus Kollegians, 41

Journal of Heat Transfer board, 152

Katy, Texas lawsuit, 95

Katz, Donald Laverne, 59; Katz Award, 194; Katz-McKetta Method, 59, 79

Kearney, Mrs. (landlady), 60, 75

Keele, Milton Duane, 176

Klass Klassics high school yearbooklet, 32–33

Kobe, Kenneth, 110, 114

Korotchenko, Ukraine, 10, 160

"Laboratory Mishaps" poster, 102

Lake Austin property, 121–25, 180–81

"Last Psalm, The" student poem, 167

lawsuits, 95–96

lectures, energy, 94, 113, 151–59, 161, 163, 166, 173

"Let's Not Cry Wolf: Earth's Population Is Not Doomed" lecture, 158

letters of recommendation, 56

Lewis, John L., 35

Lewis, W. K., 141

lime, 81, 97

limestone, 52, 121, 182

Little Shop café, *62*, 63, 77

Livingston, Bill, 144

lye, 52, 56

Machnyk, Anna (grandmother of JJM), 10–11

madrugada, 90

magic of friendship, 203

Manhattan Project, 61

Manning, Frank, 167

Marcel Dekker, Inc., 111

marriage, JJM advice on, 140–41

McCormack, Mike, 158

McKetta, Anna Mae (sister of JJM), *9*; birth of, 10; nicknamed "Hanya," 16; associate editor of high school booklet, 33; marriage to Merle Thomas, 44; working at beauty salon, 44; trip to Yukon, 46; JJM/Pinky honeymoon stay with, 72; death at ninety-four, 188

McKetta, Charles "Chalco" (brother of JJM), *14*, *25*; birth of, 10, 13; childhood, 13, 16, 18–19, 22; going to work in mines, 31; courting, marrying

McKetta, Charles "Chalco" (*continued*)
Nellie Parris, 31–32, 44, 55; JJM partnered with in mines, 34; reading *Coal Carbonization* book, 35; death of, 45–46; Charles William named after, 78

McKetta, Charles William "Charley" (son of JJM): birth, childhood of, 78, 99, 130; becoming forest economist, 96; at Perry Lane house, 98; in Marine Corps, 159; introducing JJM to flying, 159; oldest-son question, 130; wordplay, 64

McKetta, Elisabeth Sharp (author, granddaughter of JJM), 1–2, 174, 185–86, 189, *198*

McKetta/Miketa, Frank (double cousin of JJM), 13, 22, 24, 45, 64, 146

McKetta/Miketa, Frank (uncle of JJM), 11–13, 22–23, 30–31, 44–46

McKetta, Helen Elisabeth "Pinky" (née Smith), *69, 71, 124, 134, 150, 186*; family background, 65–66; nicknames, 3, 27, 66–67; college years, 68–70; Records Office job, 70, 75; meeting JJM at Little Shop, 63; courtship, marriage, honeymoon, 3, 70–72, 76; first apartment after marriage, 75; birth of Charley, 78; as tempering agent for JJM, 134, 178; writings of, 66–68, 181–82; birth of Mike, 98; birth of Randy, 98–99; living in Houston, 106; deaths of parents, 106; birth, childhood of Mary Anne, 115–16, 194; designing Tortuga Trail home, 121–25 (*124*), 180; as "Outstanding Volunteer for the State of Texas," 116; broken leg, *150*; cancer surgery, 180; move to Westminster Manor, 181–85; in hospice care, 73; views on death, 187; at JJM's ninety-fifth birthday party, 188–90 (*188, 189*); death, memorial service, 191–93

McKetta, John J. III "Mike" (son of JJM), 99, 201; birth of, 98; "Mike" because of red hair, 98; as a child, 99; saying grace, 130; becoming a lawyer, 48, 95–96; inheriting love of spreadsheets, 147; as "landlord" of Tortuga house, 181; *tour de grandchildren* with JJM, 119–120

McKetta, John J. IV (grandson of JJM), 191–93, 199

McKetta, John J. Jr. "Johnny"

—CHILDHOOD, 1; birth, 7–8, 13; early childhood, *9*, 13–14, *14*, 204–5; first day of school, 15, 177; learning English, 15–16; nicknamed "Ivanchko," 16; family moving from town to town, 17–18; move to Brier Hill, 19–20; stealing corn, 20; altercation with priest, 21–22, 177; teaching Sunday School, 22, 25, 90; founding "Frontier Boys Club," 21, 25; first crush (Mary Bair), 22; football and boxing, 23–24, 44, 101; living with coach, 24; learning cornet, 24–25; circulation manager for high school booklet, 23–33; graduating from high school, 32–33 (*33*)

—ADULTHOOD, *25, 41–43*; becoming a coal miner, 1, 29–30, 34; on dangers of mining, 34, 37–38; joining a strike, 35; reading book on chemical engineering, 3, 35, 107; accepted at Tri-State College, 35–36, 39–40; working odd jobs, forming band, 40–41, 60, 86; in drama club, 48; graduating from Tri-State, 48; job at Michigan Alkali, 51; PhD from Michigan, 78; teaching GIs, 84–86 (*85*); living in Houston, 105–6; returning to Austin, 108; learning to fly, 158–59; postponed trip to Egypt, 159–60; offer to forego salary (1985), 170; effects of constant travel, 132–33; high-school reunions, 172; love of teamwork, 101; making and bending rules, 85; on oil embargo (1973), 158.

See also degrees and academic positions (JJM); honors and awards (JJM); humor (JJM); publications and editorial positions (JJM); speeches and lectures (JJM)

—FAMILY LIFE, *134, 186*; meeting "Pinky" at Little Shop, 63; courtship, marriage, honeymoon, 70–72 (*71*); first apartment after marriage, 75; birth, childhood of "Charley," 78, 99, 130; birth of "Mike," 98; house on Perry Lane, 98, 142; birth of "Randy," 98–99; birth, childhood of Mary Anne, 115–16, 194; visit to ancestral home, 160; move to Westminster Manor, 181–85; *tour de grandchildren*, 119–20; ninety-fifth birthday, 187–89 (*187–189*); getting a pacemaker, 187; response to Pinky's death, 191; meeting Susan Clevenger, 193, 197; hundredth birthday celebrations, 194–99 (*196, 197*); cribbage, 76, 78, 99; daily exercises, routine, 44, 47, 72, 114, 166, 183–84, 194; death of father, 145; "Djiedo," 27; sudden deaths of mother, brother, uncle, 45–46, 85, 194

McKetta/Miketa, John J. Sr. "Pop" (father of JJM), *17*; birth of, 11; passage to America, 11–12, 202; name change, 12; paying for brothers' passage, 12; courtship, marriage to Mary Gelet, 12–13; working in the mines, 11, 15; becoming an electrician for mines, 16–18, 145; as Brier Hill chief electrician, 19–20, 30, 145; purchasing Yukon farm, 30; wife's, son's deaths, 45–46; injured in fire, 46; death of, 145

McKetta, Julia (née Gelet, aunt of JJM), 12, 45

McKetta, Mary (née Gelet, mother of JJM), *25*; marriage, 10; Gelet sisters marrying McKetta brothers, 12–13; family life, 10, 18–20, 22; birth of JJM, 7–8; meeting Nellie Parris, 31; death, 44

McKetta, Mary Ann (niece of JJM), 32

McKetta, Mary Anne (daughter of JJM), 78, 115–17, 191, 193, 194

McKetta, Robert Andrew "Randy" (son of JJM), 64, 96, 98–99

McKetta/Miketa, Steve (uncle of JJM), 11–12

McKetta Challenge, vii, 4, 177, 190

McKetta Method, 4, 59, 79, 93, 154

"McKetta Method" for women student engineers, 137–38

McKetta Rules, 86–88, 107, 178

McKetta's Boys, 168–69

Melnyk, Catherine (great grandmother of JJM), 10

Menser, George, 24

mentors and mentoring, 3, 23, 51–52, 82, 125, 194

Merz, Ed, 60

Michigan Alkali, 51–52, 54–56

Mikan, Frank, 22

Miketa, Ivan (great grandfather of JJM), 10

Miketa, John. *See* McKetta/Miketa, John J. Sr. "Pop" (father of JJM)

Miketa/McKetta, Steve (uncle of JJM), 11–12

Miketa, Wassail (grandfather of JJM), 10–11, 30

mining. *See* coal mining

Moore, Gerald, 40, 44, 51–52, 208n2

Mount Bonnell, 121

mowing, 13, 99, 122, 153

My First 80 Years (McKetta autobiography), 175; book cover in orange, 176; on "Chemical Cow" exhibit, 97; on courting Pinky, 70; distributed to do-

My First 80 Years (*continued*)
nors, 177; on expert witness work, 95; on flying, 159; on learning from others' mistakes, 46; on Piedras Negras' "Boy's Town," 140; on wearing burnt-orange underpants at Texas A&M, 170–71

Nader, Ralph, 151, 162, 163
name tags: for faculty, 135–36; JJM's, 1, 183
National Acid Precipitation Assessment Program, 179
National Air Quality Management Committee, 157
National Carbon Dioxide Greenhouse Committee, 157
National Council for Environmental Balance, 157
National Energy Policy Commission, 152
National Environmental Development Association (Triple "E" award), 157
National Hazardous Waste Committee, 157
National Science Foundation, 100, 128
National Youth Association, 40
natural gas, 52–53, 58, 80, 93, 156, 209n10
Naval Reserve Officers, JJM course for, 60
network of support, JJM's, 3
Nichols, Mrs. Bert, 40
Nixon, Richard, 4, 152
Norway and North Sea oil, 162
Nova Scotia, 177
nuclear energy, 150–51, 156
nuclear weapons, 61
Nussbaum restaurant explosion, 95

offshore drilling, 93, 131, 154, 160–62
oil. *See* petroleum
orange. *See* burnt-orange color, JJM and

"outside professor," JJM as, 117–18, 127, 132–33
oyster shells, 81

"panty-raid craze," 100
Parris, Nellie, 31–32, 44, 46
Paul, Donald, 112, 170
peace through strength, 92
Perry, Ervin, 136
personal "religion," JJM's, 168
petroleum: embargo (1973), 153–54, 158; and Ernie Cockrell, 128; *Exxon Valdez* incident, 161; fossil fuels and environment, 150–51, 156; as future of energy, 52–53; and Gulf Publishing, 109–10; hydrogen sulfide in, 58; JJM on Tesoro Petroleum board, 160, 180; JJM's work with, 92–93, 105–6, 108–10, 126; offshore drilling, 93, 154, 157; peacetime applications of, 92; Permian Basin oil field, 81; San Marcos oil spill, 95; Santa Rita oil well, 81; Texas oil boom (1901), 80; worker safety in, 155; WWII need for, 83, 92
Petroleum Refiner Magazine/Hydrocarbon Processing Industry, 92, 105–8, 156–57. *See also* Gulf Publishing Company
"Pillar of Success" award, 179
"Pinky." *See* McKetta, Helen Elisabeth "Pinky" (née Smith)
piss-and-vinegar necktie, 172
plastics, 52, 86, 111–12, 209n2 (ch8)
Plitvice, Croatia visit, 177
Poehl, Michael, 171
poetry by and for JJM, 22, 31, 167
pollution from energy sources, 19, 57–58, 153, 155–56, 162–63
polymers/polymerization, 83, 86, 112, 209n2 (ch8)
Porter, Horace C., 35–36
presidents, JJM advising, 4; Bush, George H. W., 157; Carter, Jimmy, 156–57, 174; Ford, Gerald, 152;

Nixon, Richard, 152; Reagan, Ronald, 153, 179
Prince William Sound, 161
professional organizations, 83, 140
publications and editorial positions (JJM): *Advances in Petroleum Chemistry and Refining* (ed.), 110–11; editing Gulf Publishing Company, 105–10, 113, 131, 140, 145, 152, 194; *Encyclopedia for Chemical Processing and Design* (ed.), 4, 108, 110–15, 141, 172; *Hydrocarbon Processing Industry* (*Petroleum Refiner Magazine*) (ed.), 92, 105–8, 156–57; *Journal of Heat Transfer* (board member), 152; *Petroleum Refiner Magazine* (ed.), 105–7. See also *My First 80 Years* (McKetta autobiography)

quizzes, classroom, 87, 126

ranok, 90
Ransom, Harry, 142–44
Rase, Howard, 131, 139
Reagan, Ronald, 4, 153, 179
religion, 168
renewable energy, 150
research foundations, 100, 127–28, 135
"Resident Scholars Program," 139
Retired Senior Volunteer Program, 179
retirement, JJM in, 175–76; *tour de grandchildren*, 119–20; hundredth birthday celebrations, 194–99 (*195–199*); learning to use computers, 184. *See also* Westminster Manor
Richardson, Red, 3, 23, 44, 47, 194
Roush, Raymond, 40, 179
rubber, 80, 83, 92

San Marcos oil spill, 95
Santa Rita oil well, 81
Saudi Arabia, 131, 153, 154
Schneible, Claude, 57–58
Schoch, Eugene P., 80–83, 209n10

Scholz Garten incident, 87
scrubbers, 57–58
semisolid energy, 163
Shakespearean acting, 48, 101, 176
Sharpe, Howard, 67
Shell Oil, 82, 127
shoeless student, 128
significance and belonging as human needs, 54
Silent Spring (Carson), 150, 162
slap-hand teaching technique, 159
Smith, Anne (née Ewing) (mother of Pinky), 65–67, 98
Smith, Clyde, 23, 24
Smith, "Pinky." *See* McKetta, Helen Elisabeth "Pinky" (née Smith)
Smith, Robert Andrew (father of Pinky), 65–66
smoking, JJM, 37
"Sno-glo," 56
sodium hydroxide (lye), 52, 56
sodium hypochlorite (bleach), 56
solar energy, 150, 156
Spate, Monty, 127
speeches and lectures (JJM): before British House of Lords, 153, 161–62; Centennial Lecture at Texas A&M, 170–71; commencement speeches in Pennsylvania, 159; as guest lecturer, 94; last formal lecture, 172; lectures/articles on energy, 94, 113, 151–59, 161, 163, 166, 173; speeches at AIChE, 131–32, 141
Spindletop oil boom, 80
spreadsheets, tracking life through, 86, 88, 146–47, 184–85
Sputnik education crisis, 130
Stanley, Bill, 176
Stevenson, Jack L., 170
Stice, James, 135
students, JJM's relationship with. *See* teaching methods and philosophy of JJM

sulfur, 30, 80–81
sulfur dioxide, 57–58, 179
"sympathy" cards, 49
synthetic diamonds, 112
Syria, 154

tarantulas as pets, 130
taxes on oil companies, 154
teaching methods and philosophy of JJM:
adjusting to women students, 137–
38, 168–69; attending student's wedding in loco parentis, 169; birthday calls, 4, 87–88, 117, 146, 176, 184,
191, 199–200; birthday skip rule, 87,
117; block system, 138–39; chalk-
throwing at students, 88, 100, 109,
117, 125; course selection guidance,
138–39; development of block system, 138–39; farewell after last lecture, 173; fifty-second classroom quizzes, 87, 126; "Inspection Trip" class,
83; lecture titles on energy options,
158; McKetta Rules, 86–88, 107, 178;
as "outside professor," 117–18, 127,
132–33; on proper dress and hair,
126, 128, 166; requiring name tags for
teachers, 135–36; Saturday makeup
classes, 131; students as most important duty, 136–37; students house sitting, 125; supporting faculty, 138–40;
supporting undergraduates, 135–36;
Teaching Effectiveness Program, 135;
teaching methods, 86–88, 90; on
"unteachable" students, 136; writing
weight on blackboard, 88, 109, 117,
165, 172
temperature profiles of wells. See Mc-
Ketta Method
Tesoro Petroleum, 160, 180
"Texas 10" in poll, 146
Texas A&M University, 129, 170–71
Texas McKettas, 180
"Texas pennies," 5, 119, 166, 190

"The U.S. Energy Problem: America's
Achilles Heel" lecture, 158
Thomas, Merle (nephew of JJM), 44, 109
Three Mile Island meltdown, 156
toluene, 54, 92
Tortuga Trail house, 123–25 (124),
180–83
tour de grandchildren, 119–20
traveling: aborted trip to Egypt, 159–
60; "Boy's Town" incident, 140–41;
camping trips, 99; cribbage during,
76; with family, 160, 178; Galápagos trip, 177; Germany trip, 177–78;
JJM flying himself, 158–59; professional trips, 132–33, 179–80; schedul-
ing around class schedule, 131; visits
to people from childhood, 159
trees producing air pollution, 153
Trimble, John, 187
Triple "E" award, 157
triple-point, 102–3
Tri-State (Trine University), 36, 39–40,
48, 51, 152, 179
trumpet/cornet, JJM playing, 24–25, 41

Ukrainian immigrants, 16
undergraduates, support for, 135–36
underwear, UT-themed, 1–2, 170–71, 190
UNESCO, 132
Union Carbide, 82
unions, 35, 107
University of Michigan graduate school,
57–59, 75, 108
University of Texas (Austin): Board of
Regents, 142–43; celebrations of JJM's
hundredth birthday, 194–97 (195–
197); chemistry shacks and "Big Lab,"
81, 83; as "energy university," 200;
impact of GI Bill on, 84–85; UT
Tower lit for JJM, 188. See also Chemical Engineering Department (UT
Austin)
"unknown dragons," 156

"unteachable" students, 136
Upper Big Branch mine disaster, 27–28
uranium and Manhattan Project, 60–61
"US Energy Self-Sufficiency Will Probably Not Happen in Our Lifetimes" lecture, 166

Vandiver, Frank, 170
vulcanization of rubber, 80

waste chemicals, profiting from, 53, 56, 81, 82
water content of natural gases, 93
weight tracking, 88, 109, 117, 165, 172, 184
Westminster Manor: "going to Health Services," 186; hundredth-birthday party at, 197, *198*; JJM at, 49, 73, 183; move to, 2–3, 27–28, 181; number of bricks to build, 87; Pinky at, 184; plays at, 2–3; retirement to, 2–3; spreadsheet of dinner mates, 147; on wait list for, 181
"Why the U.S. Will Not Achieve Energy Self-Sufficiency" lecture, 158
W. K. Lewis Award, 141

women as engineers, 137–38, 168–69
wood pulp, 80
wordplay, 64
work ethic, 47, 54, 61
World War I, 8, 79–80
World War II, 3, 56, 60–61, 83, 92
Wyano, Pennsylvania, *9*, 146–47; birthplace of Charles, Anna Mae, 10; birthplace of JJM, 7–8; daily life for coal miners in, 12–13, 38; JJM's father as electrician for, 16–17; JJM's father's arrival in, 12; named for Y&O Steel, 7; "room-and-pillar mines" in, 9; school in, 15–16

yellow ribbons/dresses protest, 169
yogurt analogy, 145
Yom Kippur War, 154
Youngstown and Ohio Steel Company (Y&O), 7, 12
Yukon, Pennsylvania: family farm in, 30–31, 44–46; Yukon Volunteer Band, 24–25, 45, 68

"zero energy"/"zero pollution" debate, 151, 162, 163

ABOUT THE AUTHOR

Elisabeth Sharp McKetta teaches writing for Harvard Extension School and leads writing workshops around the country. She is the author of four books, *The Fairy Tales Mammals Tell* (2013), *The Creative Year: 52 Workshops for Writers* (2014), *Poetry for Strangers* (2015), and *Fear of the Deep* (2016). Her PhD (University of Texas, 2009) focused on the intersections between fairy tales and autobiography. She lives in Boise with her husband and two children. See www.elisabethsharpmcketta.com.